UPROOTING COMMUNITY

Uprooting Community

Japanese Mexicans, World War II, and the U.S.-Mexico Borderlands

SELFA A. CHEW

THE UNIVERSITY OF
ARIZONA PRESS

TUCSON

The University of Arizona Press
www.uapress.arizona.edu

Printed in the United States of America
21 20 19 18 17 16   7 6 5 4 3 2

ISBN-13: 978-0-8165-3185-1 (cloth)
ISBN-13: 978-0-8165-3418-0 (paper)

Cover designed by Lori Lieber
Cover image: Hiromoto Yoshino family, Temixco, circa 1948. Courtesy of
Dr. Raul Hiromoto Yoshino.

Publication of this book is made possible in part by the proceeds of a
permanent endowment created with the assistance of a Challenge Grant
from the National Endowment for the Humanities, a federal agency.

Library of Congress Cataloging-in-Publication Data
Chew, Selfa A., 1962–
  Uprooting community : Japanese Mexicans, World War II, and the U.S.-
Mexico borderlands / Selfa A. Chew.
      pages cm
  Includes bibliographical references and index.
  ISBN 978-0-8165-3185-1 (cloth : alk. paper)
  1. Japanese—Mexico—History—20th century. 2. Japanese—Mexico—
Ethnic identity. 3. Japanese—Mexico—Evacuation and relocation,
1942–1945. 4. Mexico—Race relations—History—20th century. 5.
Mexican-American Border Region—Race relations—History—20th
century. 6. World War, 1939–1945—Social aspects—Mexico. 7. Mexico—
Relations—United States—History—20th century. 8. United States—
Relations—Mexico—History—20th century. I. Title.
  F1392.J3S65 2015
  305.800972'0904—dc23
                                2015005381

♾ This paper meets the requirements of ANSI/NISO Z39.48-1992
(Permanence of Paper).

To my brother, Pedro Manuel Chew Sánchez, for his infinite generosity, work, and sacrifice for our community and to those who have fallen with him in an absurd war against the people of Mexico.

To the teacher students of the Ayotzinapa Raul Isidro Burgos Normal School for their insistence in educating the poor and the indigenous.

To all Asian immigrants in the American Continent because they have resisted with dignity their oppression. Thanks for the immigrants' labor and cultures.

Contents

Acknowledgments

Thanks to the workers who have sustained with their labor and taxes the educational institutions in which I have been trained to become a social scientist.

I will always be grateful to my professors for their guidance and example: Maceo Dailey, John D. Márquez, Michael Topp, Yolanda Chávez Leyva, Julia Camacho Schiavone, Paul Edison, Samuel Brunk, Jeffrey Shepherd, and Fernando García Núñez. For their selfless support, thanks to Edith Yáñez, Roberto Mora, Claudia Rivers, Daniel Orizaga, Alberto Esquinca, Pedro Chew Almanze, Enrique Minjares, Carlos Chacón De La Rosa, Victoria García, Antonio López, Gloria Hall, Lucy Meléndez, Pete Chew Sánchez, Pedro Manuel Chew Barraza, Rosita King, Elvira King de Lio, Georgina Phillips, Celerina López, Liza Bennett, Virginia Sánchez Landeros, Demetrio Anzaldo, Guadalupe Pérez Anzaldo, Rosa Gómez, Jorge Chen, Liliana Chew, Alfredo López, Héctor Enríquez, Perla De La Rosa, Alfredo Limas, Sergio Rivera, Armida Desormaux, Hortensia Echeverría, Gabriela Salas, Carlos Ruvalcaba, Michael Lewis, Susan Clark, Brigitte López, Nunsah Sánchez Santiago, Alma Yleana Acosta, Martha Reyes Tanaka, John Fahey, and Horacio and Columba Sánchez Larios. To my students, my mirrors, you are always in my thoughts.

I am in debt to my youngest sister, Martha Chew Sánchez, an outstanding woman who, earning the first doctoral degree in my family, has been my dearest mentor. My appreciation also goes to Robert Harland, Juan Sandoval, Héctor Carbajal, and Gustavo del Hierro, all wonderful proofreaders, for their valuable suggestions to edit my manuscript. I am eternally grateful to Rodolfo Nakamura Ortiz, Josefina Villegas de Nakamura, Fidelia Takaki de Noriega, Eva Watanabe Matsuo, Shyzumi Olivia Otsuka Ordóñez de Tanaka, Ángel Tanaka Gómez, Akiko Tanaka Gómez, Raúl Hiromoto Yoshino, Minerva Yoshino Castro, and their families, for their trust. Their always warm welcome and encouragement were incentives to complete my research. My deepest appreciation for Kristen Buckles, acquisition editor for the University of Arizona Press, for her advocacy of my work, and to Melanie Mallon, for her perceptive and skillful editing. Thanks also to Barbara Reyes, Karen Mary Dávalos, Gloria Cuádraz, and C. Alejandra Elenes for reviewing sections of my manuscript and providing valuable editorial recommendations. Thanks to Erika Lee, whose historical narrative on the Chinese community in the borderlands inspired my own research.

Thanks to my uncle Rodolfo Sánchez Cisneros, an exemplary human being and educator. I am beholden to my husband Doroteo Meléndez and my daughter Noli, my best friends and accomplices, for their great patience, deep love, and unyielding support; and to my sisters, Martha and Mariana, for their relentless pursuit of social justice, inspiring my teaching and research. My appreciation also goes to my parents, Selfa Sánchez Cisneros and Manuel Chew Almanze, who taught us to feel proud of our roots and to serve our community. Thanks to my nephew, Pedro Manuel, and nieces, Thelma, Ximena, and Paloma, for the hope they represent in my life, and to my uncles, Alberto, Hermilo, Lucrecio, Efrén, Mario, Francisco, and Víctor, who had such strong work ethics and earnest love for our family. And I am grateful to my grandparents, Angelina Cisneros Serra, Chio Sam Chew, Virginio Sánchez Vásquez, and Manuela Almanze, who started my journey a long time ago in different parts of the world.

I received financial support to conduct my research and to write this book from Dr. Rodolfo Sánchez Cisneros; Doroteo Meléndez; the Smithsonian Institution; the Race, Ethnicity, and Migration Studies project of the Trans-Atlantic Graduate Exchange Program; the Hispanic Scholarship Fund; the Cotton Memorial Scholarship; the Richard E. Dunlap Memorial Fund; St. Lawrence University; Dr. Diana Natalicio; and the Liberal Arts College, Department of History, and African American Studies Program at the University of Texas at El Paso.

I am sure I have forgotten to acknowledge here important people in my life, who have made possible both my education and this book. Thank you with all my heart.

UPROOTING COMMUNITY

Introduction

This book began as research into "absences" in historical memory. While browsing newspapers in El Paso, I was hoping to understand how the absence of Chinese women in the lives of many Chinese men in the borderlands had affected their social relations in the U.S.-Mexico borderlands. Combing the microfilm yielded an astonishing piece of information, unrelated to the Chinese community: I stumbled upon an article describing a military search of several homes in Ciudad Juárez on March 15, 1942, carried out under the supervision of the American consul.[1] My surprise grew when I did not recognize the Japanese surnames of the arrested persons listed in the article. My family's home was in downtown Juárez, near the addresses cited and in proximity to the house my father had lived in when he was a child. Because we were close friends with our neighbors, whom we considered our extended family, and because I am an Asian Mexican, a series of questions haunted me: Why did I not know any relatives of the men arrested in 1942? Why did I not attend school with their grandchildren? Why had my father not mentioned having Japanese friends during his childhood in what was then a small city, where practically everyone knew one another? I initiated my inquiry into the missing Japanese Mexican families in Ciudad Juárez. My research has directed me toward focusing on larger questions related to Japanese experiences along the U.S.-Mexico borderlands, as well as tracing the history of their displacement during World War II.

Japanese, Chinese, Koreans, and other Asians have simultaneously and alternately experienced racist violent attacks in Mexico. Their status as

3

subjects or slaves of the Spanish Empire in the colonial period and as peons during the Porfiriato placed Asians and their descendants among the most vulnerable populations in Mexico.[2] In addition, historical otherization processes, particularly orientalism, have cultivated in Mexicans the desire to direct anger and frustration against Asians, marked as racially inferior, nondeserving of the rights exclusively reserved for the citizens of the nation.[3] Japanese, Koreans, and Chinese have, nonetheless, specific histories that determine the social status of each Asian community in the United States and Mexico.

In racist societies, immigrants engage in particular dynamics with other racialized groups that factor in their experiences and strategies to counter oppression.[4] Although Japanese laborers were seen as Chinese on both sides of the borders, a process known as sinification, they had different reactions to the lumping of all Asians into one "Chinese" category.[5] At times they voluntarily closed ranks with Chinese immigrants. At others, they attempted to distance themselves from Chinese and other Asians, claiming a white male status. Weighing on this decision was the whiteness requirement to apply for naturalization in the United States, a condition that was removed only after World War II.[6] Embracing Japanese imperialist expansion in reaction to European and American dominion of Asia was another feature in the experience of some immigrants. The colonizer ideology imbued in some Japanese immigrants a sense of racial superiority over Mexicans and other Asian immigrants. It also gave them a purpose as settler colonizers in Mexico with a mission similar to that of white Americans.[7] Heterogeneity among Japanese immigrants, however, calls for caution in assessing their support of Japanese colonial projects. Opposition to military conscription, as well as religious and political dissension, was often expressed through migration and viewed as a problem for the Japanese state.[8] Personal agendas, group loyalties, and beliefs were factors in each immigrant experience.

Thomas Calvo argued that, fulfilling their aspirations to integrate into the receiving society, Japanese immigrants first enjoyed the status of honorary whites in New Spain; Jerry Garcia posits that a similar process positively affected Japanese immigrants in modern Mexico.[9] My research has yielded a different interpretation. Despite the financial success of some Japanese, for the most part they have been racialized with other Asians and placed in the lowest echelons in all historical periods in New Spain/Mexico. An example of white privilege not enjoyed by ethnic Japanese was taking religious habits as nuns in New Spain.[10] The prohibition to carry weapons or wear jewelry applied equally to *chinos* and *negros*, where Asians of any origin were often classified under both denominations or as *indios*. Although

Spaniards born in the American continents articulated racial hybridism as the symbol of a distinct American identity, miscegenation did not erase white supremacy as the social principle on which New Spain society was organized. The notion of *mexicanidad* developed by criollos after achieving independence from Spain exclusively recognized Spanish and indigenous peoples in the making of a national identity, very much in opposition to African and Asian individuals and communities.[11]

The war against Mexico, which ended in 1848, reinforced adherence to the European hegemonic model when Mexicans attempted to obtain official racial classification as whites. After 1865, the Black Codes and Jim Crow regulations became a powerful incentive for Mexicans to pass as white in the United States.[12] Competition for resources during the gold rush era in California brought new discriminatory practices and regulations against Asians. Although Mexicans shared the burden of racism, they learned or strengthened the orientalist perceptions cultivated in the United States.[13] The two first decades of the twentieth century were marked by sensationalist news of a possible takeover of Mexico by Japanese colonizers, published in the U.S. media. The cultivated anxiety about Japanese expansion instilled in the residents of the United States the desire to control the perceived transnational menace.[14]

The documented participation of Japanese in the Mexican Revolution and in labor movements, fighting classism and racism, as well as the losses they suffered in life and property during anti-Asian attacks refutes the notion that Japanese enjoyed a permanent high racial rank in all periods in Mexico.[15] The offensive and well-known rhyme "Chino, chino, japonés, come caca y no me des," in vogue during World War II, speaks volumes about a latent anti-Asian sentiment against any person of Asian appearance.[16] Acquainted with the notion of "Yellow Peril," some participants in the Mexican Revolution decided to exercise violence against Chinese and Japanese to eliminate the perceived threat to racial purity and economic independence.[17] During La matanza de Torreón (the Torreón massacre) of 1911, Maderista troops killed 303 Chinese and 5 Japanese persons. More than half of the Chinese population in Torreón was massacred by Revolutionary troops who shared with the local bourgeoisie their resentment against a prosperous small Asian community in the city.[18]

Because racism manifests itself in different forms and is affected by historical contexts, the anti-Japanese variant has not always been a direct reflection of anti-Chinese racism, although racial representations of the "Yellow Peril" are similar. For instance, the military power of the Japanese state, exhibited during the first decades of the twentieth century, spurred anti-Japanese activism predicated on anti-imperialism. Religion, gender, ideology, class, occupations, and internal ethnical differences also influence inter- and intraracial relations.[19]

While attempting to enforce its own hegemonic projects, Japan's diplomatic interferences were not always positive in the lives of Japanese immigrants: In addition to attempting to maintain class, gender, and ethnic hierarchies prevailing in Japan, diplomatic envoys could not provide complete protection against racism. To complicate matters, Erika Lee contends, orientalist views extended continentally to reinforce anti-Asian movements.[20] Eugenicists invoked pseudoscientific reasons to formulate and maintain laws excluding Asians in the United States. The increasing military power of Japan and its rejection of European intervention in Asia were met with the U.S. government's promotion of the Monroe Doctrine and its growing interest in achieving control over Japanese immigrants and their descendants in all regions of the American continents.[21]

P. Scott Corbett's *Quiet Passages: The Exchange of Civilians between the United States and Japan during the Second World War* describes the uprooting of 2,188 Latin American Japanese and the responsibility of the U.S. State Department, Army, and Federal Bureau of Investigation in their deportation. The civilians were interned in U.S. concentration camps after the State Department, banking on Latin American racism, "essentially offered South American countries the option of eliminating their Japanese minority by sending them to the United States." The willingness of Latin American governments to subject their citizens and residents of Japanese descent to the control of the United States ensured a firm economic collaboration with the United States. It also allowed for the direct intervention of U.S. police and military forces in the internal affairs of Latin American countries.[22]

Initially, the U.S. government ordered the eviction of Latin American men from their countries of birth or residence. This policy changed in 1943, when the U.S. State Department implemented a "family reunification" program, transporting civilian relatives of concentration camp residents from Latin American countries to the United States.[23]

Although the United States did not request from the Mexican government the internment of Japanese Mexicans in U.S. concentration camps, the U.S. and Mexican governments decided to evacuate all Japanese Mexican communities from the Mexican borderlands and coastal zones, constructing through this process a sense of national security crisis in Mexico.[24] Mexican Japanese became political hostages of the new alliance between Mexico and the United States.

The "concentration" of Japanese Mexicans during World War II seemed an innocuous program in view of the small number of Japanese immigrants living in the borderlands. Nevertheless, uprooting Japanese Mexicans meant the loss of freedom, property, and lives of Japanese immigrants and their Mexican spouses, children, and grandchildren. The number of affected persons during World War II extended beyond the number of first-generation Japanese immigrants "handled" by the Mexican government during this period. The entire multiethnic social fabric of the borderlands and the coastal zones was reconfigured in the absence of Japanese Mexicans during the war. Furthermore, Japanese Mexicans were added to the list of historical justifications to increase militarization of the U.S.-Mexico borderlands.[25]

If the prohibition against Chinese immigration in 1882 justified patrolling the borderlands in search of undocumented Chinese from 1904, as historian Erika Lee argues, the use of the army to control Japanese immigrants and their descendants contributed to the acceptance of military power in the borderlands.[26] This is one effect of the relocation program during World War II that is largely overlooked in examinations of the internment of ethnic Japanese.[27]

Mexico's new foreign policy orientation, based on the collaboration of economic and political Mexican elites, resulted in U.S. control of a large part of the economic sector.[28] Stephen R. Niblo addressed this growing loss of autonomy and argued that "the very use of the nation-state as the central analytical category [during this period] is problematic, since much of the output that was noted as Mexican was, in fact, in the hands of U.S. corporations, acquired through intracompany purchases."[29] Historian Halbert Jones posits that Mexico's intervention in World War II helped neutralize much of the opposition to establishing a political and economic coalition with a nation that had annexed a large extension of its territory during the nineteenth century.[30] Because Mexico's military contribution to the war was not significant, the making of an internal enemy became an important component of Manuel Ávila Camacho's invitation to defend *la patria*.[31] This political movement left many Japanese Mexicans homeless, unemployed, and without the protection of the Japanese, Mexican, or U.S. nation-states.

Although the displacement of Japanese Mexicans and the suspension of their civil rights took effect in the name of national security, the relocation program was a racist project: it demanded the exclusive eviction of persons who were racially defined as Japanese, regardless of their nationality. While the Mexican government also evicted several German and Italian men from the borderlands, it did so considering each case on a personal basis, not to be uniformly handled based on membership in an ethnic or racialized group. The analysis of the relocation program thus brings to the forefront the mechanisms of power that operate against racialized groups in modern societies.

Philosopher Giorgio Agamben argues that the suspension of human rights could not take place without a legal framework allowing for modern states to function dictatorially in times of political and economic crisis. Every mechanism designed to sustain democratic principles, such as the separation of powers or habeas corpus, will fail when the head of the state holds absolute power over an entire population in a state of emergency. Such a process has led to a pattern of modern "democratic" states sustaining themselves by disrupting or suspending their legal framework, often along racial lines. The relationship between racism and state power in "times of crisis" explains the vulnerable position of the Japanese Mexican community.[32] The Mexican government had invested in previous anti-Asian movements in Mexico to exacerbate nationalism. Constructing the Japanese Mexican community as an internal enemy made acceptable the suspension of civil rights of all citizens for the sake of national security. President Ávila Camacho was able to exercise an almost unchallenged control and ignore the constitutional rights of dissenters by alleging that Japanese Mexicans represented imminent danger during his presidency.

Ignoring race as a social-organizing principle contributes to the false idea that the assaults on human rights of communities of color are locally contained and sporadic events of social injustice. Thus, the research in this book examines the relocation program of 1942 as a racial project directed against residents on the periphery of different nation-states.[33] I borrow an operating definition of race from Michael Omi and Howard Winant, who claim that "the meaning of race is defined and contested throughout society, in both collective action and personal practice."[34] Race is a socially defined and unstable definition that is constantly "formed, transformed, destroyed and re-formed."[35] The idea of a Japanese race in Mexico and in the United States was, thus, not a fixed list of physical and moral attributes but a series of perceptions that changed in every community and period, determining the extent to which ethnic Japanese enjoyed or were deprived of their civil rights.

Although U.S. national boundaries were daily and harsh reminders of the limits to their freedom of mobility, Japanese Mexicans in the borderlands had established themselves as denizens on the Mexican side of the border under a less restrictive racial system, before World War II. Their uprooting interrupted the creation of cultural and social spaces in which Japanese Mexicans were negotiating their inclusion in metaphoric and real borderlands.

Rodolfo Nakamura Ortiz, about nine years old in 1942, explained in an interview that he was traumatized by witnessing the mass eviction of Japanese from Palau, Coahuila. Nakamura remembered that "just a little after my mom died, they suddenly spread the news. One Friday they started saying that all Japanese were going to be picked up. . . . You could hear the painful weeping everywhere." The Mexican government ordered Rodolfo Nakamura's father, Nakamura Umezo, to leave his town immediately, which orphaned the child. Nakamura remembered that Palau's train depot was crowded "since very early in the morning because there were too many [Japanese Mexicans] leaving." But separation of families was only one of the damaging effects of the relocation program: Japanese Mexicans also suffered loss of property, employment, freedom, health, and life itself as a result of their eviction from the borderlands and coastal zones of Mexico.[36]

In contrast with the experiences of Rodolfo Nakamura, the memories of Dr. Shoshin Murakami reflect what he perceived as a safe and free environment during World War II, away from the borderlands. In the webpage titled "Migraciones de japoneses a México," the Mexican Japanese Association (the main cultural institution of the Japanese Mexican community) presents the following quote by Dr. Murakami: "Our parents had the prettiest prison: the entire City of Mexico was their prison; they were free to walk, they could eat everything they wanted, what they could buy[,] and the people of Mexico and the government of Mexico never hurt them."[37] Dr. Murakami's narrative of the relocation program differs greatly from the personal stories of the men and women I interviewed in the course of my research. They reported their uprooting as a traumatic, disastrous event in their lives. Furthermore, most files in the Ministry of the Interior contain information on the restrictions and hardships experienced by Japanese Mexican individuals and families during World War II.[38] Yet the results of this research do not refute the validity of Dr. Murakami's memories or those of any other Japanese Mexican person shielded from the harshness of deracination during wartime. On the contrary, this book acknowledges heterogeneity and interstices in the application of the displacement program. Gender, in particular, assists our identification of agency and the creative appropriation of the patriarchal rhetoric to resist oppression; the differentiated criminalization of Japanese Mexicans, and its importance in the construction of an internal enemy; the fluidity of gendered roles and offices; and the intersectionality of sexuality, class, and race.

Sources

This book rests largely on archival documentation. I conducted my research mainly in Mexico City at the Archivo General de la Nación, Dirección General de Investigaciones Políticas y Sociales Archives. The records pertaining to this department are listed as IPS, following the nomenclature used by the Archivo General de la Nación.

President Ávila Camacho created the Departamento de Investigación Política y Social (DIPS) in 1942 to operate under the supervision of the Ministry of the Interior. This new department was responsible for the control of Japanese populations residing in Mexico during World War II. The IPS archives contain correspondence with the president of Mexico, the Ministry of the Interior, and members of the political secret police units that formed part of the Ministry of the Interior. They also contain letters signed by military officers, governors, and U.S. diplomats. These archives are a source of personal narratives from many sites of the relocation program: ministers, congressmen, police officers, Japanese Mexican men and women. Other voices emerged as well to provide a complex view of the Japanese Mexican community during the first forty years of the twentieth century, especially the critical period from 1942 to 1945. Documentation in the same file, however, is fragmented, and it requires a great effort to reconstruct the lives of the victims of the relocation program. Some Japanese immigrants did not know how to speak or write Spanish. Their views, therefore, are not recorded in the IPS files. Yet we can still find direct testimonies from Japanese Mexican men and women who wrote letters, appeals, and other documents during the relocation program.

I also conducted research at the National Archives and Records Administration (NARA) repositories in Washington, DC. I searched for documents related to the internment of Latin American residents of Japanese origin in relocation camps under the custody of the U.S. Immigration and Naturalization Service (INS). Records of their arrival to the United States, entrance permits, and related court hearings were helpful in understanding the process of their uprooting. Their arrival on American soil, their subsequent internment in concentration camps, and their ultimate deportation to Japan followed protocols that contradict democratic principles but were still "legal."

Newspapers and magazines in the United States and in Mexico were an excellent source of information, and the editorials provided a window into both local and national social aspects of the program. Some of these periodicals are *El Paso Times, El Paso Herald Times, Diario Oficial de la*

Federación, Diario de los Debates de la Cámara de Diputados del Congreso de los Estados Unidos Mexicanos, and the American *Time* magazine. These sources allowed me to identify popular notions that existed in Mexico and in the United States regarding the Japanese relocation program in Latin America.

Interviews with eleven members of the Japanese Mexican community who were affected by the relocation program were crucial in understanding the psychological and economic damages that the Mexican government inflicted on all persons of Japanese descent, not officially acknowledged as of today. Fidelia Takaki de Noriega, Eva Watanabe Matsuo, Rodolfo Nakamura Ortiz, Minerva Yoshino Castro, Diamantina Nakamura Ortiz, Mahatma Tanahara Romero, Raúl Hiromoto Yoshino, Ángel Tanaka Gómez, Shyzumi Olivia Otsuka de Tanaka, Susana Kobashi Sánchez, and María Fujigaki Lechuga gave me the opportunity to learn their personal stories and that of their families. In addition, I interviewed Hermilo Sánchez Cisneros and Alicia Bueno, who had Japanese Mexican relatives and friends and provided information on how the relocation program affected them or their relatives. I conducted these interviews between 2006 and 2010 in Mexico City, Ciudad Juárez, and Temixco. Most contacts were the result of the kind assistance I received from my extended family, the Nakamura Villegas. Interviewees provided valuable insights into their personal stories and family histories. Because victims of the Japanese relocation program were sharing painful memories, I considered a recorder an intrusive and impersonal element that could limit information to be shared and decided to take notes instead. Interviewees received a copy of the notes.

An especially insightful narrative was offered by the memories of Dr. Martín Otsuka, author of *Poems, Memories of My Home Town, and Chronicle of My Travels in Mexico.* Otsuka was arrested and incarcerated in the borderland state of Chihuahua in 1942. His book, published in 1987, was written in Japanese for a Japanese audience once Dr. Otsuka returned to his birthplace. He translated some poems into the Spanish language, which gave me the opportunity to learn his views on the Mexican community and his account of his arrest and incarceration during the relocation program.

Except where noted, I translated to English those interviews and documents produced originally in Spanish. When available, I mention the complete name of residents and citizens of Mexico once, and then I proceed to refer to them by their paternal last name. I replicated the ways in which newspapers named Mexican politicians. They avoided, for example, use of the second surname of presidents Lázaro Cárdenas and Porfirio Díaz;

however, newspapers and official documents always included Manuel Ávila Camacho's two surnames. The Ministry of the Interior records show different spelling of the surnames of Japanese Mexican men and women. When possible, I used what Japanese Mexicans wrote in their official documents.

CHAPTER ONE

Gendered Criminalization

In December 1943, Julio Novoa, associate director of Banco General de Capitalización in Mexico City, accused Flora Kikutake Yahiro, a U.S. citizen of Japanese descent, of falsifying a series of documents to fraudulently cash checks worth approximately $3,000 (pesos).[1] Kikutake had extracted the money while employed as a clerk at the same institution. As any other clerk taking care of customers' transactions, Kikutake had access to the bank's cash and records.[2] She had the opportunity and the motivation to obtain the amount she illegally extracted from the bank; nevertheless, her ethnicity and citizenship made this move particularly dangerous in view of the Mexican declaration of war against Japan as well as the U.S. mandate to force more than one hundred thousand persons of Japanese descent into internment camps. When examined in the context of World War II, Flora's motivation to commit a crime reflects not only an internal moral turmoil but also the dimension of her need to put together a sum larger than her regular income. As she was an American citizen of Japanese origin living in Mexico during World War II, her circumstances and choices can tell us a great deal about racial, class, and gender relations, ultimately refuting the idea that Mexico's rebirth as a post-Revolutionary nation inaugurated a racially democratic society.

Immediately after the bombing of Pearl Harbor in December 1941 and the entrance of the United States into World War II, Mexico became an ally of its northern neighbor. Against a previous history of popular anti-imperialist sentiment derived from the war against Mexico and subsequent invasions of Mexican territories by the United States, President Manuel

Ávila Camacho committed his administration to managing the population of Japanese in the borderlands and coastal zones. The border regions included areas in proximity to the United States, the northern regions of Tamaulipas, Coahuila, Chihuahua, Sonora, and the then-territory of Baja California. Heeding the U.S. State Department's recommendations, the Mexican government ordered the strict surveillance of those regarded as internal enemies at local, state, and federal levels as early as December 1941.[3] The transnational criminalization of Japanese and Japanese Mexicans resulted in their removal from their homes in the U.S.-Mexico borderlands and the coastal zones of Mexico. Despite the prevailing suspicions of espionage and contraband that made Japanese Mexicans vulnerable to civil and state surveillance, Flora took the risk to make personal use of the funds she was entrusted with by her employer.[4]

To learn about the lives of Flora Kikutake and other Japanese Mexicans during World War II, I conducted an extensive research at the Archivo General de la Nación in Mexico City. Records of female Japanese immigrants at the Departamento de Investigaciones Política y Social (DIPS), a section of the Secretaría de Gobernación, or Ministry of the Interior, were almost nonexistent. In many cases, their names were recorded only within the files of their husbands, without further information. An excavation of relevant documents in the Archivo General de la Nación was not sufficient to learn about their lives as evacuees. Interviews and other scholarly perspectives assisted my research; however, my own experience shapes my assessment of the importance of the Asian diaspora in the formation of gender, racial, and national identities.

The Personal: Intersection of Multiple Diasporas

As a child in a multicultural family, I learned from my elder indigenous, Korean, Chinese, and Japanese Mexican relatives how to take care and be proud of my community. In the face of discrimination, our extended family provided resources and moral support so we could survive and thrive. My parents gave and received from other members of our extended family advice, loans, food, and clothes in times of scarcity. We called the adults *tías* and *tíos*, even if they were not blood relatives but just paisanos, and their children were deemed our cousins. They expressed their delight when describing our skin tone, eye shape, or hair color, making us feel better about ourselves in a world in which those same features were often caricaturized. Cooking our meals when our *tías* visited implied lessons of Asian culture and history and the celebration of our family roots. I grew up listening to their stories in which

Asian and indigenous peoples appeared as dignified, resilient human beings, creators of millenary and sophisticated cultures. Such communal education could only take place within the interstitial spaces of hegemonic social structures, which Emma Pérez and Chela Sandoval describe as providing opportunities to construct counterhegemonic cultural identities.[5] The textbooks I received during my school years omitted the contributions of Asian immigrants to the economy and culture of Mexico. Furthermore, mass media stereotyped, humiliated, or confused us children of Asian origin with denigrating or paternalistic images, stories, and jokes about the "chinitos" that resembled our parents or ancestors. First-generation adults were more confident about their intrinsic human value even when they endured discrimination, but their children had to imagine the contexts in which people who looked like them were considered "normal." We attempted to recover from a fragmented or distorted identity through strategies Mexican American children also tried north of the Mexican border.

At my arrival in the United States, I met the bandit, the maid, the beaner, the wetback, the siesta, and other images and joke plots in which the dominant society frames the existence of persons of Mexican descent to justify discrimination and disfranchisement. In continuous déjà vu moments, which white middle-class men and women are usually spared in Mexico or when migrating, I easily recognized the struggles of Chicanas. Like them, my phenotype and culture are markers of difference and alleged inferiority; we are deemed permanent foreigners regardless of our place of birth; our histories have been obliterated or distorted in the attempt to make us feel as though we are disposable human beings; and we have had to fight the myth that we enjoy the same opportunities as anybody else when accumulative historical processes and unequal relations of power have disfranchised racialized women since birth.

I became a resident of the United States with thousands of other women who crossed the northern border of Mexico in the 1980s. Foreign investment had created geographic and economic displacement in Mexico since the 1960s. The Border Industrialization Program, inaugurated in 1965, attracted women from the interior of Mexico to supply the labor force for maquiladoras in the U.S.-Mexico borderlands.[6] In the 1970s, like many other families, mine migrated to Ciudad Juárez, where my mother worked at a maquiladora. The prospect of a better life, away from unemployment and economic instability, forced many women in the borderlands and other zones of Mexico to migrate farther. Eventually, I joined the immigrant community north of the border.

As an immigrant in the United States, I have continued the journey initiated by my grandparents in Asia two generations ago. After experiencing racism in Mexico and in the United States, I have joined the scholars of color who enrich with their transnational vision the study of transnational communities.[7] The stories of displaced Japanese Mexican women that have been rendered almost invisible in mainstream narratives recover a personal meaning in my own academic work. Not only I am a woman whose *mestizaje* and hybridity refute the official Spanish/indigenous notions of mexicanidad in both the United States and Mexico, but the history of the Japanese Mexican community is the history of my own extended family.

Displacement and Mestizaje

The notion of mestizaje, particularly from Gloria Anzaldúa's perspective and seen as both a racial and a cultural merging, merits a deep examination in view of the hybridism shaping the experiences of the Japanese Mexican community. As with any other social process, hybridism takes different characteristics according to space and time. When mestizos were recognized as a social reality by 1530 in New Spain, their existence destabilized the colonial order that sought to separate indigenous peoples from Spanish and African. Asians were initially classified as Indians, and then conflated with blacks and with the *castas*, representing a mixture of peoples in the lowest ranks of the Spanish racial system. Later, criollos articulated racial hybridism as the symbol of a distinct American identity that set them symbolically apart from the European colonial power.[8] Although the Asian presence was exhibited in the material culture of New Spain, orientalism distanced Mexicans from their Chinese, Korean, Filipino, and Japanese ancestors. The rhetoric of mexicanidad united and homogenized all indigenous and Spanish communities under one Mexican identity of mestizaje with no Asian components.[9]

Anzaldúa ponders the weight of sexual violence against indigenous women that originated mestizaje and identifies as cultural tyranny other expressions of patriarchal power implicit in the mestizo culture. Following Anzaldúa's concept of cultural tyranny, I support the argument that internalized racism in Mexico is masked by the celebration of idealized indigenous and Spanish mestizaje. The rejection of other mestizajes has invisibilized Asians denying their importance in the history and culture of Mexico. Such internalized oppression, as noted by Anzaldúa, is created through our perception of "the version of reality that [culture] communicates" and our tendency to accept dominant paradigms formulated by those in power.[10]

Although by 1942 Japanese immigrants had taken important productive positions within the labor sector, participating in the Mexican Revolution to improve the conditions of peasants and industrial workers, they were a constant target of state nationalist cultural projects that emphasized assumed essential negative racial differences.[11] As confirmed by letters submitted to officials as well as news reports, those citizens of Mexico who did not have a direct relation with Asian immigrants or their descendants saw Japanese and their children as superfluous elements of the Mexican society during World War II. Once the global conflict ended, interventions in the debate over considering Japanese Mexicans as a danger or as integral members of the Mexican society subsided. In any case, Kikutake's experience and the stories of other Japanese Mexicans have been erased from national and transnational official histories despite their importance in the economy, identity, and culture of Mexico.

In 1942 the Mexican and U.S. presidents, Manuel Ávila Camacho and Franklin D. Roosevelt, dictated the arrest and displacement of hundreds of Mexican citizens of Japanese descent. Although no Japanese Mexican was ever tried for a crime that represented a real threat to national security, many lost their property and civil rights during World War II in a process Nicholas De Genova and Giorgio Agamben refer to as denationalization. Citizens by birth, naturalized citizens, or longtime residents of Mexico who had Mexican children were deportable racialized citizens, stripped of their nationality and rights through similar legal mechanisms that targeted Jews and Gypsies during the same historical period in Europe.[12]

De Apariencia Decente: The Possibilities and Limits of Flora Kikutake

In December 1943 Flora Kikutake Yahiro had powerful reasons to deliberately face the risk of going to prison. She was an educated woman, aware of the dire circumstances Japanese Mexicans were facing at the time. As a clerk, her salary was probably enough to pay for the most basic needs of her widowed mother, who seemed to depend economically on Flora and was the only relative living with the young woman. Kikutake's was not an act of theft motivated by greed or the desire to acquire a higher standard of life. In her own words, she became a delinquent "impelida por la miseria" (forced by poverty). Confronted by Julio Novoa, who had detected the deceit, Flora explained in detail her predicament: "Because I needed to bring my little son Kiyoshi Imahashi from Japan, I acted in an incorrect manner; it is with pain that I confess having cashed falsified documents . . . to give an amount of money to a man who left in the *Gripsholm*, and then to pay the enormous interests charged by those persons who lent me money to complete [the amount required to bring Kiyoshi from Japan]."[13]

Kikutake was immersed in the Mexican culture from the time she was very young, acquiring the social and technical skills that would ensure her a job when most Japanese Mexicans were struggling to regain financial stability in the face of World War II. But the war placed her in a vulnerable position. Kikutake was born in Seattle, Washington, on January 22, 1914. The date of her arrival in Mexico is not registered, but Kikutake must have been a child when her parents dec.ded to move south of the border, for she was a student enrolled in the elementary school Josefa Ortiz de Domínguez in Orizaba, Veracruz. Flora thus had the opportunity to learn Spanish early in her life, which increased her chances of finding and holding a job. In a patriarchal world that limited educational opportunities for women, young Flora had academic aspirations, which translated into a selection of educational institutions: she attended the secondary school that formed part of the Universidad Veracruzana, and later the Escuela Nacional Preparatoria, where she was enrolled in the premedicine program. Kikutake also sought training as secretary at the Chamber of Commerce trade school in Orizaba. When she relocated to Mexico City, Kikutake was ready to take a clerical job.[14]

Kikutake's employment application of October 1941 reflects the apprehension Japanese Mexicans may have held in view of international hostilities that could affect their immigration status. Although Kikutake declared Seattle, Washington, as the city where she was born, when she applied for employment at Banco General de Capitalización in Mexico City, she wrote "Japonesa" as her nationality, perhaps conflating "race" with citizenship. The attack on Pearl Harbor had not taken place at the time the bank's administrator interviewed Kikutake as a candidate for a clerical position; nonetheless, uncertainty about the direction that Mexico would take in the global conflict made persons of Japanese origin cautious, as newspapers and politicians portrayed them as the enemy.[15]

In addition to the inconsistency between birth place and nationality, Kikutake neglected to note in her application that she had a child living in Japan. Notions of respectability that rejected single mothers could have forced her to hide her motherhood. Through her message explaining the reasons for her criminal action, we can learn that her son carried a different last name, but available information does not tell us whether she decided not to follow the patriarchal tradition of adopting her husband's last name, she was a single mother, or she was divorced. Flora also noted in her application that she was Catholic.[16]

Mexico's entrance in World War II changed Flora Kikutake's situation. Her job was jeopardized by restrictions on hiring nationals of the Axis countries.[17] The new dispositions prompted the associate director of the bank, Julio Novoa, to ask Kikutake to obtain a written authorization from the Ministry of the Interior to work at Banco General. In November 1942, José Lelo de Larrea, chief of the Departamento de Investigación Política y Social, wrote a letter to Banco General de Capitalización stating that a search into Flora Kikutake's records had produced no criminal "charges" against the *expresada señorita*."[18] Lelo de Larrea did not object, consequently, to her employment at the bank. In a period of hardship and unemployment for many Mexicans, and particularly for Mexican Japanese persons, Flora Kikutake was fortunate enough to have a job that seemed secure and comfortable. Yet, the war would take its toll on Kikutake's life.

Kikutake's Spanish vocabulary and grammar reflected her formal education and her middle-class status, favorable factors in presenting her case. She conveyed in her letters to Julio Novoa her anguish as well as her remorse in a dignified manner, stating that she had no accomplices and that she would repay in small installments the amount in question. The young woman promised to notify the bank of her new employment information to calculate a reasonable deduction from her future paycheck to cover her debt. "I recognized that these were the least honorable means through which I [could obtain the money] but my desire to bring my son to Mexico before the situation worsens in Japan was the reason that forced me to proceed in this way."[19]

Kikutake acknowledged both her duty to her employer and her responsibility to take care of her child. The owners of the bank decided not to press charges against Flora Kikutake, but they notified the DIPS about the conditions of her dismissal. Both the bank and the DIPS officers elected to avoid harsh punishment for Kikutake's actions, anticipating that she would repay the amount improperly appropriated.[20] Kikutake's technical training as a clerk made her reliable and the expectations to repay the amount were reasonable given her employability. Furthermore, in view of the state of war and under the conditions of the relocation program, Kikutake could not leave the city or the country. To ensure that she would remain in sight, the DIPS officials were notified of the arrangements. No more correspondence was filed in Flora's chart until almost one year later when, in September 1944, the DIPS chief ordered inspector Mercedes Ramírez Mendoza, the only female official registered in this institution's archives, to investigate her.

Inspector Ramírez visited Flora Kikutake's home and reported on the conditions and activities of the Japanese Mexican woman. She was a "humble" working woman who took care of her mother when at home: "The furniture is old, without luxuries, better described as humble. She lives in the company of her mother, I was informed that she works for the enterprise managing the Metropolitan Movie Theater."[21] The research Inspector Ramírez undertook reflects the "in-between" state addressed by Gloria Anzaldúa when theorizing on Nepantla. Ramírez interrogated some neighbors of Kikutake, collecting details on the Japanese Mexican woman's routine. The DIPS officer obtained most of her information from a Gonzalo Novelo M., who lived in front of Kikutake's apartment and who provided an exhaustive report on Flora's daily life. "[Mr. Novelo] informed me that she carries a decent life, she has not made any friendship with other renters [in the building], generally stays awake until very late at night, her boyfriend visits her, between twelve and one in the morning she has brothers and currently they are fighting on the side of the Japanese Government, but that she eludes any conversation about the War."[22]

Inspector Ramírez and Kikutake's neighbor Novelo did not find definitive proof of Kikutake's involvement in espionage or sabotage activities. Novelo insinuated, however, that Kikutake was part of a pro-Axis group, and he reported Kikutake's visits to a Japanese Mexican dentist who, according to Novelo, had "made [Axis] propaganda by giving free consultations."[23] Ramírez wrote her own impression of Kikutake, whom the inspector deemed "de apariencia decente, culta," and who had mastered the Spanish language to perfection. Although Kikutake had resided in Mexico since her early childhood, "she still kept an oriental look" in her adulthood, according to Ramírez.[24] Whatever Ramírez's idea of oriental was, in her view, Kikutake could not be defined as a westerner; therefore, Flora remained in the Nepantlian in-between space described by Anzaldúa in spite of her education and long residence in Mexico.[25]

Ambiguity, as well as the threat of displacement, permeated Flora's relationships with other Mexicans. Kikutake's neighbor and Inspector Ramírez insisted on describing Flora as "decente" but not to be entirely trusted, a claim that could result in Flora's internment or deportation. Novelo reported that he used to hear suspicious noises coming from her radio at about four o'clock, and then he proceeded to state that such noises could have been the product of his imagination caused by the "distrust that this kind of persons inspired him."[26] To conclude her report, the DIPS inspector wrote that Gonzalo Novelo gave her his business card and volunteered to keep close watch on Kikutake, taking note of her guests and the hours she received visitors at her apartment. Although under surveillance, and in spite of her neighbor's ill-founded insinuations of involvement in pro-Axis activities, Kikutake was able to continue her life employed at a theater in Mexico City to support her mother.[27]

Flora Kikutake Yahiro's predicament reveals the complexity of interracial gender relations as well as aspects of the gendered criminalization of Japanese Mexicans during the global conflict generated by capitalist expansion. Flora occupied a highly ambiguous social place, which represented a challenge for classification: even when she was a mother of a child, officials granted her the "honorable" title of señorita. Flora's ties to Japan were evident in the residence of her son in that country as well as the continuous visits to her Japanese acquaintances and friends. Nevertheless, her education and aspirations to become a professional in Mexico and to bring her son to her side tell us of her desire to live permanently in this country. We can even assume that her reported boyfriend was Mexican, as his racial classification was not cited by the police officer or Flora's neighbor. A member of a group considered "alien enemy" in Mexico, Kikutake was employed in clerical jobs that required the trust of her employers; she was the provider at her home, supporting her mother, a role reserved for men; and though her economic situation was precarious, and her fraud placed her in a socially disadvantageous position, her supervisor and the police officer treated her with the respect middle-class women command in Mexico. Yet her neighbor and a police officer considered her a foreigner not to be entirely trusted. Unlike the usual patriarchal procedures of gathering all information on women and children under the male head of each family, the DIPS officials opened a file for Kikutake because she was not officially associated with a man, unlike most Japanese Mexican women. Flora had no husband, brother, or son in Mexico.

Flora Kikutake's appearance was the only argument her neighbors and police had for rejecting her as a Mexican woman. Despite her status as a racialized single woman in a patriarchal world, Kikutake countered orientalist notions through her economic class, profession, skills, and demeanor, which fitted the idea of a modern citizen, a desirable trait fostered by the government of Mexico during this period, favorably affecting Flora's situation. Her cultural mestizaje shaped the complex perception that Mexicans held of Flora. She was a foreigner, but she was Mexicanized through her dominion of the Spanish language, her middle-class lifestyle, and her adherence to the norms of Mexican society that rendered her "decente."

Differential Gendered Treatment

The decision of the DIPS and bank officials not to legally prosecute Flora Kikutake stands in contrast with the harsh prosecution and incarceration suffered by Japanese Mexican men. Mexican officials punished Japanese Mexican men for crimes ranging from protesting their living conditions at the concentration camp to changing address without obtaining permission from the DIPS. Men suffered, in general, more violent forms of control than women during World War II.[28] Miguel L. Yshida, for example, was incarcerated in Perote in September 1942 after being arrested in the company of his father at Agua Caliente, in the state of Chihuahua. Yshida was Mexican by birth, and his main crime, according to DIPS inspector R. Candiani, was speaking "perfectly Japanese and because he perfectly mastered our language," he could serve as a messenger between Mexican and Japanese Mexican communities.[29] State officials did not try Miguel Yshida in court to prove he was guilty of espionage but ordered his incarceration based on his ability to speak Spanish, in contrast with the official praise of Flora Kikutake's linguistic skills.[30] Inspector Candiani, of Italian descent, thought that when Japanese Mexican men answered questions with "sagacidad" and demonstrated "cultura," the Mexican state had enough evidence of sabotage and espionage activities to warrant the incarceration of such intelligent Japanese Mexican men.[31] Similar to Flora Kikutake, Miguel Yshida was in the process of being "completely" Japanese, Mexican, or Japanese Mexican, depending on the view of those who appraised his cultural citizenship. Notably, Candiani's freedom and status as a government agent deciding Yshida's criminality attest to the racist character of the Japanese Mexican program. The Mexican government did not order the eviction in mass of Italian and German immigrants or their descendants from the borderland and coastal zones. Inspector Candiani was therefore able to hold a position of power in the management of the Japanese Mexican community.

Since the Mexican police looked for signs of extraordinary skills to revile Japanese Mexican men, the victims of the displacement program sought to accentuate their normalcy and the ordinary but indispensable gendered function they had within their families. Jorge Sato, for example, invoked his role as head of his family, declaring that he was forced to abandon his wife and three children when the Mexican government ordered him to leave his home in Mexicali, Baja California: "As man and as father I ask you to consider allowing me to go to Baja California in order to reunite with my family since, I repeat, my children are minor and they cannot work yet and I cannot get a job here to support them."[32]

Japanese Mexican men insisted in their official letters that the economic sustenance of their household was derived exclusively from their work, although many Japanese Mexican women performed unpaid labor at home and at their family's small businesses.[33] Although the intent of Japanese Mexican men was to evoke the empathy of the Mexican officials who ordered their displacement, obliterating the equally important productive role of women in their families supported patriarchal values. In addition to emphasizing their role as providers, Japanese Mexican men volunteered to guard Mexican sovereignty, arguing that the defense of their country fell to the men in their homes: "Yo y mis hijos, aunque ellos no están en la edad militar, estamos dispuestos a empuñar las armas a la hora que la Patria lo solicite."[34] As Sato offered in his plea to remain at home, the men in his family were trained to be providers and protectors. By promising to take arms in the name of the nation, Sato was enforcing patriarchal notions endowing men with authority and power.

In tune with racist notions prevalent in the United States, among complex popular ideas in Mexico of Asian men was that Japanese men were a sexual threat to Mexican women and to their capability to reproduce.[35] In June 1942, *Revista Tiempo*, a magazine published in Mexico City, equivalent to *Time* magazine in the United States, published an article titled "Japs in Mazatlán."[36] The article, whose syntax is unorthodox in Spanish and thus seems to be a translation from English, attacked Dr. Toshio Shimizu. It is important to transcribe a large portion of the published text because of the innuendos, metaphors, and other tools the writer used to depict Dr. Shimizu as a strange, despicable human being:

> Dr. Toshio Shimizu is dedicated to the medical field. His specialty is obstetrics and, within this [medical] branch, premature births are a strong point [*sic*]. Japan is a prolific and overpopulated land. The strength of this country resides in its overpopulation. The expansive sense of Japanese politics is determined by the need to find land for so many human plants. Dr. Shimizu is a patriot. Even when he has become a Mexican national, his geographic love goes across the ocean and it is placed at the feet of the emperor. Mexico is a rich coveted land. The best a Japanese doctor in Mexico can do is to place his professional skills at the service of the imperial cause. And, after thinking a lot about it, Toshio Shimizu dedicated himself to make Mexican women abort. Every abortion meant one less enemy for Japan. Each abortion was an urgent need in the thinly populated country that gave him asylum. . . .
>
> Between the skillful fingers of Shimizu some Mexican generations disappeared. In the meantime, in his country, governments fomented the

increase in the birth rate and factories threw hundreds of thousands of yards of cloth to dress millions and millions of soldiers. . . .

At the same time Shimizu was winning the battle of births in Mazatlán and his chests were filled with gold. Each trace of a child who disappeared was translated into an amount of pesos that oscillated between 15 and 50. Then forty years passed. . . . Only Dr. Toshio Shimizu remains untroubled at home, his fingers trained for the abortions and his eye opened to calculate [how to make money].[37]

The magazine accused Dr. Shimizu of practicing abortions, which were illegal in Mexico, in an attempt to steer populace and officials against him. The Mexican state, however, did not try Dr. Shimizu in court for these charges or any others. Because there is no evidence in the DIPS files of accusations against Dr. Shimizu by other residents of Sinaloa, or in any other source researched, we can discount *Revista Tiempo*'s insidious article as a calumny (one that is discussed in more detail in chapter 6).

The notion that Asian men were more dangerous than women predates the onset of the war, but nationalists and opportunists revived racial prejudices based on gender during World War II. Crispín Ayala and J. Asunción Alba, members of the Unión de Comerciantes en Pequeño (Small Businesses Union), in León, Guanajuato, requested in October 1940 the investigation of Alfonso Ayshikawa and Carlos K. Yoshikai, accusing them of being spies paid by "Imperialism."[38] Ayala and Alba thought Ayshikawa and Yoshikai were "foreigners who try to humiliate us as Mexicans" through the alleged sexual abuse of Mexican women. Ayala and Alba believed that Mexican women embodied the honor of the nation and accused the Japanese Mexican men of violating it: "The innumerable group of young women who have rendered their services to these foreigners as modest employees . . . have been forced, because of their inexperience or needs, to fall into the claws of these pusillanimous [men], being victims of bestial appetites these beautiful Mexican women deserving of better luck."[39]

Ayala and Alba's intentions were to take over the property of the two Japanese Mexican businessmen. At the onset of World War II, Ayala and Alba escalated their accusations against Ayshikawa and Yoshikai, claiming that the Japanese Mexican men used women as "bait" to attract Mexican men to their businesses.[40] The letters some Mexicans wrote in defense of Japanese Mexican men attempted to counter this popular idea that Asian men in general sought to "dishonor" women through sexual relations. They insisted consequently on emphasizing the honorable character of their defendants recurrently, stating that the Japanese Mexican men they vouched for were family oriented, productive, and law abiding.[41] Nevertheless, during World War II most uprooted Japanese Mexican men were unemployed, partially employed, or employed in subservient positions that curtailed their capacity to provide for their families, diminishing their value in a patriarchal society that required men to be the breadwinners.[42]

Claiming national security reasons, the Mexican government denied gendered privileges to Japanese men during World War II; however, the history of racism in this country included orientalist contradictory views of Asian males, showing either a tendency to feminize them or a proclivity to make them appear as abnormal, dangerous sexual beings. Both notions supporting heteronormativity limited Japanese Mexican men's full enjoyment of rights attached to maleness in Mexico.

Un Pueblo Humilde, pero Fuerte en Unificación

If some aspects of the relocation program perpetuated a patriarchal system in Mexico, other elements of the same program opened the opportunity for some women to acquire a decisive role in representing their families and administering their possessions. Although Mexican culture dictated that the ideal space for women was home, many working-class women took up jobs, whether temporary and informal or permanent, to complement the salary of their husbands, or to provide entirely for their dependents. Yet, however extended the practice of working outside their homes, Mexican women did not see their social status increase when they performed productive roles. Family and financial matters as well as property stayed in the hands of their husbands, when married.[43] Before World War II, such was the arrangement within Japanese Mexican families. In 1942, husbands, parents, and sons obeyed orders to leave their homes in the borderlands, seeking difficult-to-obtain employment in the interior of Mexico. The women in borderland Japanese Mexican communities then took on more assertive roles as heads of households.[44]

The case of Margarita Fude Jorita de Kawano—who did not have a file of her own at the DIPS—illustrates other gender dynamics taking place during World War II. Mrs. Fude de Kawano saw her husband and oldest son leave for Mexico City in 1942, with lamentable consequences for her whole clan. In July 1942, authorities removed Margarita Fude de Kawano's husband, Manuel (Tosita Masato) Kawano, and her son Manuel Guillermo Kawano Fude from Portugués de Gálvez, a municipality of Navojoa, Sonora. Both men were naturalized Mexican citizens.[45] In her struggle to keep her family's residence in Sonora, Mrs. Fude de Kawano acknowledged with clarity, in a letter addressed to the minister of the interior, that the relocation program had been implemented "after the Government of this great and noble country had to comply with its international agreements," committing the nation to uproot Japanese Mexicans, but when ordered to leave her town along with her son and her husband, she would not follow presidential orders. Manuel Kawano was gravely ill when ordered to abandon his home. On his arrival in Mexico City, his condition worsened, and he was admitted to the Huipulco Sanatorium. Not only was the fifty-nine-year-old man's appeal to return to his family denied, but the DIPS officers insisted on expelling his wife from Sonora along with their children.[46]

Margarita Fude de Kawano's resistance to the relocation program was not limited to a passive act of civil disobedience. She actively opposed her relocation orders, gathering the support of at least 175 Mexican residents of Portugués de Gálvez, "un pueblo humilde, pero fuerte en unificación" (a humble town but strong in its unity), which assertively resisted the relocation program, as many other Mexican communities did. To obtain the sympathy of federal officials, the signatories used the official discourse that highlighted acceleration in production through the application of male labor.[47] They stated that by requesting Mr. Kawano's return to his original town, they were following the orders of President "General Manuel Ávila Camacho who recommends MORE PRODUCTION" as the hallmark of masculinity and warfare.[48]

The message from the pueblo did not initially affect the stance of the officials in charge of the relocation program. Margarita was forced to continue fighting the Ministry of the Interior orders to leave Sonora immediately. She appealed, like other affected Japanese Mexicans, to the notion of family as the basic unit of the nation. In a letter to President Ávila Camacho, she stated her circumstances:

> To avoid forcing this family into ruin and misery, even more when my children and my grandchildren are children of this fortunate country, for which certainly tomorrow, when they learn this just determination you are taking, and that I hope to deserve, they will apply themselves with more strength to be useful to a country where they not only saw the first light, but in which its officials, models of human responsibility, were kindly and legitimately fair, of elevated principles and unblemished charity.[49]

Either the DIPS officials realized that the Kawano family would live under severe financial stress if forced to travel to or live in Mexico City or the bureaucrats were impressed by the support the family received from their community. The Ministry of the Interior granted an extension of ten days for Margarita to leave town.[50] After several extensions, the final decision arrived on December 30, 1942: Margarita Fude de Kawano could stay in Sonora permanently. Yet her family continued to face serious difficulties. The children did not get to see their father ever again: Manuel Kawano died in Mexico on March 3, 1943, from a kidney condition.[51]

Despite the state's harassment, Margarita and her daughters were able to manage their business. DIPS agent Molina visited their town to verify that Margarita Fude de Kawano's operations were legal and ethical. He observed that "this family is mostly composed by women born in Navojoa who work to support themselves and it is obvious that they do not abuse any [employee] or make improper profits."[52] Notwithstanding women's capability to operate businesses and work in agricultural fields, among other occupations, Mexican society at large continued to view idealized women's main function in society as mothers and housekeepers. The idea of women as domestic human beings affected the official decision to allow Margarita Fude de Kawano and her daughters to stay at home. DIPS Inspector Molina considered Mrs. Kawano inoffensive in the absence of a male head of household; thus, the Mexican state did not enforce the relocation orders in her case. In contrast, among complex popular ideas in Mexico of Asian men was the notion that they were a threat to national security and cultural values; therefore, the relocation and confinement of Japanese men was, in most instances, mandatory.[53] Facing the prospect of losing a significant portion of their income, some Mexican women refused to divide their families. They left their homes to follow their Japanese Mexican husbands or sons when unsuccessful in their effort to cancel the relocation orders.[54]

Mexican women married to men of Japanese origin were more willing than Japanese Mexican women to express their opinion about the injustice of the relocation program during World War II. They were Mexican nationals by birth, and their indigenous/Spanish mestizaje made them feel entitled to the protection of a state, which claimed that mestizos were the pillars of the nation. One of the most provocative messages addressed to the minister of the interior came from the pen of Herlinda Cruz de Yanagui, a woman from Rosario, Sinaloa. Herlinda Cruz's letters submitted on behalf of her husband reflect her political awareness: "I remember that Mexico paid Spain three centuries of slavery by providing hospitality to many Spanish children [brought by President Cárdenas as refuges from the civil war]. To England and the United States, a whole history of grave mistakes [our country has paid] with the effective help [we provide to those countries] taking a toll on our wealth and that of our children. That is how my mother country has paid all the injuries suffered in her rights."[55]

Herlinda claimed her citizenship status and that of her children to assert her right to denounce the effects of Spanish, British, and U.S. imperialism over Mexico. She demanded a uniform policy of hospitality and forgiveness from her government and underlined the feminine quality of her nation, invoking family values and the need of a man in each household to support his wife and children: "Why not allow today our husbands to return to our side, to give their love and support to our children? I ask you in the name of my motherland, in the name of my children, I believe that not all these men are guilty of this situation, that many of them live apart, distant from any issues stemming from the war."[56]

Herlinda Cruz was not alone in the struggle to free a loved one from the effects of the relocation program.[57] Other women affected by the program were also vigilant and kept themselves informed of all news concerning their situation, using it to write letters to the authorities in hopes of freedom for their husbands, brothers, or sons. Trinidad Rodríguez demanded the return of Senator Kamura in 1944 when she heard the news that "the Citizen President of the Republic signed a decree stating that any foreign persons with more than 5 years of residence in the country must be considered a national."[58] Rodríguez had proof that her husband had fulfilled and exceeded the length of residency required to keep his Mexican citizenship and submitted such proof to the minister of the interior without any positive result.[59]

Lack of effective political power and anti-Asian historical processes, not passiveness or ignorance, curtailed the efforts of women to demand the return of their husbands and sons during World War II and afterward. The wives, sisters, mothers, and daughters of displaced Japanese Mexican men took public spaces that were not ordinarily theirs and organized their resistance against the relocation program. As activists, women who were part of Japanese Mexican families mobilized other citizens to protest relocation. This was no small deed in view of the state of war that demanded complete adherence to the nation's projects. When challenging national policies, or convincing other men and women to sign petitions to cancel government orders, Mexican wives of Japanese immigrants functioned as cultural brokers between their husbands and children and the communities who received them. Japanese Mexican cultural and interracial mestizas lived in at least two cultural places and, as borderlanders, understood the specific patriarchal social codes and expectations of the dominant society operating in Mexico: they skillfully deployed notions of mestizaje and mexicanidad to attempt to cancel social injustice.

Navigating Three Cultures

In searching for appropriate methodologies to study immigration processes, pioneer scholar Sucheng Chan asserts the importance of analyzing the creation and maintenance of cultural, political, and economic networks across national borders. Eiichiro Azuma has critiqued the casual use of transnationalism, emphasizing cultural trans-Nationalism, which highlights hybridity. In addition, Azuma calls for the analysis of structural-based trans-National processes, underscoring global capitalist processes in the creation of new social relations. Azuma focuses on the "strategies of assimilation, adaptation, and ethnic survival [that] took shape through the (re)interpretation, but not repudiation, of the bounded identity constructs" of both Japan and the United States. Azuma's strategy is appropriate to examine Issei and Nisei generations in the United States of the twentieth century; however, the level of miscegenation allowed in Mexico, and the intervention of at least three different cultural and political systems in their lives, directs me to identify distinct processes characterizing adaptation, integration, and resistance to oppression in the United States–Mexico borderlands.[60]

During the period preceding World War II, children of Asian immigrants in Mexico, particularly those whose mothers were Mexican, represented a kind of mestizaje that departed from the official national identity. This hybridism demanded the reorganization of the notion of "otherness" and introduced new social tensions and possibilities in the dynamics of racial relations in the borderlands. Thus, Japanese Mexicans in this area created hybrid forms of cultural identification that challenged hegemonic ideas of nationality, citizenship, and mestizaje. Furthermore, the social fabric that borderlanders of Japanese descent wove across borders further helped them to soften the social and political limits dividing racialized communities in the U.S.-Mexico borderlands region.

Despite the degree of agency that members of the Japanese Mexican community had in the creation of their images and their sexual and cultural practices, the dichotomies imposed over the bodies of mestizas and mestizos in terms of gender, race, and sexuality have been painful and costly. While Anzaldúa recovers some aspects of the celebration of the "raza cósmica" and calls for the recognition of Spanish/indigenous mestizaje as a powerful force to transform racial relations in the borderlands, it is important to acknowledge and politicize other hybridisms that are forced by global economic projects.[61] As the Mexican women and men who resisted the displacement of their Japanese friends and relatives have proved, the conscious acceptance of multiracial identities opens the possibility to form stronger community coalitions against racism, sexism, and economic exploitation.

In their efforts to counter the effects of World War II, Japanese Mexican men and women altered normative gender roles to accommodate state, family, and individual agendas. The multiple experiences reflected in this book indicate how fluid and intricate notions of gender affected the status of Japanese Mexicans from 1942 to 1945. Sometimes the victim would pursue change to ameliorate conditions. At other times the state, as victimizer, pursued changes to promote its interests even when disrupting traditional notions of family, thus destroying patriarchal relations through the displacement of the heads of family. In either case, Japanese Mexican women and men endured systematic discrimination along gender, race, and class lines in spite of their adaptation to new gender roles. The historical impact of their economic and cultural contributions, often unregistered in the official narratives, is discussed in the next chapter.

The Formation of Japanese Mexican Communities in the U.S.-Mexico Borderlands before World War II

Early Immigration

The presence of Japanese immigrants in Mexico and the United States before World War II was the product of changes in the global economy and the expansion of capitalism. Since the end of the sixteenth century, imperialist Spain had connected Asia with the American continents, facilitating contact through commercial routes with China and Japan, mainly through its Manila galleons.[1] Despite the resistance of Japanese rulers to the religious missions of Spanish Jesuits in Japan, a group of Japanese envoys arrived in 1614 in Acapulco aboard a ship christened *San Juan Bautista*. Their objective was to assess the possibility of expanding business relations with Spain and its colonies. Pressured by the news of anti-Christian policies in Japan, Japanese men in the diplomatic group requested baptism in Mexico City. In the face of religious violence, Japanese Catholics saw Spanish colonies as a refuge.[2]

The treatment of Japanese immigrants in colonial Mexico fluctuated according to historical conditions. Individual social status varied with international economic and political processes and their corresponding racial hierarchies. The Spanish conquest of the Philippines in the sixteenth century determined the subaltern position of their indigenous peoples as well as that of Chinese immigrants and their descendants in those islands. Other Asians, however, arrived in New Spain through the Philippines. Maritimal contact and exchange took place through the annual trip of a galleon departing from Acapulco since 1565.[3] According to Edward Slack, slaves who had been shipped since the seventeenth century from "India, the Malay Peninsula, Japan, and China," as well as free persons, were very visible in New Spain and indistinctly referred to as chinos. The importance of Asian artisans, merchants, laborers, sailors, and slaves in New Spain colonial society is illustrated by the laws that intended to limit their social mobility as well as the organized anti-Chinese movement formed in early seventeenth century. In 1635, criollos already sought to ban the practice of chino barbers in Mexico City functioning as medical care providers. Japanese immigrants were not specifically mentioned in the anti-Asian campaign rhetoric in New Spain, perhaps because they were considered chinos, included by default in the anti-Chinese claims.[4]

Researcher Thomas Calvo interprets the relative financial success of certain Japanese persons in colonial and postcolonial Mexico as an indication of their status as honorary whites.[5] Yet, the Spanish racial hierarchy barred Japanese mestizos from social and economic places exclusively assigned to Spaniards and criollos.[6] The protection that the Japanese state could and desired to extend to Japanese residents of New Spain became difficult to invoke with the rejection of Catholicism in Japan. Furthermore, Japanese emigration was officially banned starting in 1638, when the Tokugawa dynasty decided to close its borders, considering it a capital crime. Only when Japan became engaged in the global economic marketplace, competing with European and American industries and their attendant capitalist and colonial model, did the nation lift emigration restrictions in 1865.[7]

Transnational Capital in Need of Laborers

Among Japanese immigrants to the American continents there were middle-class intellectuals, students, and entrepreneurs; however, Japanese immigrants in the U.S.-Mexico borderlands at the end of the nineteenth century arrived primarily to supply the labor American companies required on both sides of the international border. To examine the history of Japanese Mexicans, it therefore necessary to look at immigration and transcultural processes on both sides of the border and to attend to international issues affecting Japanese Mexican status.[8]

American investors considered Asian immigrants easy to manage and a temporary, disposable labor force. The first groups of such Japanese immigrants in North America did not establish themselves in the borderlands initially. U.S. companies with interests outside the United States imported most Japanese as contract laborers to the companies' Hawaiian and Mexican plantations. Although Hawaiian sugar plantations started hiring Japanese men in 1865, it would be another forty-two years before Japanese immigrants arrived in Mexico.[9]

The international labor market was not entirely exploitative. Japanese men saw several advantages in migrating to work in the United States and in Mexico. The promise of earning higher wages and returning to Japan in three or four years with their savings was attractive, although low salaries made it almost impossible to fulfill their initial plans. Different working conditions, social expectations, and laws in Mexico and in the United States would transform their lives significantly—their sexuality, growing families, mobility on the economic ladder, citizenship rights, and interracial relationships. In Mexico's borderland, Japanese immigrants found fewer legal restrictions but not a life free from racism; anti-Asian attitudes targeted them and made them vulnerable. In the United States, their low social status was more evident and legally sanctioned.[10]

The first emigration publicly supported by the Japanese state in the nineteenth century comprised thirty-four Japanese immigrants. They arrived in Chiapas, Mexico, in 1897 to establish a coffee plantation and a colonizing mission linked to Japan's imperialist plans. Although the immigrants' personal agendas may have differed from those of the Japanese state, Japanese officials expected this and other colonies on the North American continent to be a prosperous extension of Japan, eventually contributing to the economy of the metropolis. As a show of their support for the colonists, the Japanese government created the Sociedad Colonizadora Japón-México to provide colonists with loans and land.[11]

Japanese and Mexican officials treated the pioneering Japanese sojourners with great respect. They referred to them as colonists, not as immigrants, and the Japanese government selected the members of the commercial adventure in Mexico according to their skills in agriculture. The newly arrived Japanese technicians, however, found it difficult to establish themselves in land that had not been cleared or developed. After some failed attempts at producing coffee, the Sociedad Colonizadora Japón-México stopped financing the colonists' effort to establish a plantation in Chiapas. The colony lost all opportunities to recover its costs from the failed enterprise when the Japanese administrators suspended payment for the land, which was then repossessed by the Mexican government. Disheartened, nine Japanese colonists returned to their country of origin.[12]

The twenty-five Japanese men who remained in Mexico formed a second cooperative, Compañía Japonesa Mexicana, in 1901. Marriage to

Mexican women and the resulting mestizaje of their children solidified their relationships with their receiving communities. The social services they provided for their communities also assisted their integration into Mexican local societies. In rural Mexico, where medical care and other government services were almost nonexistent, the cooperative provided free medicine, paid for the construction of bridges, and funded schools.[13]

The characteristics of Japanese immigrants in Mexico would change in the following years. As the pioneers established themselves in the Mexico-Guatemala borderlands, other groups of Japanese men were traveling to the U.S.-Mexico border. The new cohorts of immigrants would receive different treatment; the Japanese and Mexican states were not as interested in their welfare as they were in that of the Chiapas colonists because these subsequent waves of immigrants were contract laborers, belonging to an economic class that did not have important leverage in Mexico or Japan.[14]

In the U.S.-Mexico borderlands, American companies had already been importing Chinese immigrants as contract laborers to work in the railroad, mining, and agricultural sectors since the 1840s, and their treatment of the Japanese workers would not be different.[15] Chinese immigrants faced increasing restrictions: segregation, fines, taxes, and physical harm aimed to curtail their economic prosperity. When the United States passed the Immigration Act of 1882 (also known as the Chinese Exclusion Act), prohibiting the entry of Chinese workers into the country, U.S. industrialists were already hiring Japanese transmigrants from Hawaii, but now they started to import Japanese contract laborers to substitute, in part, for Chinese workers, as they also did in Mexico.[16]

American investors dominated the Mexican industry and altered the demographic composition of northern Mexico with the introduction of Chinese, African American, and European American workers during the last two decades of the nineteenth century. Protected by dictator Porfirio Díaz, U.S. capitalists aggressively took over livestock, mining, timber, and plantations in Mexico, displacing Mexican entrepreneurs and landowners. By the end of the nineteenth century, Americans owned between 22 and 27 percent of the Mexican landholdings. American mining companies invested $120 million between 1902 and 1907, channeling more than 57 percent of this capital to northern Mexico's mines.[17] As their co-nationals did in California, Japanese immigrants arrived in Mexico's borderlands along with Chinese men to supply some of the labor U.S. companies required during the Porfiriato.[18]

U.S. capitalists and their British competitors in the U.S.-Mexico borderlands expected Asian workers to have minimal needs to cover. Married employees would need adequate housing, schools for their children, and medical care for their families, increasing the costs of labor. Consequently, companies operating in Mexico imported single men from China and Japan.[19] Funded with American capital and operating under the advice of U.S. experts, the henequen industry in the Yucatán Peninsula imported more than a thousand Korean immigrants under slavelike conditions in 1905. Unlike their Chinese and Japanese counterparts, Korean laborers brought their families with them. They shared with other Asian immigrants the burden of the peonage system.[20] A total of 11,000 Japanese immigrants entered Mexico between 1901 and 1907, of which 8,706 were contract laborers or imported workers who agreed to work for a fixed salary and number of years before seeking employment anywhere else.[21]

Japanese contract laborers in North America faced heavy restrictions on their geographic and social mobility. They did not have enough money to pay for their travel expenses, back or forth. They often received a loan to pay for their ticket to the North American continent, signing contracts for up to four years, and they were not free to look for better salaries at other places to pay their debt at an earlier date.[22] By 1910, 4,407 Japanese men traveled to Mexico under labor contracts with U.S. and British companies operating sugar plantations in the southern region of Mexico, particularly Oaxaca and Veracruz. Another 3,000 Japanese workers were hired to work in the coal mine of La Esperanza in Coahuila. An additional group of 500 immigrants was hired at the coal mine of El Boreo in Baja California in 1904. Between 1906 and 1907, the American Central Railroad Company hired 1,400 Japanese laborers to work in Colima. They also migrated to northern Mexico when the construction of the railway line ended.[23]

Between Mexico and the United States

Working conditions in mines, on plantations, and on railroads were harsh and unhealthy. Low wages, dust, heat, accidents, long working days, and diseases were incentives for workers to break their contracts and look for a way to cross the border to the United States.[24] Japanese contract labor immigrants in Peru found the same harsh environment. Some of them migrated to Mexico before 1910, with the hope of eventually moving to the United States to earn higher wages.[25] While Japanese men earned $0.50 (pesos) a day in Mexico, they could earn $1.35 (dollars) in the United States in the agricultural fields near Los Angeles, California. Consequently, they crossed into Nuevo Laredo, El Paso, and Piedras Negras to reside in the United States as "illegal migrants."[26]

Japanese migrant workers earned higher salaries in the United States, but they met a harsher racial system in their new places of residence. As in other Asian communities in North America, Japanese men and women faced legal obstacles to their integration into the larger society, as laws in the United States promoted racial segregation, impeded interracial marriages, and made Japanese and other people of color ineligible to become citizens. To combat economic oppression along racial lines, Japanese and Mexican workers formed the Japanese Mexican Labor Association (JMLA) in 1903, which successfully staged a strike against the Oxnard beet business in that year.[27]

Although collaboration between Japanese and Mexican laborers proved beneficial, Chinese and Japanese workers had failed to form, in general, a united front against racial economic oppression in the United States by the first years of the twentieth century. In the previous century, they had fought for resources, competing against each other for employment in the railroad, mining, lumber, and agricultural industries. According to historian Roger Daniels, Japanese laborers in Santa Clara, California, would accept fifty cents per hour when Chinese workers received one dollar. This competition would end after the 1882 Chinese Exclusion Act made replenishing the Chinese labor force very difficult. Eventually, the Chinese population declined further due to death, sickness, and age and stopped being important competition for Japanese workers. On their part, a constant flow of Japanese immigrants from Hawaii and Japan increased their number in the continental United States at the end of the nineteenth century. Japanese laborers began to demand higher wages once Chinese laborers were almost completely displaced in California, improving Japanese workers' quality of life to the extent that racist laws would allow it.[28]

Among those Japanese immigrants who had bettered their economic situation in the United States, some decided to acquire citizenship rights through naturalization. The Naturalization Act of 1790 stated that only white persons could become citizens, and Japanese applicants assumed they fulfilled this racial requirement. Because race is a fluid notion that is constantly negotiated and reconstructed, and diplomatic relations between Japan and the United States provided some degree of protection for Japanese naturalization applicants during this period, immigration officials classified 420 Japanese persons as white before 1906 and granted them U.S. citizenship. Social restrictions impeded actual assimilation of Japanese immigrants into larger society, however, and local laws deterred the formation of interracial families that could have ended the isolation of the Japanese communities in the United States.[29]

The sexual lives of Japanese immigrants in the borderlands were shaped by different factors and would eventually determine their degree of integration into the United States and Mexico. South of the border, Japanese women immigrants were almost nonexistent during this period; however, Japanese men did not suffer significant legal miscegenation restrictions. They were able to marry Mexican women or be temporary or permanent sexual partners in spite of the racial prejudice that made such unions challenging. By contrast, in the United States the prohibition for interracial marriages and the imbalance in the number of Japanese men and women made prostitution the main occupation of Japanese female immigrants at the end of the twentieth century.[30] Most of the 985 Japanese women living in the United States during this period worked temporarily or permanently as sex workers, as did many other immigrant women from Asia and Europe.[31]

Asian women sold sexual services to Asian male laborers for economic survival, but they also serviced the desires of other nonwhite and white men in the United States. According to historian Eithne Luibhéid, racist European American women and men saw sexual contact between Asian women and white men as a source of moral and physical sickness. Accordingly, the 1891 Immigration Act and the Page Law of 1875 aimed to protect allegedly pure white families and laborers from physical and moral contamination by prohibiting immigration of sex workers. Race, sex, sexuality, and criminality were intertwined, resulting in the legal exclusion of Asian women from the United States.[32]

Although U.S. scientists and the general public confined Japanese and Chinese to the same racial category, the Japanese state protected Japanese immigrants to a larger extent through diplomatic negotiations until the end of the nineteenth century. In 1906, the anti-Japanese riots in San Francisco and the placement of Japanese children in segregated schools signaled a new era of exclusion.[33] The Gentlemen's Agreement of 1907 between Japan and the United States forced the Japanese government to restrict issuing visas for travel to the United States. In Mexico, the government negotiated similar policies with Japan. To comply with the U.S. request to halt illegal entry from Mexico, the Japanese government stopped issuing travel documents for Mexico. Consequently, in 1908 the flow of immigrants from Japan to Mexico stopped completely, only to resume again in 1909. The same agreement, however, allowed the wives of Japanese men to enter the United States. Men who had the means to pay for the travel expenses of "picture brides" (fiancées selected with the help of photographs) were able to start a family in the United States, and the ratio of married Japanese women to men in the United States grew after 1907. In Mexico, Japanese women continued to constitute a very small percentage of the population.[34]

Revolution

The Mexican Revolution, started in 1910, reduced the number of Japanese residents in the country. They numbered 2,623 immigrants, of which only 167 were women. More than half of the Japanese persons established in Mexico lived in the northern borderland states of Sonora, Coahuila, and Chihuahua, whose mines and agricultural fields were devastated between 1910 and 1920.[35] Like other residents of Mexico, some Japanese immigrants crossed the border northward to find a refuge from violence in the United States. Other Japanese men in northern Mexico remained in the country to fight in the Revolutionary and federal forces during the military conflict, and a few of them were promoted to commissioned officers.[36]

Gary Y. Okihiro and David Drummond explain that legal impediments to the integration of Asian immigrants channeled Japanese and Chinese into a low-wage labor sector. When the Chinese Exclusion Act of 1882 settled the "Chinese problem," Japanese immigrants met with increasing resistance to their assimilation from white America, who saw them as the new Asian threat. The Japanese growers represented a loss of human capital for the largest agribusiness investors as well as competition for European American small farmers. Consequently, employers of Japanese workers, politicians, and small growers made possible the passing of the Alien Land Law of 1913, prohibiting persons ineligible for citizenship from owning property. To circumvent the provisions of this regulation, Japanese immigrants transferred their property to their children born in the United States. On both sides of the borderlands, however, Japanese immigrants and their descendants faced instability as they accommodated to different economic and legal environments during the first two decades of the twentieth century.[37]

In 1914, Japanese ambassador Shotuko Baba visited Mexico to find a solution for the troubles Japanese immigrants were experiencing as a result of the Mexican Revolution. In the midst of the conflict, groups belonging to the various Revolutionary factions or to the federal army took Japanese immigrants' property and lives. Ambassador Baba's objective was to obtain a temporary permit for Japanese to reside in the United States until the end of the Revolution. Enforcing the exclusionary provisions of the Gentlemen's Agreement, the U.S. government refused to grant visas. The Japanese diplomat thus negotiated a contract for a group of Japanese men to work in American-owned cotton plantations in the Baja California peninsula, a relatively isolated area of northern Mexico.[38]

Alongside farming, fishing became an important economic activity in the Baja California peninsula for Japanese immigrants. During the 1910s Japanese entrepreneur Seiji Kondo, whose fishing company was based in San Diego, California, hired Mexican employees and brought fishermen from Japan to catch and pack tuna and abalone in Ensenada. The upheaval of the Mexican Revolution allowed Kondo's Japanese employees to enter Mexico without being documented by immigration officers.[39] In January 1912, two Japanese residents of the United States attempted to buy two thousand acres in Baja California, eliciting the public disapproval of Mexican and American politicians. Based on the hemispheric security principles of the Monroe Doctrine, the United States demanded the annulment of any effort by Japanese to acquire large extensions of land in Mexico. The affair confirmed in Mexico the notion that Asian immigrants were not entitled to exercise control over Mexican resources.[40]

Certain political moves by the leaders of the Revolution shaped once again the demographic characteristics of the Japanese community in Mexico. President Venustiano Carranza sought to exterminate the Revolutionary forces of leftist generals Francisco Villa and Emiliano Zapata. To face his enemies, Carranza needed to buy armament and the favor of the U.S. government; thus, some American corporations operated in Mexico in relative safety under the protection of Carranza's government. Gradually, Japanese immigrants found work at U.S. companies in Sonora and Sinaloa that supplied cotton and other products for the U.S. Army during World War I.[41]

In 1917, Carranza's political decisions affected the Japanese community in Mexico through a bilateral agreement with Japan accepting licensed Japanese medical doctors, dentists, pharmacists, obstetricians, and veterinarians to practice in Mexico.[42] Signed when the Mexican Revolution had not concluded, the treaty reflected his decision to keep an avenue open for the purchase of armament through Japan and allowed for the diversification of occupations within the Japanese Mexican community.[43]

Despite the introduction of professional immigrants in Mexico, nationalist activism imposed more limits to the assimilation of Japanese Mexicans and the exercise of their rights, affecting mainly working-class Japanese Mexicans. In 1919, President Carranza modified article 106 of the labor law. The new provisions established that naturalized citizens were not considered nationals under the law that regulated labor in Mexico; therefore, they were not entitled to its protection.[44] In consequence, Japanese Mexicans found it more attractive to work in their own businesses, even when their profits were minimal, because they could not enjoy the nominal benefits and stability of the nationalist labor laws.

Distinct racist legal frameworks continued to operate in the northern Mexican borderlands at different levels. In 1921, a new law prohibited the entry of contract laborers, reducing the possibilities of poor Japanese workers to migrate to Mexico. Only investors or relatives and friends of already established immigrants received permits to migrate to Mexico.[45] In 1924, local regulations prohibited the marriage of Chinese men and Mexican women in Sonora.[46] Although directed to men of Chinese descent, the antimiscegenation law portrayed all Asian men in a negative light since Mexicans usually did not acknowledge any difference between Chinese and Japanese persons through a sinification process.[47]

At the end of the Mexican Revolution, scholars in Mexico of the caliber of philosopher and minister of education José Vasconcelos claimed that racial mixture was a positive aspect of the Mexican population. Discussions on Mexican mestizaje were, nevertheless, predicated on the belief that essential qualities characterized different human groups, therefore, that biological races did exist. In essence, Vasconcelos's theoretical structure was based on the possibility of racial progress and hierarchies; thus, underlying the concept of "raza cósmica" is the idea that certain European elements are superior and vital to the development of an allegedly improved race.[48]

José Vasconcelos introduced the concept of raza cósmica to praise the advantages of miscegenation; he believed, however, that it was "not fair that people like the Chinese who . . . multiply like mice, should come to degrade the human condition." Vasconcelos, in agreement with stereotypes formed in both the United States and Mexico, thought the "yellow race" was immersed in mystery and had a "strange angle" provided by their "slanted eyes."[49] The Mexican philosopher envisioned the ideal human being as a racially mixed individual with strong European characteristics, less noticeable indigenous features, and no visible traces of black or "mongol" heritage. Those Mexicans who did not form close ties with Asian immigrants or their children accepted dehumanizing stereotypes and considered Asian/Mexican mestizajes as unnatural.

In spite of the damages Japanese immigrants suffered during the Revolution, they persisted in their economic activities during the 1920s. In addition to cotton production in Sonora and Sinaloa, Japanese kept a strong presence in the fishing industry. The port of Ensenada intensified commercial activity during this period thanks to Japanese fishermen, who caught whale, shark, seal, turtle, lobster, shrimp, abalone, oyster, and many other maritime creatures and products. International commerce fanned out from this area, catering mainly to the North American, Chinese, and Japanese markets. Nonetheless, Japanese investors and their employees would have to look for other geographic areas or occupations once Mexican competitors claimed to have priority over foreigners.[50]

In the 1920s, members of the political elite who were also businessmen from northern Mexico or had strong connections with investors in the borderlands, saw certain Asian immigrants as their competitors. Furthermore, the civil war had resulted in extensive unemployment, which politicians and businessmen evoked to spur nativists against Asians. The immigrants became scapegoats for the deteriorating conditions of the working class.[51]

The nationalist fervor that ended up affecting Japanese immigrants was not exclusively a product of the Mexican Revolution. Anti-Asians in Mexico had a model in the racist legal system operating in their neighbor to the north and in the treatment of Chinese and Japanese workers by transnational companies.[52] The United States' main racialized target among Asians consisted of the Japanese immigrants who had taken advantage of the porosity of the U.S.-Mexico borderlands to improve their quality of life by crossing the border north or south.[53]

Defeating Binational Racism

Despite Japan's role as an ally of the Entente Powers against Germany during World War I, Japanese immigrants in the United States remained labeled as the "Yellow Peril." Alarming newspaper reports on the conspiracies of "Japs" to colonize areas of the United States and Mexico upheld tense racial relations in both countries. Sensationalist news also forced the Mexican ambassadors to assure the American public that no official support was given to Japanese colonization.[54] The exchange of racial ideas in the borderlands continued to affect Asians on both sides of the borders, and such American representations of Japanese must have contributed to the deployment of anti-Chinese organizations in Mexico. Mostly located in areas contiguous to the United States, these associations promoted murders, incarceration, and massive deportations. In 1921, they mobilized for a law to stop Chinese immigration, escalating their physical assaults on Chinese immigrants and their families. Sonoran president Álvaro Obregón not only supported but also extended the scope of the anti-Chinese movement, prohibiting the import of Asian contract labor in 1921. According to the new provisions, visa applicants needed to have an affidavit from relatives or friends in Mexico committed to supporting them. This was a difficult requisite for working-class Japanese immigrants: fewer than two hundred immigrants per year from Japan arrived in Mexico during the 1920s.[55] Japanese Mexican communities, nevertheless, were already rooted in the country.

Previous arrivals established stakes in borderland communities through the marriage of Japanese men to Mexican woman and also through their naturalization as Mexicans. Their children, the Nisei generation, had few ties with Japan in spite of the Japanese schools and associations in Sinaloa, Sonora, and Baja California that kept Japanese culture alive.[56] Economically, Japanese immigrants sought to gain a foothold in the country. Some Japanese fishermen saved enough money to buy their own boats and worked independently on a small scale in Baja California, Sonora, and Sinaloa. A number of farmers stopped working for wages and became tenant farmers in the same area, taking care of the land and tending to the stock and machinery of the mostly American landholders, who in exchange would allow them to use a portion of the land for themselves. Some Japanese tenant farmers, former U.S. residents, hired other Japanese and Mexican workers. By 1925, Japanese farmers cultivated 70 percent of the total land in Mexicali, Sonora. Most worked for the Colorado River Land Company in the cotton fields.[57] Japanese men also operated laundries and barbershops in the borderlands. Women and their children labored as unpaid workers to help keep these Japanese Mexican family small businesses running.[58] Frequently, Japanese men worked in partnership with their compatriots, sharing expenses in order to make their businesses prosper.[59]

On the U.S. side of the border, Japanese American families had also steadfastly established roots despite the laws and the racist climate restricting their social mobility. By 1919, Japanese farmers owned 74,769 acres through their children and leased an impressive 383,387 more in California, hiring Japanese and Mexican workers on their farms. The same year, gross income for their crops was valued at $67 million, or 10 percent of the total agricultural production in California.[60]

Although Japanese immigrants resided in various parts of the United States, they concentrated mainly in the West Coast in rural areas. In 1920, 45,414 Japanese men and 26,538 Japanese women lived in California. These numbers represented 70 percent of all Japanese immigrants in the United States. They resided mainly in the agricultural areas of Fresno, Sacramento, San Francisco, Alameda, and San Joaquin.[61] Almost a third of the Japanese population of California lived in Los Angeles County. Communities in other areas continued to experience rejection.[62]

The children of Japanese immigrants were growing up as Japanese Americans: like other youth of the diverse communities of color in the United States, second-generation ethnic Japanese had nominal citizenship rights and were exposed to the values and culture of the dominant society. But the social status of their parents and the laws sanctioning racial discrimination made citizenship of men and women of Japanese descent a second-class status. The issue of U.S. citizenship and race was eventually decided by the 1922 Supreme Court decision *Takao Ozawa v. United States*, which declared that Japanese were ineligible for U.S. citizenship through naturalization. The Supreme Court ruled that since Ozawa was neither a "free white person" nor an African by birth or descent, he did not have the right of naturalization as a "Mongolian."[63]

For the next two decades, European Americans continued to enforce their economic and social privileges through the application of local and federal laws. The complete integration of the first and second generation of Japanese in the United States was halted by the 1923 California Alien Land Law prohibiting Japanese immigrants from controlling the assets of their children or holding them in trust. Once again, they countered the effects of this racist law by hiring white American attorneys, who administered the land that Japanese immigrants or their children rented or owned. Several Japanese immigrants living in the Imperial Valley, however, crossed the border southward to invest in the agricultural sector in Baja California while keeping their residence in the United States. Others migrated from the United States to Baja California and Sonora permanently during this period.[64]

The presence of Japanese immigrants continued to be strong in Mexicali, across from Calexico, California. In 1925, more than one thousand Japanese men and women worked as tenant farmers or owned small shops in this city.[65] Japanese tenant farmers harvested two-thirds of the cotton production in the Mexicali area. Issei, first-generation Japanese Mexicans, maintained contact with the Japanese community of Imperial Valley, California, despite the United States' attempts to impede the entrance of Japanese immigrants. Hichiro Soejima, like other Japanese rejecting white supremacy, designed a settler colonization agenda in North Mexico. He acquired five hundred acres near Hermosillo, Sonora, bringing with him other Japanese remigrants from the United States. Soejima and another Japanese man were killed by a robber in 1928 during the anti-Chinese period in Sonora.[66]

In the 1930s, the prohibition against manufacturing, selling, importing, or exporting alcoholic drinks in the United States intensified the visits of U.S. residents to the Mexican borderlands for the purpose of consuming alcohol. By then, Japanese families in Mexicali owned restaurants, shops, barbershops, and brothels, and they benefited from the visit of American patrons. This particularly prosperous community of Japanese immigrants and their descendants managed to reproduce to a large degree their Japanese cultural practices, including family structure and hierarchies.[67]

Across the border in California, Japanese Americans continued to form a mostly rural population in the 1930s despite the vibrancy of cultural urban centers in San Francisco and Los Angeles. Fifty percent of the total population of Japanese men and 33 percent of the total population of Japanese women worked in the agricultural, lumber, and fishery sectors. Twenty-five percent of all the Japanese population worked in the wholesale and retail trade. Seventeen percent were employed in the personal service sector. A larger number of Japanese women than white women worked outside their homes during this period; however, many women worked in their family business without receiving a salary.[68]

Racial relations in the U.S.-Mexico borderlands were complex and often involved confrontations among nonwhite communities. In previous decades Japanese immigrants shared with Mexican workers common grievances against capitalists. Nevertheless, in the 1930s Japanese individuals and families had achieved higher economic status as tenant farmers, and their relationship with Mexicans changed. Japanese growers were under the pressure of their landholders, who continuously raised the rent on land. On the other side, Japanese tenant farmers hired Mexican and Mexican American workers to do most of the labor-intensive tasks. When Mexican workers demanded better wages, some Japanese employers faced organized labor with the same tactics white businessmen used to subdue the Mexican laborers: they called for the intervention of police and immigration officials to remove from their farms those considered communists or illegal. In addition to the support state institutions lent to Japanese growers, they relied on their own ethnic group to operate their businesses. Japanese farmers survived the 1933 El Monte Berry Strike thanks to the work of friends and relatives who arrived from different areas of California to substitute for Mexican protesters. Relatives continued to provide unpaid labor at all times, and in 1933 Japanese children stopped attending school to help on their parents' farms. In subsequent labor movements, some Japanese joined labor strikes, but other Japanese functioned as scabs, weakening the claims of Filipino and Mexican workers in the American Southwest.[69]

Japanese Mexicans vs. Mexican Nationalism

In addition to class conflicts, state miscegenation laws and the legal classification of Mexicans in California as "white" diminished the possibility of establishing deeper bonds between Japanese and Mexican men and women through the formation of interracial families in the United States. Furthermore, Japanese in communities in the United States tended to marry among themselves, and on both sides of the U.S.-Mexico border, Japanese men considered marriage to a Japanese woman a sign of prosperity and higher social status; however, U.S. and Mexican racial hierarchies held Japanese below whites regardless of their social class.[70]

National and international events affected Japanese communities in the Mexican borderlands in the 1930s. Prior to World War II, economic depression and the deportation of ethnic Mexicans from the United States raised the level of aggressive nationalist feelings and nativism for various reasons. Government officials and local racist groups attributed unemployment and lack of resources to the presence of Asian immigrants. The Third Migration Act responded to this anti-Asian wave. Formulated by President Pascual Ortiz Rubio in 1930, new regulations established "race" as a primordial element of assimilation and therefore as a category of exclusion in the case of Asian immigrants, since Mexicans considered them "exotic" agents of millenary cultures, unable to blend in Western societies.[71] Because immigration officials were endowed with the power to apply this new law at their discretion, some Asian immigrants were able to enter Mexico despite the new regulations, particularly when invited by a relative or friend, but also through the use of the traditional *mordida*, or bribe.[72]

If President Ortiz Rubio openly acknowledged race as an organizing social principle when signing the new immigration law, other policies he signed appeared to be color blind and formulated to strengthen the nation's economy by expulsing foreign interests. But the most severe effects of nationalism came in the form of land confiscation affecting Asian sharecroppers and tenant farmers. Ortiz Rubio approved in 1934 the agrarian reform acts to nullify the privileges of American, British, and French investors, whose exploitation of the Mexican working class had spurred the Mexican Revolution.[73] Once in power, the leftist president Lázaro Cárdenas enforced the agrarian reform law to redistribute land in Mexico among the peasant communities in the northeast.[74] Japanese tenants lost their investment when the land they rented changed hands before the harvest. Since the Compañía Industrial Japonesa del Pacífico lent them money to invest in farming, Japanese Mexicans had to struggle for several years to repay their debts when the Ministry of Agriculture forced them to vacate the land they were cultivating.[75]

The pressure from private and public sectors to marginalize "foreigners" of color in Mexico grew stronger as patriotism demanded that economic resources be in the hands of those regarded as Mexicans. The Liga Nacionalista Mexicana del Territorio Norte de Baja California (Nationalist Mexican League of the Territory of Baja California) campaigned to evict Japanese, Jewish, and Chinese persons from the peninsula. Some government officials also felt compelled to "protect" Mexico from what they considered an inferior race. Anti-Japanese activism actually had concrete results when Japanese Issei who owned property in Tijuana lost it in 1935 on the grounds that ownership of land within one hundred kilometers of the territorial limits of Mexico was forbidden to foreigners.[76]

Incidents of clandestine fishing helped nationalists to mount a campaign against all Japanese persons. Contravening Mexican laws that prevented foreign companies from fishing in national waters, both Japanese- and Anglo-owned ships registered in the United States would fish within Mexican territory and return to their base on the U.S. coasts. In 1940, in view of what they perceived as an assault on their rights, nationalist entrepreneurs pressed the federal government to remove the permissions granted to fishing companies and return control of the fishing industries to Mexican owners in the territory of Baja California and in the states of Sonora and Sinaloa.[77] In the same year, the Compañía de Productos Marinos fired Japanese fishermen and employed almost exclusively Mexican workers to comply with the regulations on hiring solely nationals. Out of work, Japanese fishermen were thus forced to fish independently on a small scale or to cultivate land as tenant farmers to support themselves. Before World War II, nationalist policies had economically damaged the most important Japanese Mexican communities, Ensenada and Mexicali. Unemployed fishermen and displaced growers sought to develop farmland or to open small businesses in other areas of the Baja California peninsula; however, most Japanese Mexicans did not have time to recuperate from their losses before World War II.[78]

World War II Arrives

By the onset of World War II, the Nisei generation continued to face racism in the United States, which translated to economic and social isolation. When trained in vocational schools, Japanese American men and women could work only in civil service. White-owned private companies and the military would not hire them; consequently, many second-generation Japanese Americans worked permanently in their family businesses. Segregation and limited career opportunities coexisted with a certain degree of financial success; Japanese American agricultural enterprises proved to be highly productive. In 1940 Japanese immigrants and their descendants operated 5,135 farms on 220,094 acres in California, with a value of $65.8 million, growing about 43 percent of the state's commercial truck crops.[79]

When President Franklin D. Roosevelt signed Executive Order 9066 mandating the internment of approximately 120,000 Japanese and Japanese Americans in concentration camps, this ethnic group was a large contributor to the agricultural development of the nation. As Japanese Americans entered the camps, the U.S. government made sure their interests in agriculture were mainly transferred to European American hands during World War II. Japanese immigrants and their descendants, however, were also employed in other industries and suffered great economic losses in both the United States and Mexico during wartime.[80]

Although Japanese Mexicans in the borderlands had integrated into their host communities through marriages, naturalizations, and businesses, they were as vulnerable in any social and economic crisis as Japanese Americans were in the United States. After the attack on Pearl Harbor, the Mexican government redefined patriotism to portray Japanese Mexicans as the enemies and the United States as the ally. On December 11, 1941, a group of blacklisted Japanese Mexicans received orders to abandon their homes in Baja California. On January 2, 1942, at the request of the U.S. State Department, all Japanese Mexicans in Baja California relocated to Guadalajara and Mexico City. During the following months, the Mexican government supervised the evacuation of approximately 2,700 Japanese immigrants from the U.S.-Mexico borderlands. A number of Japanese Mexicans were able to delay their relocation through bribery, the protection of powerful friends in various levels of the government, or surreptitious behavior, but most members of this vibrant community were uprooted by April 1942.[81] Because the United States was not interested in controlling the Mexico-Guatemala border area, the relocation program did not affect the Japanese Mexican residents of the southern borderlands in the same way. Some Japanese Mexicans in that region were able to remain in their original place of residence for the duration of the war without experiencing large losses in their lives.[82]

At the end of World War II, 50 percent of all Japanese Mexicans lived in Mexico City, and most of the remaining population resided in assigned zones in the interior of the country. Only a small number of those persons displaced during the war returned to northern Mexico, where demographics changed, and the memory of the Japanese Mexicans during the so-called Good War was almost lost.[83]

World War II extended the hand of the United States into Mexico to expel Japanese Mexicans from the borderlands in the name of national security for both countries. The facile compliance of the Mexican government and its enforcement of U.S. racial policies was a new chapter in Mexico's history. It had severe implications and results for Japanese Mexicans, and it is this story of "absent historical memory" that is very much in need of exploration.

CHAPTER THREE

The Impact of World War II and Hemispheric Defense on Border Communities

Much "modern" power in democratic societies is persuasive and manipulative rather than coercive.

—TEUN A. VAN DIJK

United States Military Forces on Mexican Soil

Unaware of the international agreements that dictated his coming arrest, Keiji Matsusaka, a Japanese Mexican merchant living in Ciudad Juárez, celebrated his son's birthday on March 15, 1942. The special occasion could help his family momentarily forget the hard times that Mexicans of Japanese origin were experiencing along the U.S.-Mexico borderlands. Suddenly, the local police interrupted the birthday celebration to arrest. Matsusaka and several other guests. As they left Matsusaka's home, the apprehended men realized that other soldiers surrounded the building. Among those persons detained was Dr. Tsunesaburo Hasegawa Araki, a Mexican national by naturalization and a prominent member of the ethnically diverse community, and Yoshio Sato, former president of the extinct Colonia Japonesa (Japanese Association). With the incarceration of these men at the local armory, the Japanese Mexican community in Juárez lost its cohesion and leadership and thus, the possibility to negotiate the terms of their relocation, if they ever had that opportunity.[1]

On March 16, several soldiers escorted Dr. Hasegawa from the armory to his home. Upon his arrival, this Mexican citizen of Japanese origin was ordered to assist the U.S. soldiers who had been trying without success to open Hasegawa's drawers. The search was not in the hands of the Mexican military. U.S. officials were also present at his home, and Douglas Henderson, the U.S. vice consul at Ciudad Juárez, directed the binational

49

military operation with the help of a translator. In addition, agents from the Mexican police, dressed as civilians, helped search Dr. Hasegawa's and fourteen other Japanese Mexican households.[2]

Mexican and American soldiers had joined in their hunt for items to substantiate allegations that Mexican Japanese were involved in acts of espionage and sabotage; nonetheless, they did not uncover definite proof of the existence of a Fifth Column in the borderlands.[3] The presence of U.S. military personnel on Mexican soil, exercising control over a group of civilians, was a strong signal that an enormous transformation in the relations between these two neighboring countries had occurred. The new coalition would have deep economic and political consequences for the United States, Mexico, and Japanese Mexicans.[4]

Strained Relationships

Presently, the alliance between the United States and Mexico during World War II seems a natural consequence of their decision to defend the world from expansionist powers. In 1941, however, the general Mexican citizenry deemed U.S. businesses and military forces as the largest threat to the integrity of the Mexican territory and sovereignty.

Japanese were aware of the history of conflicts between Mexico and the United States and deemed Mexicans more sympathetic to Japanese immigrants. Hisao Ito, arrested by U.S. soldiers during the March raid in Juárez, wrote in his memoirs that Japanese Mexicans had been grateful for the help they had received from many Mexicans during the process of establishing their new communities. Japanese immigrants resented their exclusion from the United States and thought they shared grievances with the Mexican citizenry against the northern country. Nevertheless, in March 1942, Ito noted with sadness that the Mexican soldiers were behaving "like Americans" while they, along with a U.S. platoon, searched the homes of several Japanese Mexican families. Days later, when Mexican soldiers escorted the arrested men as they left their barrios in the company of their wives and children for Mexico City, their neighbors gathered to show their support shouting "¡Viva Japón! ¡Viva México! ¡Mueran los gringos!" With these words, Mexicans in Juárez were expressing not only their anger over the eviction of their neighbors, but also their shared memory of the multiple offenses the U.S. government had inflicted on Mexico since the nineteenth century.[5]

The Mexican government was fully aware of the anti-American sentiment in Mexico and tried to delay information on the raid. National newspapers in Mexico did not publish news of the transnational operation, although they included the victories of Japanese troops during the first months of 1942, news that some Mexicans received with pleasure.

Historian Gabriel Trujillo Muñoz states that during this period, despite their anti-fascism, "Mexicans saw in the attack on Pearl Harbor and in subsequent victories [for Japan in Singapore, Philippines, and Shanghai] some kind of vengeance for all the atrocities the United States had inflicted upon Mexico. . . . Japanese, in the eyes of many Mexicans, were the new Pancho Villa, the new Joaquin Murrieta of the world."[6] Even when Ávila Camacho had declared war against Japan, the American search of Japanese Mexican homes was a U.S. intervention in Mexican affairs many Mexicans would not have easily tolerated in March 1942 had they been informed of the transnational operation in timely ways.[7]

A history of tense affairs between the United States and Mexico developed when the United States supported the independence of Texas in 1836, motivated in part by the Mexican government's refusal to allow Anglo colonizers to import the slavery system into the neighboring nation, something forbidden in Mexico since 1821. Relationships deteriorated further when the United States annexed Texas in 1845 and launched a military invasion in 1846 that resulted in the loss of more Mexican land and the displacement or subordination of the Mexican residents of the conquered territory.[8] According to historian David Montejano, both Texas independence and Mexican war were "essentially the reflection of 'manifest destiny.' The Anglo-Saxon nation was bound to glory; the inferior, decadent Indian race and the half-breed Mexicans were to succumb before the inexorable march of the superior Anglo-Saxon people."[9] At the conclusion of the war, the United States continued to menace its southern neighbor's quest for economic independence; however, antagonism between the governments of the United States and Mexico subsided at the end of the nineteenth century, when Porfirio Díaz took power.[10]

Dictator Díaz, president of Mexico from 1876 to 1911, allowed the extension of U.S. and British investment in Mexico at the expense of indigenous peoples and the working class. This represented an interregnum in the history of strained relationships between the two governments. During this period of friendly relations, the two nations collaborated to remove rebel indigenous populations fighting in the U.S.-Mexico borderlands.[11] In disagreement with Dictator Díaz's collaboration with the United States, Mexican nationalists and labor leaders continuously rejected foreign intervention and perilous working conditions imposed by both American and European companies over their Mexican employees.[12]

On the U.S. side, Americans continued to take over the land of Mexican ranchers, forcing persons of Mexican origin into subordinate positions and impoverishing most Mexicans living in the U.S. occupied territory.[13] Furthermore, Mexicans were alerted to the racist treatment of their compatriots and of the Mexican Americans residing in the United States.[14]

The Mexican Revolution exploded in 1910 and ended the association between Díaz and U.S. businesses and government, but the U.S. government continued its attempts to control the nation. At the onset of the Revolution, several factions had anti-imperialist agendas and demanded the expulsion of powerful North American and European companies. U.S. diplomats remained in the Mexican capital nonetheless, actively involved in designing a new government in favor of American businesses. The intervention of the United States in Mexican affairs added to the complexity of the social unrest. Ambassador Henry Lane Wilson's maneuvers resulted in the assassination of Francisco I. Madero, the first Revolutionary Mexican president, in 1913 by Victoriano Huerta, who also murdered other members of Madero's cabinet. Wilson's decisive support of Victoriano Huerta and his coup d'etat in the same year spurred most Mexicans' condemnation of any U.S. interference in their country's internal affairs.[15] In the United States, racial relationships between Mexicans and European Americans tensed further when colonized individuals resisting oppression in Texas called for insurrection through the Plan de San Diego, the first of three versions signed in January 1915. The plan called for unity among Mexican Americans, African Americans, and Japanese. The insurrection did not take place, but Texan forces and vigilantes killed hundreds of Mexican Americans without due process in response to the potential interethnic insurrection.[16]

While Japanese immigrants were forming ties within the Mexican community, the gap between Mexican nationalists and U.S. interventionists grew larger. The footprints that American troops left in Chihuahua during the 1917 search for General Francisco Villa left a deep scar in the Mexican memory that, as of today, has not healed.[17] As cultural studies scholar Claire F. Fox argues, the Mexican Revolution not only made visible the struggles for power at the beginning of the twentieth century, it also elevated local actors to the level of national characters. Many Mexicans viewed Villa as representing the entire country's desires for independence; therefore, most Mexicans interpreted General John J. Pershing's persecution of the northern general as a direct insult to Mexicans. A new American incursion into Mexican soil would require a major catalyst for a collaborative effort between countries, such as the ominous presence of a common enemy. In the meantime, the gap between Mexico's general population and American interests in Mexico grew in the post-Revolutionary years.[18]

At the end of the Mexican Revolution, during the years between World War I and World War II, Mexico gained a considerable degree of economic and ideological independence that the United States considered a menace. The possible spread of Mexico's revolutionary example among Latin American countries increased the tension between Mexican and U.S. governments.[19] Furthermore, economic depression exacerbated racism in the United States, resulting in the eviction of approximately half a million persons of Mexican origin in the 1930s, an expulsion that Mexicans took as an offense, to say the least.[20]

In response to the unrest of the working class in Latin America, President Franklin D. Roosevelt signaled a reconsideration of the Monroe Doctrine and its interventionist character. He also demonstrated his awareness of the anti-imperialist sentiment of labor leaders in Latin America. On March 4, 1933, Roosevelt declared that he would "dedicate this nation to the policy of the good neighbor—the neighbor who respects his obligations and respects the sanctity of his agreements in and with a world of neighbors."[21]

President Lázaro Cárdenas (1934–1940) profoundly tested the Good Neighbor policy and the diplomatic relations between the United States and Mexico when he ordered the nationalization of the oil industry in March 1938. American, British, and Dutch owners of petroleum property, who had benefited from their association with Dictator Díaz, were forced to leave their businesses in the hands of the Mexican government.[22] American oil investors who lost their property and businesses in Mexico as a result of the expropriation unsuccessfully demanded U.S. military intervention to restore their investments. Since the United States needed to gather all its resources to prepare for a possible war against Germany, Italy, and Japan, its military intervention in Mexico to recover American oil property was not strategically possible in 1938.[23] Weakened by the recent economic depression and foreseeing the need to obtain raw materials from its southern neighbor, Roosevelt's United States tried to block Mexico's sale of oil as an alternative, less brusque, means to pressure Mexico to negotiate the terms of the expropriation.[24]

The ensuing international embargo orchestrated by the United States against its southern neighbor made the sale and distribution of Mexican petroleum difficult. American corporations required that their international partners refuse transportation, storage, and acquisition of Mexican oil. Furthermore, British agents impeded its delivery in Sweden, making clear that the boycott against Mexico would be enforced at any port in the Atlantic Ocean, further distancing the Latin American country from its northern neighbor. These international maneuvers against Mexico fed a strong popular nationalism in the country and reduced the possibility of an alliance between the United States and Mexico.[25]

In the end, the U.S. economic embargo against Mexico forced Cárdenas to strengthen commercial exchanges with Japan, Germany, and Italy and reduced further the influence that the United States had over Mexico.[26] Consequently, Mexico gained certain leverage in its dealings with the United States when its trade with Japan became more consistent. After all, as State Department undersecretary Sumner Welles recognized during the First Meeting of Ministers of Foreign Affairs of the American Republics, held in 1939 in Panama, the United States had to make plans for the imminent war because "the struggle that is going on confronts us with difficulties of both an immediate and an ultimate character. We are already experiencing dislocations in our usual commerce."[27]

Although military intervention in Mexico was not advisable in 1939 in view of the global conflict, the U.S. government and the American public remained distressed by the ideological struggles taking place in its neighboring country, which in some cases implied opposition to U.S. interventions in Mexican affairs. President Cárdenas nationalized, in addition to the oil industry, some services deemed to operate for the good of the public, such as telephone, electric energy, and water. Furthermore, the Cárdenas regime promoted the organization of unions, seeking to control them through the official party, and allowed open political activity of the Mexican Communist Party as well as other leftist individuals and organizations.[28] The United States sought to exert a larger influence south of the border to impede the total adoption of what Roosevelt's administration considered a socialist regime in Mexico modeled after the Soviet Union. As reflected in the description of post-Revolutionary Mexico in *Time* magazine:

> The most effective slogan used by Lenin & Trotsky to rally rural Russians to their Red standard in 1917 was "Land to the Peasants!"
>
> Today the rulers of Mexico, styling themselves collectively "The Revolution," are at last taking seriously and actually carrying out the basic Mexican Constitutional law of 1917 which is simply a fulfillment of this same slogan.[29]

Not only was President Cárdenas an ardent antifascist attempting to create a more balanced distribution of resources among peasants and workers, but a recalcitrant popular sentiment against foreign investors remained a strong element of the Cárdenas post-Revolutionary administration. Anti-imperialist sentiments would fade when the populist Mexican president left office in 1940. Cárdenas's presidential successor, General Manuel Ávila Camacho, calmed the fears of the American public and the U.S. government through his public decision to support capitalism in Mexico.[30]

Although a highly popular figure in the United States, Ávila Camacho confronted disapproval in his own country. Elected in 1940 in the face of extreme social unrest, Ávila Camacho had the task of controlling an armed opposition of sympathizers with General Juan Andreu Almazán. Thus, the 1940 presidential inauguration was marked by violent confrontations between police and rebels: "Two nights before Ávila Camacho's inauguration came a function which Camachismo particularly enjoyed. Government police and soldiers raided Communist headquarters in Avenida Brasil. In the inevitable gun fight, an Army major was killed and two Communists wounded."[31]

According to the American news magazine *Time*, the Mexican police and army arrested fifty persons accused of conspiracy. The Mexican government confiscated during this search "rifles, machine guns, ammunition, bales of propaganda, and alleged evidence of a plot to assassinate Ávila Camacho." In addition to the leftist challenge to the new president, a group of "young intellectuals and fanatical women" from the right wing staged a protest during the presidential inauguration at the U.S. Embassy in Mexico, chanting and shouting "Viva Almazán." The magazine was unsympathetic to this rally, stating that "this was a crowd of supporters of the defeated Presidential candidate [Andreu Almazán and who] disapproved U.S. recognition of Ávila Camacho." Conservative president Ávila Camacho thus faced resistance from left and right but enjoyed the approval of the United States.[32]

To gather resources to control the insurrections, the Mexican president established a firmer alliance with Roosevelt's government, which he announced during his inauguration speech: "Nothing divides us in this America of ours. Any differences that may exist between our peoples are overcome by a lofty desire to secure the permanence of a continental life of friendliness based on mutual respect and on the victory of reason over brute force, of peaceful cooperation over mechanized destruction." Ávila Camacho translated friendliness and mutual respect between the United States and Mexico into commercial agreements and acceptance of foreign investment in Mexico. He assured American investors that Cardenism was no longer a threat to American or national capitalists, stating that "whenever [enterprises and investments] comply with our laws, every legitimate profit they make shall be respected. The companies willing to work with constant effort, and willing to risk the dangers any business may encounter, may count on guarantees from our institutions."[33] This modernization program challenged the new president's political skills since it involved not only American investment but also the technical military support of the United States for the suffocation of armed and peaceful political opposition, a move that could trigger vigorous protests from nationalists and labor leaders.[34]

War propaganda was crucial in building a gradual shift in the perception Mexicans had of the United States as an abusive nation. With the financial assistance and supervision of American private and public institutions, Ávila Camacho's administration downplayed the imperialist shadow the United States had cast for more than a century over Mexican land and resources. In order to comply with the U.S. demand to control the Japanese Mexican community, Ávila Camacho portrayed Japanese Mexicans as an imminent danger to national security.[35] At the same time, and under the same war rationale, he canceled the civil rights of all Mexicans to preempt any attempt to resist his plans for Mexico. Eventually, these and other factors, such as anti-Nazi sentiments and the solidarity of most Mexicans with the Republic of Spain, worked in favor of Ávila Camacho and his business partners.[36]

The Mexican president took careful steps in building a close relationship with the United States even before he became the candidate of the official party. In exchange for the right to use its territory, Mexico would receive armament, training, and financial support for its army from the United States. To avoid more insurrections or strong protests by nationalists in the face of American intervention, Ávila Camacho avoided making public his agreements.[37] Not until March 1941 did the minister of foreign affairs, Ezequiel Padilla, publicly hint in a speech before Mexico's congress at the possibility of joining the United States against a German attack, a move that caused ample protests from anti-American citizens. On April 1, 1941, the Mexican government made a bolder move when it seized eleven German and Italian vessels stationed in different Mexican ports, arresting their 555 sailors, whom the Mexican authorities accused of, but did not try in court for, "planning sabotage activities."[38] Nevertheless, Ávila Camacho and members of his cabinet continued to state that, in case of war, Mexico would not allow the entrance of American troops into Mexican territory.[39]

Censored newspapers in Mexico did not report the U.S. military incursion into Juárez in March 1942. Most Mexicans would not have taken this operation lightly because of the long history of U.S. interventions in Mexico. Nevertheless, the U.S. military raid across the border confirmed a solid deal between both national states. U.S. confidence in Ávila Camacho and in the Mexican Army grew to the extent of planning its modernization and adoption of American military operations to eventually operate under the command of the U.S. Army. In addition, the United States registered Mexican nationals in its military, establishing very successful recruiting stations in Mexico: the number of Mexican citizens serving in the U.S. Army during World War II is estimated at 250,000.[40]

Indeed, the United States had achieved cooperation from most Latin American governments in its war efforts. In January 1942 most American republics agreed during the Third Meeting of Ministers of Foreign Affairs in Brazil to the uprooting of Japanese Latin Americans. Although this book does not examine the transference of Latin American Japanese to the United States, their abduction formed part of the same hemispheric operation that canceled the rights of persons of Japanese descent, including Japanese Mexicans, across the American continents. Such suspension of civil rights was planned in the United States and Canada long before the Pearl Harbor attack occurred. President Roosevelt called Japan "a menace" in 1938 when expressing his regret for the Philippines' gradual independence from the United States.[41] As early as 1938, Canada created the Defence of Canada Regulations (DOCR), which contemplated the arbitrary detention and confinement of Japanese immigrants and Canadian citizens of Japanese descent. Acting in unison, Canada's Privy Council Order 1486 was published only five days after President Roosevelt's Executive Order 9066 in February 1942, and Canada subjected Japanese Canadians to internment in concentration camps.[42]

A Call for Continental Solidarity

The United States was clearly concerned about geopolitics in the Americas, as indicated in three major conferences held in 1939, 1940, and 1942. At the request of the United States, Latin American and U.S. diplomats conferred during the First Meeting of Ministers of Foreign Affairs of the American Republics in Panama in 1939. In view of the global conflict starting on September 1 with the German invasion of Poland, the American republics agreed to remain neutral and to study the possibility of organizing the economy on a continental basis. In addition, they committed their police and judicial authorities to prevent or repress "unlawful activities that individuals, whether they be nationals or aliens, may attempt in favor of a foreign belligerent state."[43] Participating in this and the two subsequent conferences were Mexico, Ecuador, Cuba, Costa Rica, Peru, Paraguay, Uruguay, Honduras, Chile, Colombia, Venezuela, Argentina, Guatemala, Panama, Nicaragua, the Dominican Republic, Brazil, Bolivia, Haiti, El Salvador, and the United States.[44]

Continuing the conversation on hemispheric matters, Latin American and U.S. diplomats held the Second Meeting of Foreign Ministers of the American Republics in Havana in February 1941. During this conference, the signatories resolved to support the neutrality of the American republics in the ongoing military conflicts. Latin American officials agreed on the restriction of activities of diplomats representing countries involved in the war, rejecting the intervention of belligerent nations in their domestic affairs.[45]

The Japanese attack on Pearl Harbor on December 7, 1941, provided the United States with the occasion to call, once again, for hemispheric solidarity.[46] To effect the planning of war strategies, including the organization of economy at a continental scale, President Franklin D. Roosevelt ordered the organization of the Third Meeting of the Ministers of Foreign Affairs of the American Republics. At the conclusion of this meeting in Rio de Janeiro in January 1942, the U.S. and Latin American diplomats agreed to economic measures that would benefit the elites of each nation, and to confine all Axis nationals in concentration camps or exclusive zones, canceling the citizenship of naturalized Latin American citizens born in Germany, Italy, or Japan. Days before, Mexico had set up an example in the management of the Japanese population: President Manuel Ávila Camacho had uprooted most Japanese immigrants and their descendants from the U.S.-Mexico borderlands.[47]

The American republics took other measures of durable impact during the Rio de Janeiro meeting at the expense of Latin American Japanese. Mexican minister of foreign affairs Ezequiel Padilla and other diplomats convened on the creation of the Inter-American Defense Board, "composed of military and naval technicians appointed by each of the governments to study and to recommend to them the measures necessary for the defense of the Continent."[48] This board urged President Roosevelt to fulfill his promise to deliver a total of $459,422,000 in armament to the Latin American governments during World War II. Brazil and Mexico, the main supporters of the United States during the Rio de Janeiro conference, were among the nations that received the largest amount of assistance to outfit their military forces.[49] Such assistance increased the control that Ávila

Camacho needed to suppress armed opposition to his programs in Mexico. President Ávila Camacho justified his acceptance of American arms and training by claiming that they were to fight the Axis powers and a possible Fifth Column formed by Mexican Japanese. *Time* gave a public explanation of the American intervention in Mexican affairs and military maneuvers: "If the Japanese should attempt an invasion of the U.S., a convenient place to land would be Mexico. Mexico's 4,200-mile-long western coastline has hundreds of sheltered bays and inlets, in many places could offer no more formidable resistance than a few bewildered fishermen."[50]

The Mexican state, however, used U.S. military equipment to control indigenous men and women demanding better conditions, as well as other rebels. Thanks to the armament provided by the United States, the Mexican government effectively suppressed a number of guerrilla movements organized in the face of inflation, conscription, and unfulfilled land distribution promises.[51] In exchange, it opened its territory to American investors and even authorized U.S. soldiers to search the houses of several Mexican citizens of Japanese descent, in Mexican territory.

Although a small raid, the American military operation in Juárez in March 1942, which resulted in the arrest of fifteen Japanese Mexicans, is of great significance in the history of U.S.-Mexico relations. The incursion of American troops into Mexico was grounded in the Rio de Janeiro meeting Resolution XVII, which established that World War II demanded "the fullest cooperation in the establishment and enforcement of extraordinary measures of continental defense." Japanese Latin Americans paid the price of hemispheric economic and military collaboration. Those Japanese Mexicans living in the U.S.-Mexico borderlands were subjected to the intervention of the U.S. Army in their lives.[52]

War and Economy

World War II represented a great opportunity for the United States to reinforce its neocolonial practices and the Monroe Doctrine, later furthered under Cold War ideological logistics. Yet, the elites of the United States were not the only ones to benefit from hemispheric organization of economic resources and production during World War II; national dominant groups in each Latin American country profited from international agreements.[53] The United States was able to not only fulfill the needs of its war industry through the supply of raw materials from Mexico and other American republics but also solidify its leadership role in a war perceived as a just intervention, ensuring a more lasting political and economic interference in other American republics. Sumner Welles, retrospectively, continued to appreciate the collaboration of the Mexican government in achieving the U.S. objectives: "How different would our situation be today if on our southern border there lay a Republic of Mexico filled with resentment and with antagonism against the United States, instead of a truly friendly and cooperative Mexican people seeking the same objectives as ours, guided by the same policies, and inspired by the same motives, in their determination to safeguard their independence and the security of the hemisphere, as those which we ourselves possess."[54]

Mexico, as well as other Latin American countries, promised to make a priority of expeditious delivery of the products and articles that the United States considered necessary to conduct its war against Japan, Germany, and Italy. The U.S. Board of Economic Warfare became the central institution in charge of organizing the industrialization processes of each American republic. Hence, it approved new administrative procedures and transportation routes, promoted the sale of raw materials to the United States, and distributed U.S. war funds among American and Latin American companies.[55]

Signatories to the resolutions during the Third Meeting of Ministers of Foreign Affairs agreed to the permanent character of the policies formulated during the perceived continental security crisis. The Latin American diplomats promised that, at the conclusion of the war, the United States would continue to enjoy inter-American trade under the same regulations and low prices. U.S. manufacturers obtained protection against the possible development of industrial processes in Latin America in the postwar period. According to the logic and interests of U.S. corporations, Latin American low-priced goods would be unfair competition to U.S. manufacturers even after the war. The *Final Act of the Third Meeting of the Ministers of Foreign Affairs of the American Republics* included the commitment to protect postwar U.S. businesses "against competition from goods produced in countries with a low standard of living."[56]

As the war continued, Mexico and other Latin American nations faced internal upheaval caused by the demand to produce more at lower real wages. Ávila Camacho imposed economic measures that demanded more sacrifices from the working class and the political skills of the elites to contain insurrection. With the march of World War II and the implementation of the resolutions passed in Brazil in 1942, agriculture fell under the control of the Mexican-U.S. Commission for Economic Cooperation, created in 1943 in total coordination with the U.S. Board of Economic Warfare.

Accordingly, this board established crops in Mexico that inhibited the production of grains essential to the Mexican diet, with a consequent rise in malnourishment among the most unprotected populations.[57]

The result was that while poor Mexicans were close to famine during World War II, the United States received the resources it required from Mexico. During this period, foreign investment quadrupled. The administration of important resources in the agricultural and mining sectors was mainly in the hands of U.S. corporations or decided by binational committees. Labor shortages in the United States were solved through the employment of more than 220,000 Mexican laborers, who arrived through the Bracero Program. They, as well as an undetermined number of undocumented Mexican workers, substituted for U.S. citizens fighting the war abroad. Although the United States' goal was to provide supplies for its army and civil population, control over Mexican production and exports extended beyond World War II.[58]

Despite the benefits to the United States of raw materials and human labor, exported to the detriment of the economic growth of Mexico and every other Latin American country signing the Rio de Janeiro act, Sumner Welles regarded the terms of inter-American trade established in Brazil as the product of uninterested assistance to Latin American countries: "Because of our material resources, it was obvious that the main brunt of the hemisphere effort to maintain the inter-American economic and commercial structure would have to be borne by this country. . . . The assistance rendered by agencies of this government . . . helped to stabilize the national economies of our neighbors and enabled them to pass through the most serious crisis they had ever faced."[59] The Mexican government advertised as well the infusion of American capital in Mexico as a positive aspect of the modernization of Mexico without noting how low real wages had fallen during this period. As Stephen Niblo found in his study of Mexico's economy during World War II, Mexican institutions altered statistics in order to embellish the results of industrialization. Perhaps the best summary of the situation was formulated by a resident of Tepoztlán, in the state of Morelos, who described the results of modernization in Mexico during the 1940s: "We have a new road and many tourists but our children are still dying." The signs of modernity and industrialization, which included the construction of highways, did not necessarily reflect substantial improvement in the quality of life of most Mexicans.[60]

If workers and peasants did not benefit from the trade agreement between the United States and Mexico during World War II, the economic and political elites did. Payment for Manuel Ávila Camacho's collaboration with the U.S. government and businesses arrived in the form of American financing of his friends' and relatives' businesses. U.S. investors also profited from the implementation of new economic projects in Mexico, among them Samuel R. Rosoff, whose company was in charge of constructing the Valsequillo dam. At its conclusion, this project allowed the irrigation of estates in Puebla owned by President Ávila Camacho and other officers of the Mexican government. Rómulo O'Farrill, married to the president's niece and owner of the Automotriz O'Farrill (Packard and Mack trucks), was highly favored through the import of Mack trucks into Mexico. Approved by the U.S. War Production Board, the funding of these and other ventures helped to develop the fortunes of members of the presidential cabinet as well as of some of their relatives, while Mexican workers' real wages declined as the war produced inflation. In the meantime, nationalism in time of war aided the Mexican government in its management of discontents.[61]

Nationalism and War

The new terms of the relationship between the United States and Mexico did not involve only economics; cultural production was a key element in building the consent of large populations to the collaboration between the two nations. This cooperation included modernization programs demanding low wages, higher production, and improvement of transportation, but also the production of mass media in both countries. Cultural artifacts, such as films, radio programs, and posters, demonized Japanese as a way to construct a more cohesive national identity based on race. If before the war, Mexicans in general constructed a national ideal of citizenship in opposition to U.S. imperialist projects, during the war, Japanese embodied a racial enemy.

According to communication science scholar Seth Fein, full collaboration between the Mexican and U.S. governments "affected not only industrial and agricultural development, for example, the modernization of Mexican railroads to facilitate the delivery of Mexican resources and labor during the war, but also shaped ideological production." The Americanization of Mexican society, which took off during World War II, thus implied a profound change in the ways in which production and consumption were organized, including new notions of who the enemy was and how to combat it.[62]

To control the content of mass communication in Latin America, President Roosevelt created the Office of the Coordinator of Inter-American

Affairs (OCIAA) in July 1941. This department controlled mass media in Mexico during World War II. Combining entertainment with a favorable image of the United States as an ally, Nelson Rockefeller, as chief of the OCIAA, commissioned American entertainment and propaganda industry investors to intervene in the production and distribution of films, radio programs, and television shows in Mexico. Under the supervision of the OCIAA, American producers used Mexican artists or cultural elements that could contribute to softening any resistance in Mexico to the intervention of the United States in national affairs. They had to work on the Americans' anti-Mexican stance.[63] Walt Disney toured Mexico as an American cultural ambassador and celebrated pseudo-Mexican folklore through the creation of *The Three Caballeros*, in which, according to "the persons of Donald, Jose and Panchito, the United States, Brazil, and Mexico were three pals, none more equal than the others." Disney has had a profound effect on how Latin America has been represented in the United States. Before the war, American cultural products demonized Mexicans; at the onset of the war, Disney and other mass media enterprises changed representations of Mexicans to create a friendlier image of them in relation to Americans.[64]

Cartoons, actors, singers, and other ideological tools exalted nationalism and a sense of national emergency at the expense of Japanese. Mass media productions cultivated a degree of "self-discipline" in the face of the imminent danger Japanese represented during World War II, and this awareness of an enemy, embodied in the Japanese Mexicans, helped to suffocate nationalist and labor demands. As historian Stephen Niblo notes, Mexican labor leaders occasionally expressed their dissatisfaction with the prevailing working conditions, "however, they made the assessment that it would be parochial and wrong to do anything to hurt the war effort." Unionist demands thus had to be postponed until the threat of the war disappeared.[65]

Historian Monika A. Rankin's research on modernity and propaganda assists our understanding of the control over dissenters that the Mexican government exercised during World War II. She argues, "World War II provided a platform for shifting economic development strategies that privileged industrialization" in Mexico. Halbert Jones addresses the difficulties of keeping latent anti-American sentiments subdued during World War II.[66] Within this political and economic framework, the Mexican government promoted the idea that the entire country was actively attacking the enemy not only through the confinement of Japanese Mexicans, but also by meeting the United States' demands of war production.

Indicating the urgency of addressing the status of Japanese Mexicans, President Ávila Camacho reported to the nation his government's actions against "the enemy" in his presidential address of 1942. In Ávila Camacho's words, Mexico was spun as a heroic people facing open war against Italy, Germany, and Japan "because the entire nation has demonstrated with its attitude that, when the time arrives, each Mexican knows how to be a soldier determined to defend the motherland, by taking the arms or at their place of work; through productivity or through sacrifice (Applause)."[67] The "defense of the motherland" consisted of the expulsion of Japanese Mexicans and their descendants from the borderlands and the coastal zones.

Among the measures to relocate persons of Japanese descent, Ávila Camacho signed a presidential decree suspending individual constitutional rights that "could constitute an obstacle for the expeditious and easy defense of the nation." Accordingly, his speech heard throughout Mexico over the airwaves explained that "German, Italian, and Japanese who resided near the coasts and the border, or in faraway places where their presence was deemed undesirable, were transferred to the capital of the Republic and to other places of the interior. Meeting centers belonging to a group of foreigners, our country being in a state of war against theirs, were closed [and other] efficient measures taken in order to avoid the distribution of enemy propaganda and other activities that affect the security of the nation."[68]

Although Ávila Camacho included German and Italian residents of Mexico in his speech, the main target of these measures was the Japanese Mexican community. Federal deputy and congressional president Manuel Gudiño Díaz replied to the presidential address on the same day with more false accusations against the Japanese Mexican community. Gudiño Díaz emphasized "the danger they represent[ed]" and, without specifying their alleged crimes, mentioned their "disloyalty to the same country that has offered hospitality to them." Similar condemning statements were made in the United States and Canada, where Japanese were considered "disloyal at the core."[69]

Whereas during previous decades, the Mexican citizenry had often associated nationalism with the struggle against U.S. ownership and exploitation of valuable natural resources, World War II precipitated the creation of a new kind of nationalism. According to Rankin, "public discussions of the war allowed leaders to fuse those economic strategies with more abstract definitions of democracy and shifting concepts of *la Patria*."[70]

Labeling Japanese Mexicans as an "internal enemy" partially contributed to Ávila Camacho's success in achieving national unity. His concept of nation was inextricably linked to racial notions of citizenship. In 1943, Ávila Camacho argued that "because of the war . . . [Mexico needs] a rigorous selection of immigrants, giving preference to those who are capable of assimilation because of their racial and ideological affinity."[71] In consequence, when Ávila Camacho removed Japanese Mexicans from the borderlands, he reinforced the idea that Japanese immigrants and their Mexican children were not capable of assimilation and that their inability to integrate into their communities made them agents of the Japanese state. All the while, mass media productions and the official discourse in Mexico emphasized a strong ideological affinity between the peoples of Mexico and those of the United States.

Despite narratives claiming that the relocation program was a necessary operation to defend the American continents, Japanese Mexicans were not tried on individual bases to prove their involvement in espionage, sabotage, or military operations. Instead, the Mexican government demonized and uprooted Japanese Mexicans to comply with the United States' requests. Such deracination had durable and damaging effects on their lives.[72]

Dr. Tsunesaburo Hasegawa Araki, arrested in 1942 on Mexican soil by U.S. and Mexican soldiers under the direction of the U.S. vice consul, never returned to the borderlands. The Mexican government did not produce any official document canceling his naturalization; nor did he recover his citizenship officially.[73] Like Dr. Hasegawa, thousands of Mexican Japanese remained away from their homes in the borderlands, having lost their property, family ties, and some even their lives during World War II. As of today, however, neither the Mexican nor the U.S. government has ever offered individual reparations to the uprooted Mexican Japanese for their losses.

CHAPTER FOUR

Citizenship Revoked and the Realities of Displacement during World War II

The small number of Japanese immigrants in Mexico by 1942 may obliterate the deep consequences of their eviction from U.S.-Mexico borderlands on the notions of what constitutes a democratic society and the meaning of citizenship.[1] As is the case with the Japanese American community or any other social group whose civil rights were suspended during World War II, the implications of targeting a racialized sector in times of crisis are enormous if principles of equality and freedom are to be held as permanent and universal.[2] Historians of the Japanese diaspora in Mexico believe that the number of Japanese immigrants in the borderlands ranged between 2,700 and 4,700 in 1942. Regardless of their number, the relocation program left all members of the Japanese Mexican community—including those born in Mexico, naturalized citizens, and the Mexican children and wives of Japanese immigrants—without the protection of the Mexican Constitution.

Unstable Citizenship

Citizenship indicates affiliation in a social class that holds a legal relationship with the state. Enjoying the protection of the state is a privilege citizens of Mexico are entitled to, whether the citizenship status is acquired through birth or naturalization. Although Mexico had extended citizenship to several Asian immigrants, their civil rights were negated by the anti-Asian movements. While citizenship was a notion tied to race, the protection granted to Asian immigrants was quite limited, as proved by the expulsion of Chinese, some of them naturalized citizens of Mexico, from Sonora in the 1920s.[3] Their relationship with the state remained unstable as the social view prevailed over their legal status as citizens of Mexico; phenotypical Asians, even if citizens of Mexico, were considered foreigners, not Mexicans. At the onset of World War II, the Mexican state was able to proudly announce the official cancellation of its duty to protect all Mexican citizens of Japanese descent.[4]

On June 1, 1942, President Manuel Ávila Camacho signed a decree to suspend individual rights, claiming the legal frame was "an obstacle to facing the situation created by the state of war in an immediate and direct way." Having an enemy at home in the ethnic Japanese population facilitated the breach in constitutional safeguards. Among the rights the Mexican president temporarily nullified or restricted were freedom of speech, the press, peaceful assembly, and petition; the right to be secure against unreasonable searches and seizures; and the right to a swift and public trial.[5]

Ignacio Koba and Luis Tanamachi of Nogales, Sonora, were among the residents of Mexico who had their civil rights taken away at the onset of World War II. The Mexican government had forced other Japanese Mexicans in more populous areas into sealed trains escorted by soldiers, into packed buses, or into truck beds since January 1942, to be taken to the interior of Mexico. Tanamachi and Koba, however, refused to go along with their uprooting as late as September of that year.[6] When they heard the news that the government of Mexico had ordered all Japanese subjects to present themselves before federal authorities in Mexico City, neither Ignacio nor Luis thought the measure applied to them. After all, Tanamachi and Koba had documents to prove they were citizens of Mexico. Both continued to operate the small barbershop they owned in partnership in Nogales.[7]

In an effort to cancel federal and local orders for them to leave Nogales, Tanamachi and Koba wrote a telegram informing President Ávila Camacho that they both were Mexican citizens. The men felt that their forty-year residence in the country made them "Mexicans by feeling, more than by naturalization," noting that having emotional ties to Mexico was more important than being officially citizens of that country. They had both their citizenship documents and the weight of many years living peacefully in their Mexican town.[8]

Tanamachi and Koba believed that once President Ávila Camacho acknowledged their citizenship rights, they would not be obligated to leave their few possessions, family, and friends for relocation. Aside from the violation of their constitutional rights, the move to the interior of Mexico would be too costly for them, since no government entity would cover their travel expenses. Additionally, they were required, in compliance with the relocation orders, to pay the expenditures for their housing, clothing, and meals for the duration of the war. This arbitrary imposition was in itself a damaging act against the integrity of individuals and families affected by the relocation program, for even criminals who were tried and sentenced were taken care of by the state while their freedom was taken away.

Although the Mexican government insinuated that Japanese Mexicans formed a Fifth Column, it did not officially declare Japanese Mexicans prisoners of war, spies, or civilian internees. All persons in the United States under these classifications were protected by international agreements on war procedures such as the Geneva Convention, but the joint Mexican-U.S. Defense Commission, which determined the conditions of the uprooting of the Japanese Mexican community from the borderlands, did not follow the protocols of a "civilized" war.[9]

Japanese immigrants and their descendants soon reacted to the loss of their civil rights. Naturalized citizens and citizens by birth were initially confused by the orders to evacuate the borderland. Hundreds of them submitted telegrams to various Mexican officials, protesting their relocation. Concerned persons objecting to their deportation, or that of their relatives or friends, from the borderlands during World War II usually received swift official responses to their telegrams. The painful pleas of the Japanese Mexican families to remain undivided and at home was, in most cases, expediently denied. Japanese Mexican men and women who were not married likewise endured separation from their community, property, and means of support.[10]

A Vulnerable Population

Luis Tanamachi Yide, a younger man apparently unrelated to Luis Tanamachi of Nogales, Sonora, managed to stay at home in Navolato, a small community in the northern state of Sinaloa, until 1943, under the protection of local residents and the governor of Sinaloa, Rodolfo T. Loaiza.[11] Both Tanamachis were barbers, but younger Luis seemed to have had a more difficult situation than Tanamachi from Nogales. Luis Tanamachi Yide, from Navolato, wrote to the minister of the interior Miguel Alemán to provide details of his hardships. Tanamachi Yide was forced to perform "agricultural activities on a small scale because, due to the rising prices of staples [he] needed to undertake other kinds of labor, in addition to practicing his [barber] trade." He sought to support "in an honorable manner" his wife and his son.[12] The younger Tanamachi also stated he had a family who would have been in difficult circumstances and "forced to live from public charity" should he obey his relocation orders. He wrote that he did not have anything "to do with the current international situation, having resided in this generous country—which I dearly love—for a long time."[13] Both Tanamachis based their arguments on their sworn loyalty and their lack of financial resources.

President Camacho did not reply directly to any Japanese Mexican requesting an exception to the relocation orders. In the case of Koba and Tanamachi, Adolfo Ruiz Cortines, then the chief officer of the Departamento de Investigación Política y Social (DIPS), answered their plea. Ruiz Cortines, who would be president of Mexico from 1952 to 1958, explained in a telegram to both Mexican citizens that they could remain at home with one condition: the governor of Sonora had to become the party responsible for them.[14] Thus, the fate of Japanese Mexicans could be decided on a personal basis by members of the national elite.

Japanese Mexicans in Sonora saw their chances to remain at home decreased by the political alliances of their governor, Anselmo Macías Valenzuela. Macías, who held the rank of colonel, fought during the revolution against the forces of Emiliano Zapata and Francisco Villa and supported anti-Asian former presidents Plutarco Elías Calles and Álvaro Obregón.[15] The governor refused to side with the working-class Japanese Mexican men who requested his authorization to remain in their town. Nogales was a border community that could not afford residents of Japanese origin for security reasons, he argued, and Macías could not personally vouch for the "foreigners" Koba and Tanamachi.[16]

Legal Recourses Voided

Ignacio Koba and Luis Tanamachi did not accept the official answer to their plea from the governor of Sonora. Although Governor Macías supported the government's order to uproot them, the two men were relentless in seeking to maintain their civil rights and citizenship status. A first recourse was provided by articles 103 and 107 of the Mexican Constitution, in which citizens were given the right to request protection from a state court against state abuses through the writ of amparo.[17] Tanamachi and Koba petitioned a judge to suspend any official act against their civil rights while the legality of the government orders was investigated. The procedure was costly, as they had to pay an attorney to file their documents in court, but despite their scant resources, they had much more to lose with eviction.[18]

Processing the amparo delayed their transference for some days; nevertheless, the effort proved futile in the end. The judge in charge of overseeing their case denied them protection from the government's injunction. On October 30, Anacleto Olmos, mayor of Nogales, ordered Koba and Tanamachi to present themselves at the DIPS, Ministry of the Interior, located in the Mexican capital.[19]

The situation for Japanese Mexicans became more troubling still. The Mexican government ordered that Japanese Mexicans carry documents at all times indicating their official place of residence. Mexican citizens of Japanese descent and Japanese nationals suffered continual harassment and had no place to hide. The threat of violence loomed while Japanese Mexicans tried to establish their right to remain at home: police and soldiers could enforce relocation orders at any time. And officials of different ranks and departments had to be informed where Japanese Mexicans were at all times and why.

In small communities, Japanese Mexicans had the support of their neighbors, and mayors usually petitioned for the cancelation of relocation orders without success. Local officers had to expel Japanese Mexicans from their communities against their own will. As Tanamachi and Koba exhausted their legal recourses, federal and local authorities hurried them to leave for Mexico City. Mayor Olmos set their departure date for November 2. Emphasizing the power of federal institutions over local power, on November 3, Adolfo Ruíz Cortines, then director of the DIPS, inquired as to the whereabouts of these two Mexican citizens and demanded their immediate presentation in Mexico City.[20]

The recently created DIPS gave a number of inspectors the task of secretly visiting remote populations in search of members of the Axis countries. Such federal employees acting as undercover agents occasionally wrote anonymous reports, identifying themselves with numbers. Inspector number 135, in charge of surveying North Sonora, diligently sent a telegram on November 4, 1942, to the Ministry of the Interior informing that, on the same date, Ignacio Koba and Luis Tanamachi, described as "Japanese subjects" despite their Mexican citizenship, had taken the train in the direction of Mexico City in the company of Hitsa Matsuo de Tanamachi, Luis's wife.[21]

Even with the uneven pace of the relocation program, no amount of time was sufficient to allow Japanese Mexicans in the borderlands to prepare for their displacement. They knew that they would be left to their own means, but many relocated persons of Japanese origin did not have property to convert to cash to fund their removal from their communities. Tenant farmers had serious difficulties, as they had invested most of their resources in crops they would not be able to harvest because of the order to abandon their homes. They attempted to delay their relocation to avoid total bankruptcy.[22] Hiroshi Tanaka Ykeda, Suematzu Tanaka, and Sigueru Sata, who lived in the state of Sonora, requested permission to remain working in their fields until the end of the harvest season.[23] Tanaka Ykeda explained their situation in detail to the Ministry of the Interior:

> I arrived in this country in 1917, residing in the Yaqui region since 1927, to become a small scale farmer. Once in this region, I married a Mexican national, Maria Petra González. . . . Because the past years have not been fruitful in terms of farming, I have no money. The only hope I have is the harvest of wheat and vegetables I planted in 20 hectares located in Sapochopo. Having invested everything I have in the fields, I have worked in partnership with Suematzu Tanaka and Sigueru Sata who are also in very bad financial shape, but hopeful to recover through this year's harvest. It is because of this situation that . . . I beg you, and with me Sigueru Sata and Suematzu Tanaka, the latter having a wife Kimie Tanaka and five little children born in this country, to postpone the deadline set for us to leave this place.[24]

Although at the foundation of the modern nation is the idea that abiding existing laws will guarantee equal opportunities for all citizens, the suspension of laws in states of emergency create or reinforce unequal relations of power. The Mexican government interned Japanese nationals; they also uprooted and stripped citizens by birth and naturalization of their civil and human rights. Such cancelation of human and individual rights resulted not only in the erasure of the political participation of Japanese Mexicans, but also in material losses that deprived them of their livelihoods.

Despite their pleas, Mexican Japanese farmers were now forced to abandon the fields they had tended with great effort. Other small businesses owners transferred or closed their shops, with negative consequences for the communities in which they resided with their families.[25] Initially, the Mexican government gave most Japanese Mexicans in the borderlands only two alternatives in their relocation to the interior of the country to keep them under the control of centralized police and military offices: they could reside in Mexico City or in Guadalajara, the two largest metropolitan centers in the country. Upon their arrival in these two cities, uprooted Japanese Mexicans faced unemployment, homelessness, and separation from their families.

Mexico City

The rising unemployment rate in Mexico City was the product of rural migration to large urban centers in the 1940s; Japanese Mexicans, however, had specific obstacles to overcome. Legislative measures forbade "enemy aliens" from accepting employment if their hiring would displace a Mexican citizen.[26] The Ministry of the Interior required Japanese Mexicans to present themselves regularly at its offices on Bucareli Street. Some displaced men had to be counted every day, and others weekly.[27] Few business owners would grant permission to their employees to miss a work day, much less excuse their absence when the DIPS subjected them to interrogations that lasted several days.[28] Even those who were bedridden due to sickness had to overcome their medical problems to sign their name at the DIPS offices as mandated by the Ministry of the Interior.[29] In general, poor residents of all ethnic backgrounds were already having a hard time trying to make ends meet in Mexico City as inflation elevated prices for staples. Several Japanese Mexicans were blind or disabled, and therefore had even fewer opportunities than other newcomers to find a job in the capital.[30]

Hunger was prevalent from the first days of the evacuation for Mexican Japanese from the borderlands. Numerous written testimonies describe malnourishment in the army facilities, police stations, jails, concentration camps, and other designated areas in which Japanese Mexicans were confined.[31] The lack of food significantly and disproportionately affected children, women, and sick and elderly persons, whose support had been previously provided by Japanese Mexicans forced to leave their employment or small businesses in the borderlands. Once in Mexico City, men separated from their families were responsible for two households, theirs in the interior of the country, and those of their relatives in their places of origin.[32]

The high rate of unemployment among relocated persons in the capital was noted by generals Alfredo Delgado and Ramón F. Iturbide. Both generals observed that "the crowding of foreign persons relocated to this capital is becoming a grave economic problem, since they are exhausting their means of support and they have to compete in a desperate struggle with our nationals in order to survive or to be left to the compassionate care of state or private institutions. In addition, would it not be easier to have them under control in the interior of the country than in an urban center as densely populated as the City of Mexico?"[33] To complicate Japanese Mexicans' search for jobs, officers at the Ministry of Interior followed to the letter the order to constrain their mobility within the limits of the federal district. The borders of Mexico City were not always clearly defined in relation to the Estado de México, the state surrounding the national capital. When officers in charge of processing employment authorizations could not identify the address of a potential employer as being within jurisdiction of the federal district, they denied the requested permission, arguing that the place was within a restricted zone.[34]

Even though Mexico City was one of the zones where Japanese Mexicans from the borderlands were ordered to stay, DIPS inspectors arrested and imprisoned Japanese Mexican men who were caught without written authorization from the DIPS in Mexico City.[35] Francisco José Kameyama Kynosuke's experience illustrates the problems Japanese Mexicans faced in the federal district. Months after his arrival in April 1942 from North Mexico, Kameyama found a job as a mechanic and had permission to work at the shop employing him. His employer then moved the shop Francisco José worked at to Tlalnepantla, Estado de México. This municipality was only ten miles away from Mexico City and had officially been part of the federal district until 1856.[36] No visible division separated Tlalnepantla's streets from Mexico City. The shop was not located within the area of confinement, however, and Kameyama met with trouble at his new place of employment when DIPS inspectors asked to see his permit. Because Kameyama had a book in Japanese at the time of the inspector's search, and he did not have a permit to live in Tlalnepantla, Francisco José was charged by the federal police with being a spy. The forty-two-year-old man, who had been living in Mexico since he was a toddler, spent four days in jail until he was able to demonstrate that his book did not include subversive material. It was a religious text that a priest had given him as a baptismal present.[37]

Policemen in Mexico City could corroborate almost immediately individual permits of Japanese Mexicans, because certified copies were filed at the DIPS offices in the same city. They chose to harass displaced Japanese Mexicans, however, and curtail their chances to hold their jobs or find employment. Yadao Yamashita Yamashita, from the state of Coahuila, exemplified the troubles Japanese Mexicans met when they misplaced their documents. When a DIPS inspector interrogated Yamashita in the street and found out that the Japanese Mexican man did not have his documents with him, he escorted Yamashita to the DIPS office. Yamashita was detained until he produced his permit to reside in Mexico City. The inspector could have verified Yamashita's relocation documents by simply examining his file at the same DIPS offices where Yamashita had been arrested. The burden of proof fell on Yamashita, however; therefore, he spent time detained until somebody else brought his documents to the DIPS facilities.[38]

Not only were Japanese Mexicans subjected to physical abuse by officials who threatened them with arrest in order to collect bribes, but they were also vulnerable to exploitation in their place of work. Employers of Japanese Mexican persons living in Mexico City assumed the role of guards as they were "committed not to authorize [their Japanese employees] to move out of their place of work and residence."[39] Thus, Japanese Mexican workers were forced to keep their jobs, even when mistreated, until the Ministry of the Interior authorized them to leave them.[40] When their new employers were particularly powerful, as was the case with the seven Japanese Mexicans hired to work in April 1942 at the ranch of the minister of economy, Francisco Javier Gaxiola, Jr., their obligation to remain at their place of employment undoubtedly felt weightier.[41] Japanese Mexicans frequently worked at military households and haciendas performing housekeeping, gardening, or agricultural chores.[42] Even former president Lázaro Cárdenas employed at least two uprooted Japanese Mexicans during World War II.[43] Since many Japanese Mexicans had achieved self-employment by 1942, albeit some with very small businesses, becoming dependent laborers reduced not only their salaries, but also their social status and self-esteem.

Unfamiliarity with their surroundings could also have been a reason to stay or to leave a job. Living in the city required more than knowing the names of the streets.[44] Japanese Mexicans who had spent many years in northern Mexico had to learn to be streetwise. Thefts affected Japanese Mexicans greatly since uprooted persons had to carry their original permits with them at all times. When their documents were stolen, policemen suspected Japanese Mexicans of lying, and the procedure to replace their permits was long and arduous: police officers visited their homes to conduct an exhaustive investigation before the DIPS could grant a duplicate permit.[45]

Uprooted Japanese Mexicans were not the only ones to endure tight state control during World War II. Japanese Mexicans who had an established life in Mexico City before 1942 were also affected by state policing at the onset of the war. For example, the DIPS placed Daniel Okada's restaurant at 44 Luis Moya under surveillance because inspectors considered it a "place where we know persons of the same nationality meet, with the danger of becoming a center of activities supporting the Axis." Their reasons to consider Okada a spy were that he was blacklisted by U.S. officials; he purchased American supplies for his restaurant through a Mexican woman;

he owned "his own house and car"; and he maintained business transactions with a L. U. Funatsu, whose name had also been blacklisted in 1942.[46] Luis M. Takano and Benito Takizawa were also established denizens of Mexico City who faced harassment during World War II. They derived their support from driving a taxicab. In August 1942, the Japanese Mexican men were forced to surrender their driver's licenses and car's license plates to police officers who thought persons of Japanese origin were barred from being taxi drivers.[47]

Middle-class Japanese Mexicans who had managed to keep some of their possessions or capital found other types of restrictions on the conduct of their businesses. Professionals and businessmen who needed to travel to other cities in the interior of the country to acquire supplies for their offices or shops were forced to request permission in advance.[48] Even some Mexican Japanese who enjoyed certain economic comfort in their new places faced instability and emotional distress due to their relocation, as Hisashi Narihiro, a doctor, described: "Very often we hear rumors that we will be transferred once again to other places and since this [new displacement] implies a grave disturbance in my professional practice and since my financial resources have been affected by the different moves I have been subjected to and having the imperious necessity of working in order to survive decorously, I beg you to order . . . this city as my permanent address."[49]

Seeing resources of Japanese Mexicans reduced, Japanese Mexican entrepreneur Alberto Yoshida begged Minister Miguel Alemán to soften restrictive financial regulations:

It is true that a disposition dictated by the Treasure Department allows the monthly withdrawal of up to five hundred pesos . . . but this measure does not alleviate their desperation and moral suffering . . . for they will have to spend all their savings to live in misery and hunger. . . . I beg you in the name of many of the persons affected [by these dispositions], being a just and a humanitarian measure, the individual release of all frozen bank accounts, so they can choose freely their employment or occupation.[50]

Yoshida proposed a new regulation that would affect only middle-class and wealthy persons, among them Yoshida himself, since the poorest members of the community did not have bank accounts from which to withdraw money.

Yoshida also requested permission to publish a weekly bulletin "in Japanese language and in Castilian, taking in account that most of our compatriots do not know how to read Castilian." The publication would inform the community about possible jobs and provide orientation on how to comply with the national measures applying to Japanese Mexicans, "excluding absolutely all political comments about the international situation." In addition, Yoshida reminded the minister of the interior that Japanese Americans interned in concentration camps in the United States had food, employment, and medical care while under the custody of the U.S. government.[51]

Not only did the Mexican government not provide shelter and meals for uprooted Japanese Mexicans, but it denied these people, often without explanation, the opportunity to work in order to support their families. Thus, the Ministry of the Interior sabotaged the earnest efforts of Japanese Mexicans to find employment.[52]

Unemployment added to the problems of some uprooted Japanese Mexicans. Destitute and extremely sick, George Yamanouchi, from Rayón, Sonora, faced his own imminent death as soon as he was ordered to leave his ranch in the borderlands. Yamanouchi was a sixty-seven-year-old man with a heart condition, arthritis, and severe edema, all problems worsened by the altitude of Mexico City.[53] In a series of letters addressed to various offices, George Yamanouchi requested to "be allowed to die at the piece of land I lived at for so many years, and where with my work and thousand sacrifices I acquired some land I love more than life itself. I am very old, Sir, and I only have a few days to live, I will always thank you for the favor [to let me die at home], for which I appeal to your generosity and humanitarianism."[54]

The Japanese Mexican elder man did not receive permission to return to Sonora to spend his last days at home. Fortunately, other Japanese Mexican men tended to him in Mexico City for a while. When, for reasons of employment, his roommates were forced to abandon the elderly man, the Comité Japonés de Ayuda Mutua (CJAM), an organization that mediated between the uprooted Japanese Mexicans and the government, asked the Ministry of the Interior to intern Yamanouchi in a nursing home.[55] Confronted with the moral obligation of the Ministry of the Interior having to pay for Yamanouchi's care at a nursing home, Eduardo Ampudia, DIPS chief, gave permission for the ailing Japanese Mexican man to return to Sonora on March 16, 1944.[56] It was too late. Yamanouchi could not make the trip back home because of his grave medical condition.[57] George Yamanouchi entered a concentration camp, where he died in August 1944.[58] He shared with other Japanese Mexicans common circumstances of poverty, illnesses, and death during the relocation program.[59]

The program also affected other Mexican denizens of Asian descent. That Korea had been invaded by Japan and Koreans were victims of

Japanese imperialism did not matter to Mexican officials who sought to control the Japanese Mexican community already displaced and living within the limits established for them. In November 1942, Mexico City police chief general Miguel Martínez arrested José Hahn Kim, secretary of the Korean Association in Mexico City. Colonel Daniel P. Fort accused Hahn Kim of "having a conversation [with an unidentified person] that was contrary to democracy."[60] The policemen's qualms grew larger when they searched Hahn Kim and found two documents in languages they did not know. One of them was written in Korean, but the officers thought the text showed Japanese characters. The second document was typed in English. This text, signed by Chi Kin, chief of the executive committee of the local Korean Association in Mérida, Yucatán, once translated from English to Spanish read (as a DIPS translator reported): "At the present time America and Japan are at war and Mexico has declared war against Japan. This is a good opportunity for Koreans: one in thousand years. After we lost the sovereignty of our country, people in the world called us slaves of a ruined country. . . . The matter we shall worry is that during this bitter war between America and Japan, if the unlawful persons mistake Koreans by Japanese: how should we do concerning the unreasonable and violent actions [*sic*]?"[61]

The Korean community's fear of falling victim to the anti-Japanese campaign proved justified. José Hahn Kim was detained because a civilian passing him in the street suspected Kim of being Japanese due to his appearance. His accuser, Daniel P. Fort, did not have to explain in detail what kind of statements Hahn Kim had made in order to warrant his arrest. It was Hahn Kim's responsibility to establish his innocence and to prove he was legally in the country. It appears that General Martínez released Hahn Kim from jail after a General Rojo vouched for the Mexican Korean. Nevertheless, Japanese and Korean Mexicans lost any civil or human rights they had when Mexico declared war against Japan.[62]

In Giorgio Agamben's examination of the mechanisms through which modern nations operate, he recognizes that the enjoyment of human rights is dependent on the projects of the state. Counter to the idea that modern states protect each of their citizens, Agamben argues that citizenship does not imply permanent access to human and civil rights; rather, the state dictates the conditions under which some citizens will enjoy their rights and when they will have access to the protection of the laws. In *State of Exception*, Agamben studies how states take actions that in principle violate human rights but that become legal practice during states of emergency. The philosopher concludes that the suspension of laws predicated on the excuse of national crisis allows a state to cancel the citizenship of those who challenge the rule of the state in order to exclude, exploit, or exterminate or them.[63]

The 1942 relocation program contributed to the normalization of state violence against the same citizens it was purportedly created to protect.[64] A common element in the management of populations cited in this and other chapters is the targeting of individuals in terms of legally defined racial characteristics. The territorial exclusion of populations of color that took place in the U.S.-Mexico borderlands, with the consequential loss of their rights, reinforces the idea that effective citizenship is limited to persons racially classified as "Mexicans." Furthermore, the construction of negative images that surround the uprooting of racialized persons and communities separates human beings into deserving and undeserving citizens. Both the U.S. and Mexican governments alienated ethnic Japanese through their racial classification in 1942 and deprived them of their civil rights.[65]

The Mexican government forced Japanese Mexicans to travel south in order to relocate to Mexico City. Yet, the evacuation program had a transborder character that involved many more persons from other regions. Thousands of Latin American families traveled in various directions within and outside the American continents. The U.S. State Department and Department of Justice would take control of the lives of thousands of Latin American Japanese during World War II to control and isolate them in concentration camps in the United States for the duration of the war and beyond.[66]

CHAPTER FIVE

The Road to Concentration Camps

Villa Aldama and Batán

[Alberto] Shunji Yoshida and Sanshiro Matsumoto . . . founded a farm in Temixco, Morelos, where the Japanese were concentrated during the First Great War [sic].

—SERGIO GONZÁLEZ GÁLVEZ, MEXICAN AMBASSADOR

Current friendly relations between Japanese Mexican leaders and members of the Mexican government have aided in the impression that Mexico protected all Japanese Mexicans from the United States' control during World War II. Confirming this affable relationship, on December 3, 2008, the Mexican Ministry of Foreign Affairs organized the academic symposium Ciento Veinte Años de Amistad entre México y Japón (One Hundred and Twenty Years of Friendship between Mexico and Japan). In Mexico City, Mexican and Japanese diplomats, scholars, and businesspeople celebrated what, in the official news reporting the event, has been a long-lasting, uninterrupted "relationship of deep respect, sincere friendship, and mutual collaboration" between Japan and Mexico.[1]

The speeches Mexican officials addressed to the audience during this conference reflect the will to ignore the damage the Mexican government inflicted on the Japanese Mexican community during World War II. Mexican ambassador emeritus Sergio González Gálvez praised the virtues of those Japanese Mexicans he regarded as memorable heroes of the Mexican Revolution. Among them, González mentioned Shunji (Alberto) Yoshida and Sanshiro Matsumoto, who, according to the educator and diplomat, "founded a farm in Temixco, Morelos, where the Japanese were concentrated during the First Great War [sic]." González Gálvez stated that the uprooting of Japanese Mexicans occurred during World War I, not during World War II, and insisted on denying the effects of their eviction from the borderlands.[2] Distancing himself from the reality of the Japanese Mexicans' experience, the ambassador not only described Temixco camp as a farm and the product of Sanshiro Matsumoto and Alberto Shunji Yoshida's entrepreneurship, but he merged the names of these two businessmen with those of the Japanese Mexicans who participated in the Mexican Revolution against social injustice, placing them in the pantheon of heroes of the civil war.[3] In sum, the concentration camp was a farm, and the privileged Japanese Mexicans who ran the camp for the Mexican state were heroes of the Mexican Revolution according to this Mexican diplomat.

Contributing to the misinterpretation of the relocation program, Dr. González Gálvez omitted the fact that most displaced Japanese Mexicans did not enjoy Matsumoto and Yoshida's freedom to administer the finances of Temixco's concentration camp and other businesses during World War II. Furthermore, González Gálvez stated that the eviction of the Japanese Mexicans from the borderlands occurred during World War I, a conflict in which the Mexican state did not take part directly. If his time frame was an involuntary mistake, Ambassador González Gálvez elected to omit from his narrative the existence of other concentration camps in Mexico, the material losses of most Japanese Mexicans, and the suspension of their basic civil rights, which resulted in hunger, homelessness, and even death. The Mexican diplomat, and those who applauded him in December 2008, refused to recognize the responsibility of the Mexican and U.S. governments in the dislocation of the Japanese Mexican community during World War II.[4]

Refuting González Gálvez's declaration, hundreds of files in the DIPS archives and the direct testimony of some displaced Japanese Mexicans attest to the violence and coercion that defined the lives of uprooted borderlanders during World War II. Immediately after the Mexican state evicted Japanese Mexicans from the borderlands, the victims endured lack of economic resources and uncertainty. Their internment in concentration camps gave a different dimension to the experience of Japanese Mexicans during World War II, characterized by forced labor, lack of freedom, and class conflicts.[5]

In view of the presidential suspension of civil rights and Ávila Camacho's decision to ignore the Geneva Convention's protocols during World War II, no individual or institution in Mexico had enough power to protect working-class Japanese from the Mexican state's orders to evacuate the borderlands. The emergent Comité Japonés de Ayuda Mutua (CJAM; Japanese Committee of Mutual Assistance) represented the Japanese Mexican community and negotiated some aspects of its relocation, however. Although the association tended only to the most urgent needs of the displaced borderlanders during World War II, its main objective, as ordered by the Ministry of the Interior, was to assist the Mexican government in managing Japanese Mexicans. In this capacity, the CJAM operated the concentration camps in Temixco, Villa Corregidora, and Rancho Castro Urdiales, three of the five known camps in Mexico, and requested the closure of the first concentration camp in Villa Aldama, Chihuahua.[6]

The CJAM intervention in the operation of concentration camps during World War II, except for the Villa Aldama camp, has supported the widespread idea that Japanese Mexicans formed a self-governed society in the camps. The research in this chapter uncovers the lack of power and the degree of coercion Japanese Mexicans were exposed to in World War II. Although the CJAM assisted the uprooted population in various instances, particularly in the case of Villa Aldama's camp, the CJAM's involvement in lives of the internees was quite complex. Since legal recourse to protect the Japanese Mexicans was not possible, the CJAM navigated the same system of corruption and personal favors that permeated the relationships between U.S. and Mexican officials during World War II.[7]

Managing the Camps

In January 1942, the Mexican government, showing its support for the U.S. nation, ordered the deportation of all Japanese diplomats, leaving Japanese immigrants without effective diplomatic representation in Mexico.[8] As hundreds of empty-handed Japanese Mexicans arrived in Mexico City with their children, the Mexican government realized that, without the means to cover their most urgent needs, the displaced persons would become a visible problem in the capital. Having forbidden the operation of Japanese clubs or associations and intending to transfer to a third party the responsibility of feeding and housing the "citizens of an enemy nation" as well as their descendants, the Mexican state granted a special permission for the establishment of the CJAM in March 1942.[9] Although local Japanese associations had provided direction and cohesion for immigrants and their descendants before 1942, the CJAM acquired an unprecedented role when the Mexican government allowed the intervention of its leaders in the management of Japanese Mexicans during World War II.[10]

The CJAM originated out of the relationship Japanese diplomats had with some members of the Japanese Mexican elite. Before leaving for Japan in January 1942, Ambassador Yoshioki Miura left three of the most prominent

Issei in Mexico in charge of the Japanese Mexican community: Sanshiro Matsumoto, former gardener of the presidential palace and owner of a chain of nurseries; Heiji Kato, manager of El Nuevo Japón; and Kiso Tsuru, owner of the oil company La Veracruzana and other enterprises.[11] The three men received one hundred thousand pesos from Kyoho Hamanaka, Japanese naval attaché in Mexico. In turn, the Japanese Mexican entrepreneurs deposited this amount in cash in the hands of attorney Abelardo Paniagua Lara, a close friend of Alberto Yoshida. Paniagua made financial transactions on behalf of the CJAM board members when the Japanese Mexican entrepreneurs could not personally sign certain contracts due to the restrictions on Japanese businesses.[12]

Although the Mexican and U.S. government had blacklisted Kiso Tsuru and Heiji Kato as collaborators of the Japanese state, the two wealthy Japanese Mexicans received the initial monetary funding for the CJAM operations from the Japanese state. They also became members of the board, deciding the financial affairs of the CJAM.[13] Kiso Tsuru, Sanshiro Matsumoto, Heiji Kato, and Alberto S. Yoshida were the highest authority within this Japanese Mexican association, and in that capacity and within the limits the Mexican state imposed on them, they negotiated most aspects of the relocation program with the Mexican government and administered the CJAM resources.[14]

The financial support the Japanese state gave to the Japanese Mexican elite, as official diplomats left Mexico, provided the CJAM with the power to manage the Japanese Mexican community. Most Japanese Mexicans were trying to solve everyday problems caused by their relocation and persecution and did not have the means or time to participate more actively in the decisions the CJAM leaders made for them. Homeless and confused, uprooted Issei and Nisei Japanese Mexicans gratefully accepted housing and meals from CJAM leaders upon their arrival in Mexico City.[15] Similar to its counterpart in the United States, the Japanese American Citizens League, the CJAM would be an interpreter and mediator between the victims of the relocation program and the government, and it would also be ready to make agreements in the name of the entire Japanese Mexican community.[16] Such deals sometimes had a negative effect and at other times a positive influence on the quality of life of working-class Japanese Mexicans.

Although personal relations and sympathy could have influenced President Ávila Camacho's decision to give the CJAM the power to manage displaced Japanese Mexicans, corruption and the accumulation of wealth through questionable operations characterized Ávila Camacho's administration.[17] In addition to money and personal connections, protection required knowledge of the way corruption operated at the highest levels of the Mexican government, and that familiarity with the mechanisms of bribery was reserved for entrepreneurs. Unlike the Japanese Mexican leading the CJAM, who were wealthy or had close relations with politicians, disfranchised evacuees were unshielded, and they suffered systematic humiliation, incarceration, and continuous displacement.[18]

In Preparation for the Relocation Program

Alberto S. Yoshida was among those Japanese entrepreneurs who had personal contact with powerful Mexican politicians. Acting on the news that Japanese Mexicans were being forced to evacuate the borderlands, Yoshida, then a businessman residing in Mexico City, wrote a letter to Congressman Jesús M. Ramírez in January 1942. He explained to Ramirez that he had learned of the creation of a commission in charge of deciding how the property of nationals of the Axis nations would be allocated. The Japanese Mexican businessman invoked his twelve-year friendship with the Mexican congressman, who was a member of that commission, asking the politician to serve as a middle man between the Japanese Mexican community and the president of Mexico. Yoshida implored the Mexican government

> to rent or to indicate the facilities where the [Japanese Mexicans] could work the land, concentrated up to [a] certain number in each hacienda in order to optimize the control over [them]. This measure would be beneficial *to us* because *we* would not live as recluses in a Concentration Camp, we would have certain liberties in our private lives although we could not avoid the natural surveillance that the Mexican authority would exercise over us. [*my emphasis*][19]

In the same letter, Yoshida suggested that Japanese Mexicans pay for expenses derived from their forced relocation. Equally important was his assurance that profits would result from the labor of the displaced persons: "For the government the benefits would be as follows: to obtain a surplus from the agricultural production as a remedy to the scarcity [of agricultural products]. In addition, [the government] would not have to pay for the food, facilities, etc. In sum, instead of being a burden for the public treasury, [the haciendas] would be a source of production for the national economy."[20]

Yoshida's proposal was very attractive to President Ávila Camacho because it meant sharing the profits of the labor and also transferring the expenses of the concentration camp to the Japanese Mexican community itself. The U.S. State Department had discussed with the Mexican government the issue of concentration camps before the uprooting of the Japanese Mexicans had begun in January 1942.[21] Harold D. Finley, first secretary of the U.S. Embassy in Mexico City, recommended that U.S. diplomats pressure the Mexican government to obtain cooperation from Mexico to open a camp exclusively for Japanese Mexicans in the Maria Islands, a Mexican archipelago in the Pacific Ocean. U.S. officials thought Japanese Mexicans deserved to be subjected to the strictest incarceration systems. This island had been home to federal maximum security prisons since 1908.[22] Eventually, President Ávila Camacho authorized camps in other parts of Mexico under the most convenient terms for the Mexican and U.S. governments: neither state would have to finance any camp in Mexico. The financial matters concerning Japanese Mexican internees were, from the inception of the concentration camps, in the hands of private parties.

During World War II, the Mexican government officially referred to the facilities in Temixco, Villa Corregidora, and Rancho Castro Urdiales as concentration camps. However, Japanese Mexican inmates did not endure the same lethal violence suffered by internees in Europe's death camps. Nevertheless, internment in Mexican camps resulted in decreased quality of life, isolation, death for some inmates, disintegration of families, and loss of other networks of support.[23]

In March 1942, Japanese Mexican families in Ciudad Juárez were not fully aware of the conditions of their impending uprooting. After the U.S. and Mexican armies searched the homes of fifteen Japanese Mexicans in that city and escorted them to the federal district, the Japanese Mexican community split. The remaining Japanese Mexican families received orders to board a train to Camargo, Chihuahua. Eventually, Chihuahua's governor, Alfredo Chávez, ordered their internment in a labor camp in Villa Aldama. Eventually, under the pressure of relatives and friends of Villa Aldama's inmates, the CJAM leaders negotiated with the Mexican government for the release of the Japanese Mexicans interned in that camp.

Villa Aldama Camp

On March 27, 1942, El Paso's newspapers informed their readers that a group of eighty "Japs" from Juárez would have to leave the border city. If there were any qualms about their uprooting, the newspapers calmed them down, stating that the Japanese Mexicans had "been offered farming land in the prosperous farming community of Santa Rosalía [Camargo], near

Chihuahua City, where they will be able to earn a living for the duration of the war."[24] In fact, the displaced Japanese Mexicans did not stay in Santa Rosalía de Camargo or receive farming land. This group of uprooted borderlanders was held captive in Villa Aldama, Chihuahua. Governor Chávez forced them to work for Tomás Valles de Vivar, a wealthy politician and Chihuahua's treasurer.[25]

In April 1942, despite their lack of resources to start a new life somewhere else, entire families took the train south of the state of Chihuahua.[26] When allowed, other men chose to leave their children and spouses in Juárez, since their fates and the length of time they would be away from their usual occupations and means of support were unknown.[27]

Japanese Mexicans in Juárez were not the first group to evacuate the borderlands. The Mexican army and police in Baja California had already removed Japanese Mexican communities in January 1942 from the North Pacific area adjacent to the United States. By April, only those Mexican Japanese who could not travel to the interior for reasons validated by the Ministry of the Interior (Secretaría de Gobernación) remained at home.[28]

When military authorities ordered Jesús Kihara to leave his home in Juárez, he did not bring his family with him to Camargo. His Mexican wife and children would fare better in the company of their friends, and they all hoped the period of internment in a concentration camp would end soon. The haste of his travel did not allow him, or the rest of his travel companions, to carry any but the essential items they would need while away from their homes for an unspecified time. Later, uprooted Japanese Mexicans from Juárez would learn that, without appropriate housing, no amount of clothing would be enough to protect their bodies from the weather they endured for several months in Villa Aldama, Chihuahua.[29]

Kihara's experience is an example of the troubles and tribulations that many Japanese Mexicans had to endure during the relocation program. Kihara and other Japanese Mexican men and women from Juárez arrived in Santa Rosalía de Camargo in the southeast region of the state of Chihuahua at the end of March 1942.[30] Because the Mexican state did not supply the necessary food or clothing for the Japanese Mexican evacuees, the displaced men and women were responsible for acquiring basic supplies to survive during the days they spent in Camargo, a city located approximately seven hundred miles south of Ciudad Juárez. Some Japanese Mexican men managed in only a few days the difficult task of getting a job in the small city to pay for some of their life expenses. Such sources of income disappeared almost immediately, however.[31]

On May 7, Kihara's group from Juárez, in addition to other, elderly Mexican Japanese individuals from Camargo, was forced to enter the city's jail.[32] Chihuahua's governor, Alfredo Chávez, had ordered the incarceration of "nondangerous" civilians in a crowded space for three days "under the strictest surveillance." Even though Chávez admitted the innocence of the Japanese Mexican detained, he ordered their arrest. The group of displaced Japanese Mexicans was then escorted out and north of Santa Rosalía de Camargo to the hacienda property of Tomás Valles de Vivar in Villa Aldama.[33]

In 1942, Valles was the general treasurer of the state of Chihuahua and would soon become senator. Adding to his titles and power, Valles had other important posts in the national public and private sector: he was appointed ambassador of Mexico in Portugal; member of the First Credit, Money, and Credit Institutions Committee; affiliate of the First Tariffs and Foreign Trade Committee; and president of the First Mines Committee and the Special Livestock Committee.[34] Valles reaped immediate benefits from the confinement and exploitation of Japanese Mexicans during World War II. He did not offer compensation for the jobs the evacuees performed in his agricultural fields. Nor did he provide housing, sanitary facilities, or adequate clothing for the type of labor and weather conditions to which Japanese Mexicans and their families were exposed.[35]

Among the forty-eight internees the Ministry of the Interior categorized as "foreigners," four were farmers. The ages of twenty-three inmates ranged between fifty-two and sixty-three; however, all men, regardless of their profession, health status, or age, were forced to work in the fields.[36] It would take several months as well as the efforts of their relatives, friends, and the CJAM to achieve the release of the internees from the concentration camp in Villa Aldama.[37]

Because of the isolation of the interned Mexican Japanese, the state of affairs at Villa Aldama's camp was not immediately known to the Portuguese Embassy (at the time, the liaison between Japanese subjects and Mexican officials) or to the incipient CJAM. The closest city to Villa Aldama was Ojinaga, a border city across from Presidio, Texas. On the Mexican side, the hacienda was distant from the main roads and urban centers of the state of Chihuahua; the postal service did not reach the camp. In the absence of a means of communication such as telephone, telegraph, or regular mail, Tomás Valles de Vivar had little accountability in handling Japanese Mexican internees.

In an attempt to obtain help, internee Arturo Tamura submitted a letter on May 20, 1942, to Yoshio Sato, who was already living in Mexico. Tamura hoped Sato would inform authorities of the circumstances Japanese Mexicans in Villa Aldama endured:

Our situation is highly critical and painful since this concentration camp is on an immense solitary plain, there are no houses or trees where to protect ourselves from the intense heat. Furthermore, we are mistreated as if we were slaves. . . . Considering that current circumstances are the result of international affairs and not personal, we believe it is fair to be treated in a little bit more humanitarian and generous terms.[38]

The lack of official communication between the Ministry of the Interior and Chávez, however, was the product not of isolation, but of federal and state officials' disinterest in reporting or obtaining a report on the conditions of the Japanese Mexicans detained in Villa Aldama. It reflects a degree of autonomy on the part of the governor and the treasurer of the state of Chihuahua as well as a desire on the side of the federal government to please local politicians in the borderlands. Nevertheless, Adolfo Ruiz Cortines, chief officer of the Departamento de Investigación Política y Social (DIPS), attempted to obtain a report from Governor Chávez in June 1942 about the living conditions of the "foreigners." A response to the chief officer's request, if ever formulated, is not filed in the DIPS archives; in any case, Ruiz Cortines, future president of Mexico, did not take any action to alleviate the situation of the internees in Villa Aldama until months later, when pressure from the internees' relatives and friends increased.[39]

In the face of the federal government's neglect, Japanese Mexicans who had been relocated to Mexico City attempted to obtain the freedom of Villa Aldama's internees. On November 4, fifty Japanese Mexican men signed a petition to the president of Mexico, asking him to order the transfer of the persons interned in Villa Aldama to Mexico City. Among the signatories were Japanese Mexican residents of Ciudad Juárez who had been apprehended, detained, and interrogated by Mexican and American military officers. Ironically, they had fared better than the rest of the Japanese community in Juárez, having been escorted directly to the capital of Mexico.[40] This group of men advocating for the internees of Villa Aldama camp committed to "provide financial assistance to [the internees] and to pay for their traveling expenses [to the capital]." They reminded General Ávila Camacho that among those Japanese Mexicans in Villa Aldama, there was "not even one criminal or idle person, all of them having lived in the Mexican Republic under the traditional hospitality of this country and dedicated to compensate such hospitality with their honest labor." In the meantime, the internee's relatives continued to seek on their own the release of the Japanese Mexican group in the camp.[41]

It is important to highlight that although Mexican authorities did not make compulsory the internment of Mexican wives of Japanese Mexicans in the camp, several Mexican women and children lived in Villa Aldama. They were unaccounted for in the official records, but correspondence between Mexican women and officials attest to their presence.[42] Mexican wives and daughters of the internees who could pay for their transportation became the intermediaries between federal and state official representatives and the inmates, traveling between Juárez and Villa Aldama, or between the city of Chihuahua and the internment camp.[43]

On November 29, 1942, Enedina López de Kihara and Julia R. de Ogata, the Mexican wives of two internees in Villa Aldama, wrote a petition to the minister of the interior on behalf of the thirty-seven Japanese men interned in the camp. Knowing that the return of their husbands to their homes in the borderlands would be impossible due to the uprooting of ethnic Japanese on both sides of the border and the general atmosphere of hatred and racism against them, but trying to remove their relatives from the concentration camp, the two Mexican women requested the transference of all internees to the capital of Mexico. Not having received a response to her prior request, López de Kihara wrote another letter to the minister of the interior on December 29, 1942. The message had a desperate tone; her husband's health was rapidly deteriorating. The woman was afraid Mr. Kihara, a fifty-five-year-old Japanese Mexican, was in danger in the absence of a doctor and "relatives who take care of his health."[44]

Other relatives of the concentration camp inmates joined Enedina López de Kihara two days later to write a new petition to the minister of the interior. On December 31, wives and daughters of several Japanese men begged secretary of the interior Miguel Alemán to free the inmates and their families. The petitioners stated that they were

> living in the open under the protection of some tents where the cold weather is extremely intense and unbearable. . . . [The Japanese Mexican] men are forced to start working from very early in the morning until the darkness covers the camp, with no salary except for the insufficient meals the men receive. Their families do not collect provisions, much less money [for their work]. Since this is happening since April, the little money we brought with us when we left Ciudad Juárez is completely gone.[45]

The general economic instability of the country worsened the living conditions of Japanese Mexican individuals and their families in the Villa

Aldama concentration camp. War inflation accelerated their economic losses because the price of basic necessities was high. Excessive cold and malnourishment exposed the men and their families to grave illnesses. Children of various ages living in the camp were not attending school or receiving any formal education.[46]

Newspapers in Mexico and the United States treated the relocation as a benign form of control and focused on the activities of the adults, obliterating the experiences of children.[47] At present, it is difficult to find written narratives on the relocation program in Mexico assessing the pain of children who had to part with their parents, in some cases both, or leave their school, their home, and their friends in their place of origin to accompany their family. The generation who endured the pain of internment is passing away. The valuable information interviewees gave me and the written appeals their parents wrote to Mexican officials allow me to state that whether in the concentration camps or at home, Japanese Mexican children, some of them newborn, experienced harassment and hunger.[48] Their families had been, in many cases, of modest means before the war started; consequently, their parents were hardly able to face the expenses involved in moving to distant places.[49]

In the Villa Aldama concentration camp, the extremely cold winter of 1942 affected all internees, and their Mexican mothers, daughters, and wives in the camp reported to the Ministry of the Interior that children and adults went "almost naked without hope to recover from their losses since their husbands . . . did not earn a cent" for their labor at the camp.[50] Desperate, they demanded the freedom of all Japanese Mexican internees. In lieu of their freedom, once again they requested adequate housing to protect the captives from the inclement weather, a doctor paid by the ministry to tend to their sicknesses, and the means to provide for their families until the end of the global conflict. Minister Alemán did not respond to these requests. Nor did he act to remove the Japanese Mexican prisoners from the concentration camp.[51]

In the meantime, unrelenting neighbors and friends of Jesús Kihara tried other personal routes to bring the Japanese Mexican man back to Juárez to obtain the medical care he urgently needed. Oswaldo Álvarez, a businessman established in the same border city, offered to place a bond to guarantee that Kihara would not become a threat to national security. Álvarez deposited his real estate property, valued at $16,730 (pesos), as part of the bond. He was willing to risk his assets so the "Mexican Government [would] allow [Kihara] to live outside the concentration camp designated for the Japanese Colony, . . . [it] being absolutely necessary to get medical attention for him." His offer did not receive an answer from the officials in charge of the relocation program.[52]

Álvarez and hundreds of other Mexican citizens confronted their government, appealing to the legal system they believed would protect Japanese Mexicans from the abuse of the state. Knowing that Kihara's sickness had been accentuated by the conditions of the concentration camp and seeking the release of the internee, Oswaldo Álvarez attempted to preempt accusations of espionage and sabotage against the internee, describing him as an honorable, peaceful, hardworking person, whom Álvarez had known for several years.[53] Additionally, another thirty-six residents of the Barrio Alto in Juárez certified to having been personally acquainted with Jesús Kihara for more than twenty years. All of them deemed him "deserving of all consideration," asked for justice, and supported his family's petition to grant all individual rights provided by the "Laws of Our Country."[54]

Other complaints from relatives and internees prompted the CJAM in Mexico City to denounce to the Ministry of the Interior the conditions in which the Japanese Mexican families lived in Villa Aldama in the now harsh winter:

> Some are planting, others are carrying stones, and so forth, and they are not provided with housing for which they have been forced to sleep under tents that [the internees] themselves have installed, under which cover they cannot remain during the day because of the excessive heat, and by night [the tents do not protect them from] the cold weather, receiving meals that are worth not even ten cents per day. As a result of such inhumane and unjustified treatment many of them are sick and exhausted. As you may well understand, that place is of the worst kind, even when compared with a concentration camp.[55]

Such comparison rested on Japanese Mexicans' knowledge about the concentration camps in the United States. Despite their losses and the diminished quality of life endured at the U.S. internment camps, Japanese prisoners in the care of the U.S. Army or the INS received food, housing, and clothing in compliance with the Geneva Convention agreements.[56]

The predicament of the Japanese Mexican families interned in the Villa Aldama concentration camp was partially resolved when the Ministry of the Interior agreed to remove the Japanese Mexican inmates from the property of Tomás Valles de Vivar, whose prestige as cattle dealer, financier, and philanthropist remains unblemished in the history of Chihuahua.[57] The Mexican government had finally heard the request of the Portugal embassy and the CJAM to relocate the internees, and transported them to Mexico City in January 1943.[58] The DIPS assigned inspector Manuel Alemán Pérez the task of traveling to Villa Aldama to escort the Japanese Mexican men from the camp to Mexico City. Without complete certainty that authorities in Chihuahua would accept the transfer of the internees to Mexico City—after all, it was difficult for Tomás Valles to let go of free labor—some members of the CJAM accompanied Alemán Pérez.[59] Their mission was to make sure that the prisoners would indeed be transported to the federal district and to pay for the expenses derived from their traveling to the interior of the country.[60]

On January 18, 1943, Inspector Manuel Alemán Pérez escorted Villa Aldama's inmates to Mexico City.[61] Once they left the Villa Aldama concentration camp, the former internees joined other evacuees in their predicaments in the federal district. They all continued to face dire conditions because the government had conveniently accepted Alberto S. Yoshida's proposition to let uprooted Japanese Mexicans pay for their own expenses while confined in designated places.[62]

Batán

The effects of the relocation program on the Japanese Mexican community were not uniform. Some Japanese Mexican businessmen who already lived in Mexico City at the onset of World War II did not see their assets affected. Thus, the evacuation program accentuated the gap between economic classes within the same Japanese Mexican community. The distance between wealthy and working-class Japanese Mexicans grew as Mexican officials increasingly shared their power over displaced borderlanders with the CJAM leaders.

The case of Sanshiro Matsumoto is an example of the class differences that determined the quality of life of Japanese Mexicans during World War II. An icon of the Japanese Mexican community since that time and member of the CJAM board of directors, Matsumoto conveniently continues to be revered by Mexican officials to this day.[63] The entrepreneur, whose father, Tatsugoro, arrived in Mexico from Japan in 1892, administered and expanded the family's flower-farming business during the first decades of the twentieth century. Clients of the Matsumotos included presidents Porfirio Díaz, Álvaro Obregón, and Manuel Ávila Camacho, along with other high-ranking politicians and generals. Undoubtedly, Matsumoto's relations with powerful clients allowed him to negotiate the destiny of hundreds of destitute persons of Japanese origin during relocation.[64]

Sanshiro Matsumoto and the Ministry of the Interior opened a camp in January 1942 on Matsumoto's ranch, named Batán and located in the southern area of Mexico City, with the understanding that internees would be financially responsible for their living expenses.[65] Considering the precarious conditions in which many arrived, however, a large part of the one hundred thousand pesos in the care of Abelardo Paniagua was probably used during the first weeks of the relocation to provide meals for uprooted Japanese Mexicans while interned in the camp or housed at the CJAM's facilities.[66]

Given the state of emergency under which Japanese Mexicans were displaced, it was difficult to accommodate hundreds of evacuees from the borderlands in a short period. The Ministry of the Interior registered 569 women, men, and children interned in Batán, although some researchers account for more than 900 persons living in the ranch during the first days of the relocation to that camp.[67] Internees of Batán were a diverse population from several geographic areas of Mexico and Japan, with different religious beliefs, ages, cultural backgrounds, economic classes, occupations, ethnicities and nationalities.[68]

Because of the lack of information about the relocation program, conditions under which Japanese Mexicans lived and worked in the ranch remain unknown. The ranch was situated in a very isolated area of Mexico City, and it was difficult for displaced Japanese Mexicans to search for other places of residence or employment. Against the official version that Batán served as a site of protection for displaced Japanese Mexicans, one of the interviewees, who was born in Mexico City within an uprooted family, stated that "there was abuse, but people do not want to talk about it. We don't want outsiders to learn what happened in Contreras [at Batán camp]." This statement reveals a code of silence that has made it difficult to construct a narrative of the internment of Japanese Mexicans from the perspectives of the internees.[69]

While the government of Mexico was ultimately responsible for the welfare of the displaced civilians, the administrators and owners of the camps were the internees' only representatives before the Ministry of the Interior, so they were "juez y parte" (judge and defendant) when disagreements or complaints arose. While internees at U.S. concentration camps administered by the army or the INS had the recourse to complain before the Spanish ambassador, no semblance of protection against illegal or unjust practices existed in the Mexican camps.[70]

Despite the restrictions the Ministry of the Interior imposed on Japanese Mexicans during World War II, CJAM leaders obtained from the ministry several travel permits to search for land to buy, but also to visit their families, or spend their vacations at resorts.[71] Thanks to their political and geographic mobility, Sanshiro Matsumoto and his partners acquired the hacienda of Temixco, Morelos, to open as a third "farm," or internment camp.[72]

If details of the conditions and activities of Japanese Mexicans at Batán are largely unknown, the camp the CJAM opened in the state of Morelos in July 1942 may reflect the complexity of the role its leaders played during World War II. Undeniably, these influential Japanese Mexicans still enjoy the praise of the Mexican government officials.

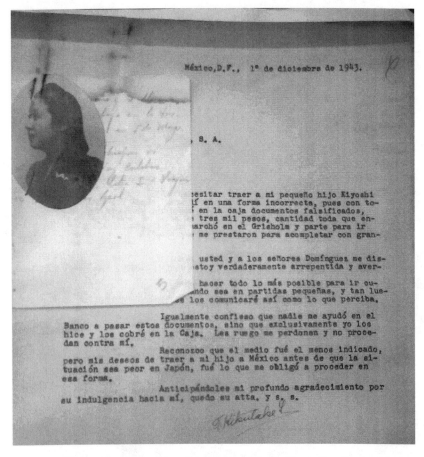

México,D.F., 1° de diciembre de 1943.

, S. A.

:esitar traer a mi pequeño hijo Kiyoshi
[f en una forma incorrecta, pues con to-
⌐ en la caja documentos falsificados,
; tres mil pesos, cantidad toda que en-
¡archó en el Orishola y parte para ir
⌐ me prestaron para acompletar con gran-

usted y a los señores Domínguez me dis-
⌐atoy verdaderamente arrepentida y aver-

hacer todo lo más posible para ir cu-
⌐ndo sea en partidas pequeñas, y tan lue-
⌐e los comunicaré así como lo que perciba.

Igualmente confieso que nadie me ayudó en el
Banco a pasar estos documentos, sino que exclusivamente yo los
hice y los cobré en la Caja. Les ruego me perdonan y no proce-
dan contra mí.

Reconozco que el medio fué el menos indicado,
pero mis deseos de traer a mi hijo a México antes de que la si-
tuación sea peor en Japón, fué lo que me obligó a proceder en
esa forma.

Anticipándoles mi profundo agradecimiento por
su indulgencia hacia mí, quedo su atta. y s. s.

F.Kikutake

Figure 1. Resignation letter from Banco General de Capitalización in Mexico City, signed by Flora Kikutake, December 1, 1943. Born in the United States, Flora lived with her parents in Veracruz, and then moved to Mexico City, taking care of her mother during World War II. Flora admitted to improper appropriation of money from the bank. She cited the need to bring her young son from Japan during World War II as the reason. Courtesy of the Archivo General de la Nación, IPS 2-1/362.4(52)/1620.

Figure 2. Kim Yano and Eva Watanabe. After losing the family business and home in Baja California during World War II, Kim Yano became the strongest pillar of her family and helped support her daughter and grandchildren by selling *manjū* (饅頭, まんじゅう), a type of Japanese bread, in the neighborhood of Portales, Tlalpan. At the onset of the war, Portales was in the outskirts of Mexico City. Courtesy of Eva Watanabe.

Figure 3. Rosa Kazue Matsuo Yano and Sumako Matsuo Yano, Ensenada, Baja California, ca. 1935. Japanese immigrants reproduced some aspects of the Japanese culture while adopting others from Mexico. Rosa Kazue and Sumako enjoyed a tranquil life and economic stability in Baja California until the Mexican government ordered the uprooting of Japanese Mexicans in 1942. Photographer: Toshio Watanabe. Courtesy of Eva Watanabe.

Figure 4. Dr. Augusto Fujigaki Lechuga and family, Mexico City, 1948. Members of the Fujigaki Lechuga, Montesinos Melgar, and Sánchez Cisneros families celebrate young Augusto's wedding. Dr. Fujigaki Lechuga was a prominent scientist who held important government positions from the 1960s on. Courtesy of Hermilo Sánchez Cisneros.

Figure 5. "I've had about enough of this." The depiction of Francisco Villa in this political cartoon is far from the always well-dressed leader of the Mexican Revolution, considered a superior military strategist. Yet it expresses the tensions present in U.S.-Mexico relations. By Clifford Kennedy Berryman, March 10, 1916, file 306154, RG 46: Records of the U.S. Senate, 1789–2011, National Archives and Record Administration, Washington, DC.

Figure 6. "Nope. Don't Want Silver Today." This cartoon by Edmund Duffy depicts the blockade the United States initiated against Mexico as a punishment for President Lázaro Cárdenas's expropriation of the oil industry. *New York Times,* April 3, 1938, 5.

Figure 7. "Materias primas para la guerra. Mexico las produce. Nosotros las transportamos." (Raw material for the
war. Mexico produces them. We deliver them.) Poster
printed by Ferrocarriles Nacionales de México (National
Railroad of Mexico) from 1943 showing pride in delivering valuable resources to the United States. From "De lo
sucedido en México durante la II Guerra Mundial," *El
Bable,* http://vamonosalbable.blogspot.com/2012/08/de
-lo-sucedido-en-mexico-durante-la-ii.html.

Figure 8. Poster distributed in Mexico during World War II, ca. 1942. These types of images helped further demonize Japanese Mexicans as the internal enemy. Published by the Oficina de Asuntos Interamericanos. From "De lo sucedido en México durante la II Guerra Mundial," *El Bable,* http://vamonosalbable .blogspot.com/2012/08/de-lo-sucedido-en-mexico-durante-la-ii .html.

Figure 9. "Americanos todos: Luchamos por la victoria/Americans all: Let's fight for victory." Poster by León Helguera, U.S. Government Printing Office, 1943-O-528719: O.W.I. Poster No. 65, UC Berkeley. Courtesy of the Bancroft Library.

Figure 10. Kim Yano, Rosa Katsue de Watanabe, and Rosa's children: Victor Katsuya, Eva Setsuko, and Luis Tadasu, Mexico City, ca. 1949. Expelled from the Mexican borderlands, Japanese Mexican women worked to support their families in a new environment. Courtesy of Eva Watanabe.

Figure 11. The Takaki family in Minatitlán, Veracruz, ca. 1941. They lost their small business when ordered to leave their home to relocate in Mexico City. Courtesy of Fidelia Takaki de Noriega.

Figure 12. Fidelia, Yoshio, and Francisco Takaki with their adoptive father, Eiji Matuda, in Chiapas, ca. 1944. Dr. Matuda was a renowned scientist and educator, who founded a school for indigenous students in Escuintla, Chiapas. He was also a professor at the National University of Mexico and assisted Octavio Paz in the translation of Matsuo Bashō's haikus. Courtesy of Fidelia Takaki de Noriega.

Figure 13. Asahiro Tanaka, accompanying the presidential family, ca. 1912. Tanaka was President Francisco I. Madero's valet. His family is very proud of the services Mr. Tanaka provided during the Revolution. In their memory is registered his obligation to taste the president's food to make sure Madero would not be poisoned. Courtesy of Shyzumi Olivia Otsuka Ordóñez de Tanaka.

Figure 14. Ángel Tanaka Gómez and family, ca. 1933. From left to right: Enriqueta Valdez Gómez, Asahirọ Tanaka Tanaka, Ernestina (Akiko) Tanaka Gómez, Ángel Tanaka Gómez, Maria de la Luz Tanaka Gómez, Jorge Alberto Tanaka Gómez, and Kawakita. Parque de Agua Azul, Guadalajara.

Figure 15. Mexican children, of Japanese descent, in an internment camp during World War II, Hacienda de Temixco, Morelos. The youngest child is Dr. Raúl Hiromoto, who considers himself the first child born in captivity. Courtesy of the Archivo General de la Nación, IPS 2-1/362.4(52)/1141.

Figure 16. The Hiromoto Yoshino family, Temixco, ca. 1948. Dr. Manuel Seichi Hiromoto and his family spent several years in the Temixco concentration camp. He was also incarcerated in the infamous Perote jail. At the end of World War II, Dr. Hiromoto established his medical practice in Temixco, near Cuernavaca, Morelos. Courtesy of Dr. Raúl Hiromoto Yoshino.

Figure 17. The Nakamura Ortiz siblings, ca. 1980. Originally from Palau, Coahuila, they endured separation from their father during World War II, after the death of their mother. Courtesy of Rodolfo Nakamura Ortiz.

CHAPTER SIX

Attempts to Challenge or Postpone Displacement

Though faced with the reality of internment and disruption of communal lives, Japanese Mexicans and their allies resisted and sought, steadfastly, to exercise their citizenship rights in Mexico. They challenged or attempted to postpone state pressures and decrees to uproot them from communities, family life, and friendships that had prevailed prior to World War II. This chapter seeks to explain the factors that enabled Japanese Mexicans to challenge state power successfully as well as factors that led others to succumb to government legerdemain and marginalization.

During World War II, Japanese Mexicans and their allies had to abandon legal recourses that had previously been available for the protection of citizens against questionable state measures. President Ávila Camacho closed that road when he suspended civil rights in Mexico and constituted himself as the ultimate administrator of justice in the country.[1] Consequently, Japanese Mexicans viewed personal appeals to the president and other state officials as their only possibility to hold their jobs, property, and families together. Such appeals often integrated the nationalist language exhibited in official propaganda.

The intent to produce an image of Japanese Mexicans as dangerous enemies of the nation was evident in Ávila Camacho's state-of-the-nation speech of September 1, 1942. Mexicans listened to the radio as the Mexican president described the uprooting of the Japanese Mexican community as an "efficient measure . . . to avoid the distribution of enemy propaganda and other activities that affect the security of the nation."[2] Federal deputy and congressional president Manuel Gudiño Díaz congratulated the head of state for "the internment of those foreigners from enemy countries, who because of their activities and origin it was necessary to set apart." Gudiño assumed that displaced Japanese Mexicans who were forced to enter a camp deserved their loss of freedom.[3]

Community Support and Disobedience

One of the many examples of communities disagreeing with the presidential program to remove Japanese Mexican members is the appeal of the residents of Cacalotlán, Sinaloa. On August 24, 1943, 180 residents requested from the Ministry of the Interior that Jesús Tarao Yanagui, doctor and farmer, be returned "to this town so he [can] continue sheltering his family."[4]

Aware of the arguments state officials used to uproot Japanese Mexicans, victims of the displacement program and their allies appropriated the prevailing nationalist rhetoric to resist the relocation orders. Cacalotlán residents claimed their own rights as Mexicans by birth to demand the return of Dr. Jesús Yanagui. His defenders noted their status as members of an ejido, an institution with political weight in post-Revolutionary Mexico.[5] They described Dr. Yanagui as a bona fide member of the Mexican community: "Mr. Yanagui married a Mexican woman eight years ago with whom he has three small children. He has been living among us for ten years and during that period we have not suspected him of concocting shady deals with spies or saboteurs in this country; we know his behavior, and during his residence in this town he has earned our love for his philanthropist and humanitarian services for which we believe that he is a person who deserves our trust."[6]

The residents of Cacalotlán asserted Dr. Yanagui's assimilation through his marriage to a Mexican woman, and his having fathered three children in this country. The time he had spent with this small community of ejidatarios was long enough to make its members feel he was not a part of any international conspiracies. Cacalotlán residents factored into their plea their right to represent the country's ideals based on their participation in the Revolution and their assertion of its expressed democratic principles: "We are a pueblo with a revolutionary and democratic history; we do not refuse to acknowledge the situation of our motherland." The inhabitants of Cacalotlán who opposed the displacement of Dr. Yanagui promised to "sacrifice themselves to defend the sacred rights of our country," and reiterated their desire to fight, using their constitutional rights, for the Japanese who were "good men, useful to the pueblos." To conclude, the signatories manifested their conviction that "an entire town expect[ed] to be tended to in its petition and wishing a favorable resolution."[7]

Like many other Japanese medical practitioners who had chosen to live in rural communities and to provide their services for free or at a very low cost while working the land, Dr. Yanagui was well respected and loved by his patients, neighbors, and relatives.[8] Although the plea of the ejidatarios was officially denied on December 21, 1943, by José Lelo de Larrea, DIPS chief, Dr. Jesús Yanagui's case exemplifies a degree of resistance that the relocation program provoked among several communities in the borderlands.[9] Other files exist with a similar number of signatures protesting the expulsion of Japanese Mexicans from their places of origin.[10]

Octavio Kazusa, a medical doctor resident of Camargo, Chihuahua, received equally overwhelming support from his community. During the first months of 1942, the Ministry of the Interior received more than seventy telegrams from individuals and institutions protesting Kazusa's relocation. The petitions came from civic associations, private clubs, public institutions, business groups, and unions. In addition, patients who received medical care at no cost, neighbors, and other citizens of Camargo testified to Dr. Kazusa's attributes as a professional and a citizen and demanded the suspension of his relocation order.[11]

Old and sick men were able to postpone their transfers to Mexico City, but local or federal authorities eventually forced elderly Japanese Mexican men to abandon their towns and relatives in spite of their ill health.[12] DIPS inspectors traveled at different times between 1942 and 1945 to rural Mexico to verify that all ethnic Japanese had been relocated. That is how the DIPS officers found that Tetsuo Taniyama Hueda had disobeyed his relocation orders. Taniyama was originally evicted from Culiacán, Sinaloa, in August 1943. Having been separated from his family for five months, Taniyama requested in January 1944 a permit from the Ministry of the Interior to return to his place of origin.[13] As was the Mexican custom when writing official reports, Taniyama wrote his petition in third person, explaining that he had left "his wife Rosario López de Taniyama, Mexican by birth, and his minor children Leopordo [*sic*], Ricardo and Amada, 8, 6 and 4 year old respectively, who are in a situation of extreme misery because of the absence of the head of the household."[14]

Taniyama did not receive authorization to leave Mexico City. Nonetheless, he defiantly left the federal district for Culiacán to tend to his wife and two of his children, who "were in a state of grave illness."[15] When DIPS agents traveled to Sinaloa demanding his return, Taniyama explained that his financial situation had worsened. He did not have money to return to the capital or to repay the money his friends had lent him to enable him to reunite with his family: "Given the circumstances that pain me and the enormous difficulties I struggle with in order to earn the bread for my wife and my children, I come to petition very respectfully from that superiority, as an act of humanity and superior justice, to grant me the permission to stay in this city, where my behavior has been immaculate."[16] Taniyama's request was denied despite the previous permit he had received from the governor of Sinaloa, General Rodolfo T. Loaiza, to stay with his family.[17]

The ambivalence of state officials allowed room for other Japanese Mexicans to resist relocation orders. Often, high-ranking officers resisted the relocation program for personal reasons, interceding on behalf of their friends or acquaintances. As commander of the first military zone in Mexico City, Rodrigo M. Quevedo wrote to the DIPS director on behalf of Toyomatsu Ito, a resident of Ciudad Juárez, Chihuahua, claiming that his good behavior and poverty were reason enough to cancel his relocation orders in 1943.[18] General Josué M. Benignos insisted on obtaining a permit for Enrique Rikaimatsu Matsumoto, whose degree of assimilation into his community was proved, according to Benignos, by his great command of the Spanish language and his inability to speak proper Japanese. In addition, Matsumoto had named one of his children Miguel Hidalgo, after the Mexican priest who led the Independence War in 1821, to express his admiration for Mexican leaders. General Benignos's recommendation only delayed Matsumoto's uprooting for some weeks.[19] Requesting the return of José Yahollosi to Coahuila in March 1943, General Brigadier Régulo Garza invoked a close relationship with the Japanese Mexican man as a friend and former coworker in the mines in Coahuila.[20]

Dr. Martín Otsuka: "The Prisoner"

The sort of leverage provided by personal relationships with powerful politicians or military officers was not available to most Japanese Mexicans. Another kind of relationship to military officials found poetic expressions in the writing of Dr. Martín Otsuka. After returning to Japan in the 1970s, the former resident of Namiquipa, Chihuahua, gave a literary account of his personal relationship with the military during the relocation program. Dr. Otsuka originally wrote his poems in Japanese, then translated some of them to Spanish. While his limited command of Spanish probably does not do justice to his Japanese verses, his readers can ascertain a frank and emotionally charged view of his arrest and how other Mexicans resisted

Dr. Otsuka's relocation. Translated to English by Robert Harland, many verses of this poem are included to allow Dr. Otsuka to represent himself in the telling of his story:

The Prisoner

Suddenly, they surrounded my room with machine guns.

There were enough men to form a platoon.

The flash of a gun barrel looked for me.

The captain unjustly demanded I surrender my radio.

He wanted to know where the money was.

He said I had funds to support seaborne Japanese soldiers.

It was a miracle: they did not find my own weapons even when they searched every cranny.

His soldiers were kind: they did not denounce me when they saw a few bullets.

The captain took me where my pregnant wife was: she was shopping at a grocery store.

When she saw my situation the surprise caused her to miscarry.

One of the richest men in town protested my arrest.

He asked for my freedom and attested to my good behavior.

The captain mulled over the rich man's offer.

The captain was sorry but he said I must follow my orders.

Thus cursed, he took me to the headquarters of the 5th military zone.

On the day of my arrest, the emperor was celebrating his birthday.[21]

Although much of the expression of Dr. Otsuka's poetic narrative certainly disappears in the translation, readers can still observe the will of the soldiers not to disclose the presence of firearms at Dr. Otsuka's home. The silence of the infantry proves their desire to avoid harsher treatment of the Japanese Mexican man. The nature of their employment forced the Mexican soldiers to search the house, but they did not blindly obey their orders to turn in any item that could support conspiracy charges against Dr. Otsuka. Later, senior military officers and the elite of his townsfolk obtained Dr. Otsuka's release—too late, however, to avoid the loss of life, as Agrícola Ordóñez de Otsuka, an expectant mother, experienced a miscarriage while trying to free her husband.

The story of Dr. Martín Otsuka's arrest has been transmitted orally in his family from generation to generation. His daughter, Shyzumi Olivia Otsuka Ordóñez de Tanaka, was too young then to have direct memories of the arrest, yet the pain emerged vividly. She tried to hold back her tears when she narrated this episode to me. According to Shyzumi Olivia, Mrs. Ordóñez de Otsuka followed her husband to the city of Chihuahua, and while she waited outside the jail for news of him, "the guards told her, 'Señora, leave, don't you see you are bleeding?' My mother answered that she knew she was bleeding, but she could not leave her husband there. . . . My father came out of jail too late. My mother had bled out, and the baby died. She was taken to a clinic right there in Chihuahua because she had to have surgery [to complete the miscarriage]."[22]

Mrs. Ordóñez de Otsuka received free medical care from a local doctor in Chihuahua, but her family was still in need of help to save her life. "The news traveled to the mountains, and from Namiquipa came down several persons to donate their blood for mother," continued Shyzumi. Yet, regular antibiotics were not effective to control a life-threatening infection, and the doctor urged the family to buy antibiotics only available in El Paso, Texas. The Otsuka family quickly sold some of their property to obtain Mrs. Ordóñez de Otsuka's expensive medicine.[23]

The Tanaka Otsuka family had many more stories to hand down from both sets of grandparents, who tell about the support Japanese Mexicans received during World War II. Ángel Tanaka Gómez, Shyzumi's husband, still remembers that in 1942, a platoon searched his home in Guadalajara. Asahiro Tanaka Tanaka, Ángel Tanaka's father, sent all the children to the basement when hearing soldiers at his door. These experiences were particularly painful for Ángel.[24]

Ángel Tanaka Gómez grew up proud of his father's participation in the Revolution; he had fought courageously alongside President Francisco I. Madero in 1911. The son was equally proud of the long-lasting friendships his father had with General Francisco Villa and Luz Corral de Villa. Although the soldiers' search in 1942 did not have any consequence, and the Tanaka Gómez family did not suffer immediate damages stemming from the relocation program, the father had to support several persons expelled from the borderlands. Ángel believes that his father's wealth was greatly diminished when he set up small businesses to help his compatriots in Guadalajara during World War II. He is also proud of his father's role in ameliorating the condition of newcomers in Guadalajara during this period, alleviating the impact of the expulsion for some Japanese Mexicans from the borderlands.[25]

A combination of personal empathy, economic interests, and political decisions created interstices for some Japanese Mexicans, softening or postponing the effects of the relocation program for a few of its victims.[26] This was the case of Governor Rodolfo T. Loaiza, who used the constitutional powers he had as governor of the state of Sinaloa to challenge the relocation program and managed to delay the eviction of a group of Japanese Mexicans.[27]

General Loaiza Defies Relocation Orders

Governor Loaiza, who publicly showed his support of people's institutions, such as the ejidos, extended his protection to Dr. Manuel Hayashi at the request of several peasant communities in Sinaloa.[28] Twelve ejidos officially resisted the relocation of Dr. Hayashi, arguing that, besides his exemplary behavior and good character, he was a productive resident of the region.[29]

Japanese Mexicans had allies, but they also endured the constant surveillance of racist, nativist groups. The Confederación de Trabajadores Mexicanos (CTM) and other zealous anti-Japanese groups and individuals in Sinaloa drew the attention of the central government in Mexico to Loaiza's protection of several Japanese Mexicans in his state.[30] The ensuing clash between state and federal powers held some promise for Mexican Japanese victims of the relocation program. This was evident in the case of Dr. Toshio Shimizu, whose resident status became the seed of a confrontation between the powers.[31]

Dr. Shimizu, whose representation as the epitome of Asian depravation is described in chapter 1, was a prominent member of the town of Mazatlán, Sinaloa. He was also a naturalized citizen who argued that his relocation would inflict "an irreparable damage" on his family should the "unjust deportation" take place. Dr. Shimizu correctly insisted on claiming his civil rights because he was not a "foreigner, but a Mexican according to the law." His relentless struggle to remain in Sinaloa could have been only one more story of defeat in the face of federal power.[32] Even so, Dr. Shimizu succeeded temporarily in his appeal. On May 14, 1942, Lamberto Ortega Peregrino,

DIPS assistant chief, granted permission for Dr. Shimizu to stay in Mazatlán. Ortega also sent a copy of the relevant documentation to the governor and to the military commander in Sinaloa. On June 18, DIPS inspector Federico Márquez visited Sinaloa to make sure all Japanese Mexicans had been removed from the state. Márquez confiscated Dr. Shimizu's citizenship certificate and residence permit as a way to ensure that the physician would obey his relocation orders and travel to Mexico City.[33]

Since Dr. Shimizu expected to stay in Mexico City for a short time, he registered at the hotel Maria Cristina, on June 25, 1942.[34] He trusted that Governor Loaiza's power as governor would get him authorization to return to his family and business soon. On the same date, the defamatory article (mentioned in chapter 1) was published in *Revista Tiempo*.[35] Not only did the magazine accuse Dr. Shimizu of practicing abortions, but the anonymous author of the article also described him as an unethical real estate speculator. But the real target was not the physician. The text ended with a message for Governor Loaiza. Although German Mexicans remained in Sinaloa, the article targeted only Japanese Mexicans. The point was to make Loaiza responsible for the presence of Dr. Shimizu in a zone from which Japanese Mexicans were excluded.[36]

In spite of his being the focus of malicious anti-Japanese innuendo, Governor Loaiza continued to show support for Dr. Shimizu and other Japanese Mexicans. On June 29, 1942, he confirmed his resolution to guarantee the good behavior of Dr. Shimizu should he return to Sinaloa, where he had "resided for more than thirty years [as head of] a Mexican family."[37] Frictions between the Ministry of the Interior and General Loaiza came to confrontation in the case of Dr. Shimizu.[38]

In July 3, 1942, Dr. Shimizu, who was well known in his community for his acts of charity and respect for impoverished people, requested permission from federal authorities to return for a short period to Sinaloa "with the only and exclusive goal to close my house and my medical office, notifying my sick patients of my leaving, and to transfer my family, completely Mexican, to this capital."[39] Dr. Shimizu was a wealthy man who had only been partially successful in his resistance to the relocation program: he convinced minister of the interior Miguel Alemán to let him return for three weeks to Mazatlán.[40]

Once in Mazatlán, Dr. Shimizu resumed efforts to oppose his expulsion. Upon his return, he met with Governor Loaiza, who stated that the minister of the interior should have respected the governor's permits. Encouraged by Loaiza, Dr. Shimizu consulted an attorney in Mexico City, asking if he could ignore the DIPS relocation orders once he had the governor's authorization. Although the attorney's advice is not filed in the DIPS archives,

Dr. Shimizu made clear that he would use every resource at his disposal to remain in Sinaloa.[41]

To the distress of the DIPS officials, Governor Loaiza insisted that Dr. Shimizu stay in Sinaloa, as Loaiza did for other Japanese Mexicans under his protection and whom he vouched for personally. Dr. Shimizu's campaign to remain in Mazatlán, however, became particularly difficult because of the intervention of Rafael Landa Ruiz, chief of Mazatlán Immigration Service.[42]

Landa's rank did not endow him with the kind of power that could prevent the governor from protecting several Japanese Mexicans, but Landa was a compadre of Minister Alemán, soon to become president of Mexico, and this relationship emboldened Landa to challenge Governor Loaiza's decisions. Against official protocols, Landa invoked his compadrazgo relationship with Miguel Alemán to demand the expulsion of Dr. Shimizu. Alemán's compadre wanted to strip Dr. Shimizu of his property, including a mine in Cosalá and real estate in Culiacán, and the Mexican immigration official requested its confiscation.[43]

Landa's insistence on Dr. Shimizu's relocation was a turning point in the history of Sinaloa and relationship between state and federal powers. When Alemán's compadre personally demanded the physician's expulsion from the state, Governor Loaiza assertively informed Landa that his orders as governor superseded the instructions of a local Immigration Service official: "As long as the Ministry of the Interior does not cancel my government's instructions, you must respect the permission I granted to some foreigners to remain in this state."[44]

The reaction from the Ministry of the Interior was to persist in its attempted relocation of Dr. Shimizu and other Japanese Mexicans and German Mexicans who remained in the state, protected by Colonel Loaiza, and who owned property Landa wanted to seize.[45] But Governor Loaiza defied the centralized political system. He angrily insisted on discussing change-of-command procedures privately in a coded telegram to the undersecretary of the interior, Fernando Casas Alemán, demanding that "whenever that Ministry judges necessary to cancel the authorizations this government granted to foreigners to remain in this state, you must inform me [personally] in order to cancel such authorizations. The Chief of the office of Immigration in Mazatlán is receiving direct orders [from your office, countering mine]."[46]

In Mazatlán, Landa Ruiz ignored the permit Dr. Shimizu had from Governor Loaiza to stay in Sinaloa and visited the physician's home, ordering him to leave for Mexico City on August 7. At the sight of the inspector, Dr. Shimizu called Governor Loaiza on the telephone. Responding to the

provocation, Loaiza asked Dr. Shimizu not to leave his residence. Emboldened by the governor's support, the Japanese Mexican physician defied
Landa Ruiz, once again refusing to leave Mazatlán.[47] Landa left Dr. Shimizu's residence, temporarily defeated, to request the support of the ministry of the interior principal officer, Adolfo Ruiz Cortines. Aware of the
consequences of further confrontations, Ruiz Cortines ordered Landa to
"leave things as they are."[48] Landa did not obey Ruiz Cortines's instructions and instead contacted the local garrison to remove Dr. Shimizu from
Mazatlán.[49] Fortunately, Landa never followed through with his threatened
use of a platoon of soldiers to arrest Shimizu.[50]

Correspondence between Governor Loaiza, Landa Ruiz, and the Ministry of the Interior officers made it clear that Landa Ruiz wanted Dr. Shimizu's property. Landa's insistence on evicting Dr. Shimizu had offended
Governor Loaiza. In turn, Loaiza's refusal to comply with the federal officers' instructions had disrupted an expected code of complete obedience
to the presidential administration, of which the Ministry of the Interior was
part.[51] Furthermore, Loaiza's protection of Japanese Mexicans compro-
mised diplomatic relations between Mexico and the United States. American consuls, when they learned of the presence of "enemy aliens" in the
borderlands and coastal zones, contacted the Ministry of the Interior to demand the immediate eviction of Japanese Mexicans. Thus, Loaiza's disobedience was particularly upsetting when friendly relations between the
United States and Mexico were a priority for the government of Mexico
during World War II.[52]

Matters between Governor Loaiza and the Ministry of the Interior did
not end when Landa gave up on the idea of using the Mexican Army to
evict Dr. Shimizu. Landa's compadre, Minister Alemán, consulted his own
legal department to confront Governor Loaiza and to uproot Dr. Shimizu
and other Japanese Mexicans in Loaiza's state. The Ministry of the Interior legal team concluded:

> [Because] the internment of Axis nationals is an exclusive power of the
> Citizen President of the Republic who carries it out via the responsible
> institution, [that institution being] the Ministry of the Interior, the Citi-
> zen Governors of the states absolutely lack the power to grant residence
> permits to the foreign residents in their respective regions. . . . Because
> the power to grant such permits is discretionary, the Ministry of the In-
> terior may revoke them at any time, without having to communicate such
> cancelation to the Citizen Governors of the Federal Institutions. . . .
>
> Dr. Shimizu, the particular case we are dealing with here, his in-
> ternment in this capital being ordered by the Citizen Chief of the

Department of Political and Social Investigation, IS TO BE CARRIED OUT [*sic*].[53]

Despite the legal team's recommendation to remove Dr. Shimizu from Mazatlán, the DIPS granted a permit for the medical caregiver and entrepreneur to remain in his home state.[54] Any deal between Governor Loaiza and Minister Alemán was probably verbal; Dr. Shimizu's file is silent on the issue. Loaiza's refusal to comply blindly with federal orders, however, had damaged his status in the Mexican political machinery.

Japanese Mexicans unfortunately lost a protector when Governor Loaiza was assassinated less than one year after he defied Minister Alemán. On February 20, 1944, Rodolfo Valdés, El Gitano, and other gangsters shot Governor Loaiza in a contract killing, paid for by unknown sources. In addition to the clashes he had with Miguel Alemán, he staged a war against growing plants to produce illicit narcotics. Although his murder was clearly politically motivated, the Mexican government did not conduct an exhaustive investigation. The identity of the person who ordered his execution remains a mystery. Loaiza had become a dispensable politician, and his family did not see justice.[55]

Governor Loaiza's resistance to the total implementation of the relocation program in the state of Sinaloa led him to disobey the most powerful institution at the heart of the Mexican state: the entrenched political machinery of the PRN (Partido Nacional Revolucionario, later Partido Revolucionario Institucional, PRI), an organization that granted power and wealth in exchange for total submission to the chain of command.

To Survive Relocation: Family Separation

In the absence of personal protection from powerful officials, most Japanese Mexicans were forced to leave their homes. Once in Mexico City, some parents realized their children would grow amid tight restrictions, economic misery, and discrimination. To spare their children the harshness of the relocation program, some parents gave them up for adoption. Such was the case of the Takaki family, evicted from the port of Veracruz in 1942.

When the Takaki family obeyed orders to leave their home and business in Veracruz, they became dependent on the assistance of other Japanese Mexicans during World War II for their subsistence in Mexico City. "Everything was lost, the *mercería* [fine hardware store] and our house, everything," recalled Fidelia Takaki. Her mother, "Doña María (Naru) Takaki, fell gravely ill and was unable to take care of her children." They stayed in the CJAM house for three months: "When we could rent a place we moved . . . The place we rented in Mexico was nothing compared to what we had in Minatitlán." Doña María died just three months after they had moved out of the CJAM quarters. "A doctor said a surgery could save her life, but we just did not have the money for that surgery." Ángel Takaki, Fidelia's father, could not obtain ⁓mployment, and the responsibility fell on his Spanish-speaking children. They struggled to find employment because they "were daughters of foreigners. There were not many places to get a job; therefore, their employees paid them very little." Clara, the third daughter, took care of her three younger siblings, but she was only fourteen years old.[56]

Fidelia Takaki remembers that although their neighbors were polite, she and her two brothers had a hard time walking to school. "They treated us like if we were the Japanese nation in war [against Mexico]. Hurting words . . . It was ugly. . . . They used to tell me 'china chale japonés come cuacha y no me des' [Chinese chink Japanese eat shit and do not give it to me]. That was new for us." Although her new friends learned to defend the Japanese Mexican children from other young attackers, the family felt the environment in Mexico was not safe for Japanese Mexican youngsters. Then they met Eiji Matuda, who was among the privileged Japanese Mexicans in the capital requesting authorization to remain in their hometowns.[57]

Dr. Eiji Matuda was a world-renowned scientist who had founded a school in Chiapas. The scientist's prestige and political relationships ensured that he kept his residence and property in the Mexican region bordering Guatemala. Dr. Matuda still had to process his authorization in Mexico City, however, and while there he learned of the troubles of the Takaki family.[58]

In an effort to shelter Fidelia Takaki and her brother Yoshio, Dr. Matuda adopted the two children. They grew up in Chiapas in the care of Mrs. Matuda. Fidelia Takaki, who later became a successful biologist, was very grateful for the protection provided to her from her adoptive parents in Chiapas. But she resented her separation from her original family and attributes the death of her mother to her inability to obtain proper medical care in Mexico City. She talks with great nostalgia about her home in Veracruz and her biological parents. When she grew up she returned to Mexico City to follow a career and resumed a caring relationship with her father, Ángel Takaki.[59]

Adult Japanese Mexicans continued to resist the relocation program in peaceful ways, but sometimes the results were tragic. Rodolfo Nakamura Ortiz, a child uprooted during World War II, during an interview remembered a Japanese Mexican man who died after leaving the concentration camp in Temixco. Nakamura blames Mexican officials for the death of the internee, who left the camp without official authorization. Mexican authorities sought the escapee in places Japanese Mexicans were known to meet, including the small business that Umezo Nakamura Nakamura, Rodolfo's father, operated with Alberto Imai in Mexico City. Rodolfo did not remember the name of the man when discussing the Japanese Mexican's efforts to avoid the police, but he recalled other details:

> By the way, they say that he was sick and died; but no . . . I know that is not true. [The policemen] came and left him here at my dad's home, already dead, all bathed, as if they had thrown water on him or something. That's it. I know that because when a group of well-groomed men came with the body, I was playing out there in the little patio. [They asked me] "Mr. Imai?" [I answered] "Yes." And he came out, Alberto Imai. He talked to them and got near the body and all that, and the men who looked like policemen took [the body] out of the car and he looked strange because he was already dead. When I wanted to enter the room [where the body was] my father did not let me in. . . . How did he die? They wrote that his death was due to illness."[60]

Rodolfo Nakamura believed that the police killed the Japanese Mexican man. His belief is consistent with the vulnerability Japanese Mexicans experienced during World War II. They did not have the civil rights that the general population or police forces were bound to respect. In this context of suspended human and civil rights, Mexican officials delivering a Japanese Mexican man's body to his friends did not warrant a full investigation of the conditions of his death.

The man who died had engaged (unsuccessfully) in another form of resistance to the relocation program: leaving a concentration camp without authorization. Haruji Yokayama Kawada left Temixco without permission in July 1943. DIPS officers searched several places to locate Yokayama. They needed to reestablish control over him and force him to pay a fine for his unauthorized departure. There is no evidence or information in his file, however, on the final results of the DIPS search for him. Because Japanese Mexicans were monitored by civilians and police at all times, Yokoyama did not have a permanent place to hide. Consistent with Niblo's report on corruption in Mexico during World War II, a plausible explanation for the lack of records reporting on Yokoyama after his escape is that he bribed the policeman to avoid penalty and incarceration.[61]

Limitations such as money and language as well as altered mental conditions in the face of emotional and physical hardships forced some persons to resist in ways that were damaging to themselves. A narrative from

DIPS officer Rodolfo Candiani conveys the desperation that drove some persons of Japanese origin to avoid the relocation program. Candiani combed the mountains of northern Mexico in September 1942 in the company of four soldiers and a sergeant. He and his military escort went through small towns and ranches in the mountains of Chihuahua in search of Japanese Mexicans. His mission was successful; he found five Japanese Mexican men working in a mine at Agua Caliente: Tomás Tokuhei Hayakawa, José Iduma, Ysac Sasaki, José Yshida, and Miguel L. Yshida López. Candiani reported that the Japanese Mexicans were "fugitives" and that José Yshida had a gun and a 30/30 rifle in his possession.[62]

After Candiani arrested the five Japanese Mexican men, he transferred his prisoners to Mexico City, where they relayed their own version of events. Tomás Hayakawa explained that before World War II began, he had rented a ranch in Sonora to work the land. The Japanese Mexican sharecropper obtained loans from the National Bank of Mexico and from private parties. At the onset of the war, Hayakawa had sizable debts plus the responsibility to pay for his family's transportation and living expenses in Mexico City under the relocation program. When he found himself without resources to comply with his orders, he left for Agua Caliente. Hayakawa had hoped to partially solve his financial problems by collecting two thousand pesos that a mechanic in Agua Caliente owed him.[63]

According to Hayakawa, the mechanic died before he could repay the two thousand pesos; consequently, the Japanese Mexican man did not have money to comply with the relocation orders. He then obtained employment as a miner to provide for his family in Sonora. Other Japanese Mexican men arrived later to work in the same mine, not having resources or the desire to obey the relocation orders and hoping to stay out of sight of the DIPS despite the small salary they received as miners. Although Inspector Candiani had confiscated some weapons, they were the kind that inhabitants of the mountains used for hunting or self-defense, and the Japanese Mexican men had not used those firearms to resist their arrest.[64]

During the same raid, Candiani learned of the presence of Dr. Manuel Seichi Hiromoto in the mountains of Chihuahua. The Japanese Mexican man was a deserter of a Japanese vessel who had established himself in Urique, Chihuahua, when World War II broke. When a Mr. Johnson, the mechanic who owed money to Tomás Hayakawa, fell ill in Agua Caliente, Dr. Hiromoto, one of the few doctors in the area, was called to tend to Johnson's sickness, but the Japanese doctor arrived too late. Johnson died. Dr. Hiromoto, pleased to see other Japanese Mexicans in Agua Caliente, stayed for some days in the mining town—until a platoon arrived in search of Japanese Mexicans living in the mountains. Indigenous and mestizos protected the doctor and alerted him of the search. Having lost his passport when he deserted the Japanese ship on Sonora's coast, Dr. Hiromoto did not want to confront the Mexican authorities. He went into hiding, and with the help of indigenous communities, neighbors of Urique, and military officials who held Dr. Hiromoto in high esteem, he managed to delay his arrest until January 1944.[65]

Transnational Elites

While most Japanese Mexicans resisted relocation peacefully and to no avail, Dr. Kiso Tsuru managed to live a life of luxury and travel during World War II. Before Mexico declared war against Japan, Dr. Tsuru owned the Compañía Internacional de Comercio, a medical products distribution business based in Mexico City. In addition, he owned other businesses, including mines, and he was the general manager and owner of the Compañía Petrolera Veracruzana, an oil company the Japanese government financed but that Tsuru presented as if it were a Mexican enterprise. Dr. Tsuru had a close relationship with the Japanese and the Mexican states through the operation of La Veracruzana and also La Compañia Mexicana de Petróleo La Laguna, both oil companies in which Mexican officials were shareholders. Japan was able to obtain petroleum at a very low cost through Tsuru's corporations between May 1940 and December 1941, while Mexican officers received bribes from the Japanese entrepreneur to authorize the import of rayon thread, even in the face of surplus. Mexico lost $600,000 as a result of the oil sale contracts and the loss through import of an excessive amount of rayon thread. Tsuru's profitable transactions with Mexican politicians, however, facilitated his financial success and freedom during World War II.[66]

Dr. Kiso Tsuru, a prominent leader of the Japanese Mexican community during World War II, supported the idea—originally proposed by Alberto Yoshida—that the Mexican government did not have financial responsibility for the displacement of Japanese Mexicans. Dr. Tsuru requested that the Ministry of the Interior send police officials to a camp he planned to open. Police would ensure that internees were "dedicated to the exclusive cultivation of the land they are responsible for." Both the CJAM and the Mexican government were to guarantee the camp's efficiency as a labor center.[67] While Dr. Tsuru's plan for a camp did not seem to materialize in San Luis Potosí, several camps opened in Temixco, Castro Urdiales, and

Villa Corregidora, under the conditions Dr. Tsuru had proposed to the Ministry of the Interior.[68]

In addition to the operation of concentration camps, Dr. Tsuru and several high-ranking officials in the Mexican government were business partners during World War II. After the United States forced President Manuel Ávila Camacho to prohibit the trade of mercury and other minerals with Japan in July 1941, several Mexican officials, including the president's brother, Maximino Ávila Camacho, continued the illegal trade of metals with Japan.[69] According to historian María Elena Paz, Dr. Tsuru was a key individual in Japan's illegal acquisition of metals from Mexico. Mexican officials involved in the clandestine trade valued Dr. Tsuru's role as a liaison with the Japanese state.[70]

Dr. Tsuru's public relationship with the Mexican state heeled the official need to satisfy U.S. demands to control the Japanese Mexicans. The Mexican government had seized 4 million pesos from Dr. Tsuru's account at the beginning of World War II, but the investments he made using Japanese state money were larger than the amount the Mexican government had taken from him. Dr. Tsuru invested 18 million yen (100 million pesos) in 1937 to finance the operations of the two commercial ventures, Compañía Internacional Petrolera (later Compañía Internacional de Comercio) and Tsuru Mining Company, which merged with the oil companies La Veracruzana and La Laguna.[71] Although the United States blacklisted Dr. Tsuru, he built strong relations with the Mexican presidential family, resulting from the deals the Japanese government made with Maximino Ávila Camacho to obtain clandestine mineral resources in 1941. In November 1942, Inspectors Juan Sánchez de Tagle and José R. Gracián reported on four men "whose activities hurt the country." Paulo Pliska, Walter Alberts, and Paul Grzesik were labeled as Nazis. Dr. Kiso Tsuru was denounced as having been in contact with Franco Baldi, allegedly the leader of fascism in Mexico. In addition, the agents stated that Dr. Tsuru had acquired merchandise from blacklisted companies.[72]

Dr. Tsuru became a national sensation when he was tried on May 16, 1943, for fraud. A newspaper article narrated a segment of the trial and referred to it as a "Scandalous Incident at the Supreme Court." The origins of the legal case lay in his business partnership with two notorious Mexican men. Military engineer Carlos Almazán and General Juan Barragán, both shareholders of Tsuru's mining company, sued the physician for his allegedly unethical business practices. According to the newspaper article, Dr. Tsuru made them believe that the mining company's seams of ore were no longer profitable, and so they stopped production and lost their investment. Then Tsuru sold the same company to his *prestanombres,* or front man, Cipriano Rodríguez Pastor, who kept official control over the administration and profits of the company, which continued to operate.[73] At the time of the "transfer" of ownership, Rodríguez Pastor signed a letter stating that the mine had belonged, at all times, to Dr. Tsuru.[74]

Dr. Tsuru's case in court and his effort to defend himself against charges of fraud were complex and involved political alliances and conflicts. Carlos Almazán was a relative of Juan Andreu Almazán, a mortal enemy of President Manuel Ávila Camacho. General Juan Barragán was a wealthy man who was active in the political arena during the 1940s. Almazán and Barragán made their case against Dr. Tsuru using the most negative language possible, evoking racist comments from journalist and judge:

> Depressed, and somehow indignant from the tone of [Dr. Tsuru's attacks when referring to his accusers], Judge Olea y Leyva stated that the honor of General Barragán was, in his opinion, above the suspicions of Tsuru, as well as that of the officers whom the inmate maliciously mentioned in his written testimony and whom he did not respect, forgetting the nature of his situation as accused, his condition of foreigner and as subject of a country with whom Mexico is at war. "Frankly," he said, "I do not grant any right to a foreigner to treat in that impolite way the officers of my country, not even in the event of his opinion having some basis [in fact], which in this case is lacking.[75]

The public treatment of the Japanese Mexican businessman was humiliating and helped perpetuate stereotypes of persons of Asian descent in Mexico. In contrast to the experience of most Japanese Mexicans during World War II, however, powerful statesmen protected Dr. Tsuru's private life and freedom of movement. The final verdict was not public, and despite the judge's nativist speech and the anti-Japanese climate, Dr. Tsuru did not go to prison.

After the trial, Dr. Tsuru continued exploiting the fluoride and zinc in his mines, notwithstanding the United States' insistence on strict control over such resources.[76] Furthermore, for the duration of World War II, the Ministry of the Interior granted Dr. Tsuru permit after permit to visit various regions of the Mexican Republic for weeks and months, including the Port of Veracruz and Acapulco, sites from which Japanese Mexicans were banned. The physician continued to supervise his businesses and property without interruption. He gave medical reasons for his trips: "Because of my health, I have to make a trip to the spa located in Ixtapan de la Sal, in the

state of Mexico . . . where I will bathe to recuperate my broken health."
Thus, Dr. Tsuru managed his business and received the care he needed
during World War II while impoverished and ill Japanese Mexicans died
in Mexico City and in the Temixco camp without medical care or any hope
of seeing their relatives again.[77]

Dr. Tsuru could travel and operate his businesses because of his wealth
and his relationships with the political and economic elite of Mexico.
Among them was his powerful friend Congressman Francisco Turrent Ar-
tigas from Veracruz, who requested from the DIPS periodic authorization
for Dr. Tsuru to travel.[78] Unlike many Japanese Mexicans who had to visit
the Ministry of the Interior offices in Mexico City daily, Dr. Tsuru did not
even have to be present at the DIPS desk to receive his permits. His employees would pick them up for him.[79] DIPS chief José Lelo de Larrea was
aware of the extraordinary relationship between Dr. Tsuru and the minister of the interior. When signing permits for the physician, Lelo de Larrea
added the phrase, "By superior orders," to make it clear that it was not in
his power to deny authorizations for Dr. Tsuru to travel practically anywhere
in Mexico.[80]

Dr. Tsuru's experience as a free individual, effectively, during World War
II is not indicative or representative of most Japanese Mexicans during this
period. While Tsuru's chauffeur took the physician in his Cadillac through
cities across the Mexican Republic on business trips, other men and women
literally struggled to stay alive. Even when not presenting active resistance
to their displacement, many Japanese Mexicans experienced deteriorating
health, which provides evidence of the lack of medical care during World
War II.

A number of illnesses may be attributed to the stress and economic conditions inflicted by the program on internees or their loved ones from the border region. As historian George Lipsitz states in *The Possessive Investment in
Whiteness*, there is a relation between health and race in racist societies.
Lipsitz explains that victims of racism are exposed to stress, depression, anxiety, and anger, which place them at risk of developing heart disease.[81] Undoubtedly, Japanese Mexican residents and their relatives were subjected to
great emotional pressures affecting their health during World War II.[82]

An Unauthorized Place to Die

During World War II, death or wealth became the only way some Japanese
Mexican men and women could escape control. Despite their attempt to

comply with the conditions of their relocation, persons of Japanese origin were dealing with a series of bureaucratic practices that required certain familiarity with legal language and official protocol. Although most Japanese Mexicans who did not comply with official paperwork requirements were not active resisters, the DIPS classified them as such. Among them, fifty-eight-year-old Minoju Satiu Fukunaga, who had been uprooted from Navojoa, Sonora, became a wanted man, sought after by DIPS inspectors and local authorities of Guanajuato and Jalisco.[83]

Unknowingly, Fukunaga raised the ire of the DIPS chief José Lelo de Larrea when he moved from Celaya to Guadalajara. Trying to follow official procedures in February 1943, Fukunaga notified the National Registry of Foreigners at Celaya of his new address in Guadalajara, Jalisco.[84] Despite Guadalajara being one of the two cities the Mexican government had ordered Japanese Mexicans to move to, Fukunaga's change-of-address notification outraged Chief Lelo de Larrea, who thought Fukunaga had not humbly asked for his authorization but merely informed him of his change of address. Larrea informed the mayor of Celaya, Jesús Ortiz Balderas, that the DIPS was the only entity with the power to authorize Fukunaga's transfer. Lelo de Larrea ordered Ortiz Balderas to force Fukunaga to return to Celaya. The DIPS official was upset because Minoju Fukunaga had not followed the chain of command and official protocol.[85]

To ensure the return of Fukunaga to Celaya, and with the authorization to use force if necessary, Lelo de Larrea commanded Inspector Loreto Orozco, stationed in Guadalajara, Jalisco, to escort the Japanese Mexican man to the place he was authorized to live in the state of Guanajuato, just across the state line.[86] At the same time, the DIPS urged Guadalajara's mayor to notify Fukunaga that he had the obligation to "return immediately to [Celaya] where he must continue residing."[87]

As a result of the DIPS efforts and investigation, finally on April 27, 1943, Inspector Loreto Orozco was able to render his report on the Japanese Mexican man who had not followed the relocation program procedures to the letter. Loreto Orozco notified José Lelo de Larrea that Minoju Fukunaga had lived his last days alone and had died in an unauthorized place on March 24, unfortunately breaking the legal paper trail that was supposed to follow Japanese Mexicans all the way to their internal exile as overseen by the DIPS officials. Following protocol, Larrea collected Fukunaga's documentation for submission to the Ministry of the Interior. In sharp contrast with the privileges Dr. Kiso Tsuru enjoyed during World War II, Minoju Satiu Fukunaga died while the Mexican government pursued him as a criminal.[88]

Lack of organized, extensive resistance against the relocation program resulted in the irreparable loss of civil rights, property, and lives for Japanese Mexican communities. Although many towns and individuals sought the freedom of their beloved relatives, friends, or neighbors, their efforts did not find a general organized response at a national level. Furthermore, supporters of Japanese Mexicans usually adhered to the nationalist rhetoric and accepted the limitations the federal government imposed on local societies. As time passed, President Ávila Camacho was able to gather the consent of the majority through assertions of supposed racial unity that included only persons of Spanish and indigenous descent. When requesting the freedom of the Japanese Mexican members of their local communities, Mexicans claimed exceptions to a rule they obeyed in more general terms. In turn, the Mexican government granted a few exceptions in exchange for the support of most Mexicans for the relocation program and other policies derived from the alliance between U.S. and Mexican elites.

For their part, Japanese Mexicans examined their place in their communities and in relation to the Mexican nation, searching for ways to avoid the effects of the relocation program. They claimed their Mexican citizenship, long residence, or having Mexican children and spouses as ways to confirm their membership in their communities. Nevertheless, in spite of the links they formed with their communities through daily experiences, their resistance to the relocation program, and the support offered at times by entire towns, only wealthy Japanese Mexicans with ties to the Japanese and Mexican national elites managed to maintain a life free from major disruptions during World War II.

CHAPTER SEVEN

Temixco Concentration Camp

Eva Watanabe Matsuo survived the poverty her family was reduced to when her parents were ordered to leave their home in 1942. She remembers that after years of misery in Mexico City, evacuees of the borderlands asked themselves why the Mexican government did not take care of their most basic needs, as they knew U.S. institutions did on the other side of the border. Her father, Toshio Watanabe, explained to Eva and her siblings that living in Baja California, he had had the choice of presenting himself, his wife, and his children before U.S. immigration officers to enter a concentration camp in California. Toshio could not stand the humiliation of being imprisoned in the United States, and thus, he obeyed the orders to move to Mexico City, initially thinking that leaving their home was a temporary move.[1]

Eva Watanabe perceives herself as Mexican, and she agrees with her father's decision. In her view, it was better to remain with their "own people" despite the scarce resources available and the anguish her family endured when they lost all their possessions. Her father saw his health deteriorate, and he never regained a stable emotional and financial status.[2]

Material conditions of ethnic Japanese in U.S. internment camps were no doubt better in general than those experienced by the Japanese Mexicans and Japanese Canadians who were uprooted. Japanese immigrants in Canada were forced to work in harsh weather, farming or clearing roads under the snow. Just as in Mexico, the government of Canada made ethnic Japanese responsible for the costs of their uprooting. The property of Canadian evacuees was auctioned by the government to pay for the expenses it incurred in their displacement. As in Mexico, the limits to mobility of Japanese Canadians was masked by their confinement in farms, even when many ethnic Japanese were naturalized citizens of Canada or were nationals of that country by birth. In Canada, state institutions used the labor of evacuees, administered their income, and sold their property to "invest" it in the needs of Japanese Canadians; in Mexico, some of those functions rested on the CJAM.[3]

The Internment Process

Government officials and historians of the relocation program mention the former hacienda Temixco as the most emblematic site of "concentration" during World War II and a model of mild population control.[4] Temixco is cited in contrast to the Perote jail, a high-security prison in which the Mexican government confined those Japanese Mexicans considered extremely dangerous. In 2008, Mexican diplomat Sergio González Gálvez described Temixco as a "farm," and other historians have defined it as "a loosely organized internment camp." Refuting the idea that Temixco was an agricultural enterprise employing free labor, DIPS files provide evidence that this was a site of confinement where inmates were forced to work under surveillance. At the same time, Temixco was a site of conflict among Japanese Mexicans and uneven distribution of power, which yielded privileges for the Japanese Mexican elite.[5]

During the first months of 1942, hundreds of uprooted Japanese Mexicans entered camp Batán, but the growing number of relocated persons made the already precarious conditions of internees impossible to sustain. In addition, many inmates were not employable due to their age or sickness. Outside Batán the state of poverty to which entire families were subjected in Mexico City spurred both the CJAM and Mexican government officials to open another camp. Displaced Japanese Mexicans could support themselves in this camp and provide housing and food for other, disabled Japanese Mexicans who had evacuated the borderlands and the coastal zones of Mexico.[6] Canada had implemented a similar program, where evacuees were given a plot of land and free seed.[7] In July 1942, leaders of the CJAM, Sanshiro Matsumoto and Alberto Shunji Yoshida notified the Ministry of the Interior that they had acquired the hacienda Temixco, in the southern state of Morelos, from Alejandro Lacy Orci, a Sonoran landowner. Only eighty-five kilometers from Mexico City, the hacienda was also only six kilometers from Cuernavaca, the capital of the state of Morelos.[8]

Military and civilian authorities participated in the creation of the camp and in the identification of every interned man in Temixco. Cuernavaca's mayor and the commander of the military zone received copies of individual permits granted to Japanese Mexicans moving into Temixco.[9] Japanese Mexicans were tightly controlled by the state and restricted to a rigidly demarcated area. The hacienda was a convenient place to isolate and manage the labor of Japanese Mexicans, which the Ministry of the Interior had placed in the hands of the CJAM leaders. In preparation for the arrival of the internees, CJAM officials Matsumoto and Yoshida received a special permit to employ the Japanese Mexican workforce at the Hacienda de Temixco. The term "employment" did not imply hiring displaced men and women for wages; rather, it referred to their use in the hacienda's economic activities.[10]

This hacienda had always been one of the jewels of the state of Morelos, cherished by powerful families in Mexico but also claimed by indigenous peasants. Although one of the objectives of the Revolution had been to make peasants the owners of the same land they worked, the Zapatista slogan being "la tierra es de quien la trabaja" (the land is of those who labor over it), politicians and their families ignored this principle to appropriate vast tracts of land, Temixco among them.[11]

Temixco's previous owner, Alejandro Lacy Orci, was able to acquire the hacienda when the state of Morelos auctioned the estate in the Revolution's aftermath. Plutarco Elías Calles was president of Mexico, and he and Orci were related through the marriage of their grandchildren. A common place of birth, political networks, and ethnocentric perceptions against indigenous and Asian peoples also bonded the Calles and the Lacy families in the post-Revolutionary period.[12]

When President Lázaro Cárdenas exiled Plutarco Elías Calles in 1935, Calles's relatives and supporters gradually returned to Sonora. Alejandro Lacy Orci decided to follow his family to northern Mexico.[13] In 1938, Cárdenas granted portions of the hacienda to the peasant communities of Palmira and Temixco. Not willing to comply with the official disposition, Alejandro Lacy transferred the problem of dealing with agrarian authorities by selling it.[14] In 1942, the CJAM leaders, unaware of the property rights and claims the indigenous communities had on the hacienda, bought the property from Lacy for the sum of $85,000 (pesos), approximately $26,435 (dollars).[15]

The CJAM faced the challenge of fulfilling the potential of the hacienda. They had acquired 250 hectares, but only 60 of them had irrigation systems.[16] Although in the past, sugarcane had been the main crop in Temixco, the CJAM decided to forego its cultivation, cashing in immediately on this decision. The CJAM leaders and new owners of Temixco sold the machinery needed to process sugarcane in the hacienda for about the same price they had paid for the property.[17]

Temixco's distribution of buildings was ideal for managing the uprooted Japanese Mexicans, as it was built by Spanish conquerors to control indigenous populations working for the hacendados. The *casco*, or main premises of the hacienda, was divided into three wings. One of them was a two-floor building. When the internees arrived, three Mexican families lived on the first floor, which was in very bad condition, lacking a ceiling. The administrator, Takugoro Shibayama, made urgent repairs to the facilities, particularly in his own family's living quarters on the second floor, and was referred to as "guard" by Mexican officials.[18]

Originally an ambulant merchant in Mexicali, Shibayama acquired an important role in Mexico City within the CJAM. While controlling internees at Temixco, he was simultaneously charged with the task of finding other haciendas so that the CJAM could "intern and place the Japanese who are currently concentrated in the capital."[19] Temixco's administrator fulfilled his mission by travelling to San Luis Potosi, Tamaulipas, and Puebla.[20]

Minerva Yoshino Castro, then a child forced to live in Temixco's concentration camp, remembers the "beautiful" stairs that led into the Shibayama family's rooms. During her interview, she recalled also that the Shibayama quarters were never open to the rest of the inmates. Only the Japanese Mexican women who helped cleaning the living quarters of the administrator and his family would have brief access to those rooms. Children living in the camp were not usually allowed to play with Shibayama's six children living in the hacienda, another indication that there were clear hierarchies and boundaries between the internees and the Japanese Mexican administrators of the internment camp.[21]

Living conditions for most internees were harsh. The hacienda had three large patios that were adapted to the needs of the CJAM. Only the third patio had a cement floor. The CJAM constructed a communal dormitory for those internees who had family with them in this area and ordered the installation of boilers in the same patio to provide hot water for parboiling the rice harvested by the Japanese Mexican internees. In addition, the casco had two empty, humid warehouses that were cleaned by the Japanese Mexicans upon their arrival. Other small rooms in this area housed eight families of Mexican peasants hired by the CJAM. Although the DIPS documents do not show in what capacity the peasants were employed, hacendados used to hire indigenous persons as maids, to tend the animals, or to farm the land. The presence of these free employees indicates that the CJAM had enough funds to pay their salaries and reflected the need for laborers in the hacienda.[22]

The camp continued to grow over time. On September 21, 1942, Luis T. Tsuji, general secretary of the CJAM, requested authorization from the Ministry of the Interior to intern a second group of forty-nine persons classified as Japanese nationals. As in the case of Villa Aldama camp, Mexican women and their Japanese Mexican children who were relatives of the interned men entered the camp without having to request individual permission.[23] In October of the same year, a third smaller group was transferred to the hacienda. The DIPS processed subsequent permits to intern other men of Japanese origin and also dealt with sporadic requests to leave the hacienda.[24] Because Tsuji and other CJAM members made frequent visits to supervise the internees living in the camp, the Ministry of the Interior granted them permanent special permits to travel between Mexico City and the state of Morelos.[25]

Although the CJAM administered the hacienda and promised the Ministry of the Interior to control the residents of Temixco, each adult male or single female internee had to obtain direct permission from the DIPS to exit the premises, either temporarily or permanently. Internees had to own a typewriter and have command of the Spanish language and writing skills to compose a legal document if they desired to apply on their own for permits to move in or out of the hacienda. Even when internees could afford to pay an expert to type their requests, the Ministry of the Interior denied employment or new address authorizations without explanation.[26] It was common for an officer from the CJAM to write such letters, reinforcing the control that the association exercised over the interned Japanese Mexicans.[27] Ultimately, the DIPS had the last word on the permits to enter or exit the hacienda.[28]

More than five hundred persons entered the internment camp from 1942 to 1945.[29] The most impoverished uprooted Japanese Mexicans regarded the Hacienda de Temixco as a refuge from harsher alternatives, such as not having a roof over their heads or a source of income at all. After all, relocation had resulted in unemployment or insufficient wages for Japanese Mexicans who had been self-sufficient before World War II, and many displaced Japanese Mexicans and their dependents turned to charity after 1942.[30] Particularly those persons with physical disabilities as well as the elderly, who before their relocation had been able to earn a living in their place of origin, found themselves in a hostile urban environment with scarce opportunities to find employment.[31]

Other reasons impelled Japanese Mexicans to accept internment. Takeshi Morita Okamura, for example, was willing to become an inmate at Temixco in order to terminate his confinement in Camp Livingston, Louisiana. A naturalized Mexican citizen, Mr. Takeshi was apprehended by the U.S. Army in the United States in 1942. He then requested assistance from the Mexican Consulate in Salt Lake City to obtain his freedom from the American concentration camp.[32] After several consultations within the Ministry of the Interior, Attorney Juan de la C. García advised its minister to accept Morita Okamura:

> Taking in consideration that [he] became Mexican by naturalization long before his country of origin was in war against Mexico; that he legally entered our country at a young age; and that in the state of Morelos, in Temixco, near Cuernavaca, the Mexican government has a concentration camp destined for the Japanese, it is fair that, as he is entitled to protection due to his [Mexican] nationality, he is allowed to come to Mexico . . . to intern him in Temixco camp, where he will be subjected to vigilance just as the rest of his countrymen.[33]

As stated by García, the camp was under surveillance. The Ministry of the Interior gave Romualdo Cházaro, an officer from the DIPS, the responsibility of making sure that all Japanese Mexicans registered as internees were within the hacienda's limits at all times.[34] Cházaro constantly submitted detailed information to the Ministry of the Interior and to military authorities in the area on the status of Japanese Mexican men in the camp, including transfers to other facilities or employment, sickness, and deaths. In his communications he usually described all internees as "enemy aliens."[35]

Internal Conflicts

The privileged accommodations of the Shibayama family created some discontent among the internees in Temixco, who, while trying to keep a community spirit, felt the direct control of the CJAM over their lives.[36] In addition to better quarters, the CJAM had assigned Takugoro an assistant, Tsumeo Somea.[37] Alberto Yoshida also had an advantaged position within the hacienda as leader of the CJAM and co-owner of the hacienda. Although he lived in Mexico City, Yoshida's presence in Temixco became more constant in December 1942. He and other CJAM members had just received their permanent permits to travel between Temixco and Mexico City, which Yoshida used to manage the funds, the sale of products, and the payment of taxes, while representing the legal and commercial interests of the hacienda.[38]

Despite the orders to bring their children and wives with them, some men just could not afford to pay for their transportation to the interior.[39] On the other hand, some interned Japanese Mexicans did not desire to see their children growing up in captivity. Rodolfo Nakamura Ortiz was only nine years old in 1942 when his only surviving parent was ordered to evacuate Palau, Coahuila, in North Mexico.[40] During his interview, he talked about the circumstances under which he remained in the care of his older siblings in the borderlands for some months. Rodolfo was very attached to his father and could not stay apart from him, particularly without receiving news from him. The child decided to take to the road on his own in search of Umezo Nakamura Nakamura. Once in Mexico City, he heard that his father was in Temixco.

I found my father, but first I had to look for him because I did not know where he was. I was told that he was in Morelos. It was very hard to find out in Cuernavaca where my father was, where all Japanese were, because I was eleven years old and nobody took me seriously. I went all the way to Temixco, and there it was pretty easy to locate the hacienda. There were no businesses; there was nothing [in Temixco]. Today there are stores, restaurants, hotels. Then there was only the hacienda, the highway. I tried not to be noticed. I entered [the hacienda] and nobody asked me why I was there. I kept walking until I met some Japanese persons to whom I asked for Nakamura.

"Nakamura!"

They were calling his name, asking for his whereabouts in Japanese language. They told me where my father was. I walked in the direction of the fields, but I did not find him on that day. I asked [the other internees] if I could stay overnight.

"Did you get registered?"

"No. They did not even notice me when I walked through the door."

"Fine. Look, you can sleep right here."

The morning after, when I opened my eyes, my father was already there. They had told him that I was looking for him.

"What are you doing here?"

"I came to look for you because we did not have news about you."

"No. I am fine. You must leave."[41]

Rodolfo Nakamura left the hacienda immediately because his father found the thought of raising him in such a restrictive environment intolerable. Soon, Umezo Nakamura requested permission to relocate in Mexico City in order to live with his youngest son, Rodolfo. The elder Nakamura lived his last years in Mexico City missing the miner community of Palau, Coahuila. He died in an accident some years later, leaving Rodolfo once again in the care of his older siblings, who by then had also been relocated to Mexico City.[42]

Although the land was rich and highly productive, proper housing was not available for all internees when Matsumoto and Yoshida bought the hacienda. In December 1942, Dr. Felipe García Sánchez, an officer from the Department of Health, inspected the hacienda and reported the immediate problems that internees were facing. Dr. García was appalled by the circumstances of the Japanese Mexicans who had installed "casetas de madera" (small wooden compartments) as "bedrooms" for approximately two hundred persons. A section of the hacienda was assigned as a dormitory for Japanese men who were single, widowed, or forced to abandon their families. A wooden platform, rising forty centimeters from the floor, was installed from wall to wall, "covered by some kind of pigeonholes, each division functioning as the space where each person sleeps. They tend their blankets over the overcrowded wooden platform, constituting a constant danger, since a contagious sickness would become general and inevitable. Such dormitories do not have doors."[43]

A section was reserved for the kitchen where men without a family in the hacienda fixed their own meals. It had a ten-meter table, with benches on the sides. The floor consisted of "tierra suelta" (dirt), with some patches remaining from a previously stone paved floor.[44] A line of *lavaderos* (special basins made of cement to do the laundry) allowed internees to wash their clothes, using rationed cake soap.[45]

Dr. García reported that the facilities were insufficient for the number of persons living in the hacienda and expressed his dismay at the sight of the dormitories, where "a great number of children [were] crowded" in unsanitary conditions. Latrines had been installed over drainage channels that could carry contaminated material to the vegetable gardens. He noted that the internees did not have bathrooms to follow personal hygiene routines, and he urged the construction of better sanitary facilities.[46]

The Japanese Mexican community led quiet lives within the hacienda of Temixco, starting their days at four o'clock in the morning. Only men worked in the agricultural fields; women took care of domestic tasks, which included preparing meals, washing clothes, and keeping their living quarters, as well as those of the Shibayama family, as clean as possible.[47] Local police officers assisted the only in-house DIPS inspector to make sure that internees remained confined. While DIPS inspector Romualdo Cházaro regularly confirmed the presence of male inmates at Temixco, women and children continued to be unaccounted for in Cházaro's daily rounds. This procedure criminalized men, reaffirmed patriarchal values, and restricted the official numbers of victims of the relocation program to the registered men. All inmates had to retire to the housing quarters by eight o'clock every evening. Mexican women who joined their families in the camp abided by the rules imposed on the inmates, just as women of Japanese descent did.[48]

Occasionally, internees had permission to visit the town, located only fifty meters from the main building in the hacienda, to acquire supplies, but they had to return quickly to the hacienda.[49] It is tempting to argue that the ability to walk through the hacienda's door to acquire supplies for the camp is a sign that Japanese Mexicans were free or that the hacienda did not function as a concentration camp. Nevertheless, soldiers and officials from the Mexican army occasionally visited the camp to verify that all persons listed in their files were present.[50]

In addition to the soldier visits, the control of Japanese Mexicans in concentration camps and other zones of confinement rested mainly on assumed racial attributes in a way that resembled slavery in the United States. Outside the hacienda, any person who appeared to be Asian was a suspect (of being illegally at the place where they were at the moment of their interrogation) and subject to the control of civilians and police.[51] In general, Mexicans supervised and restricted the freedom of poor Japanese Mexicans through their racial identification. Any person who, in the eyes of Mexicans, looked Asian was a suspect of belonging to the "Japanese race," and was thus obligated to show his or her official authorization to be in the streets or any place considered to be out of boundaries. Racial classification of Japanese Mexicans was very ambiguous—Mexicans have called any person of Asian ancestry "Chinese"—but it determined their lack of mobility. As a consequence, the Ministry of the Interior did not have to invest in facilities or a large number of guards to control persons of Japanese origin. Their physical characteristics alerted society at large, and the Japanese Mexicans themselves, that they were not free. Military and civil authorities were entitled to interrogate any person in or outside the camp.[52] In addition to surveillance, there was a powerful reason for some internees to remain within the camp: their children were also inmates, sharing the physical characteristics of their parents. It would not be easy to live in hiding, preventing them from attending school or having friends to avoid being identified as Japanese. In sum, their phenotype and economic disfranchisement made it impossible for internees to find a place in Mexico to evade the control of the Mexican government during World War II.

Internees of Temixco and other displaced Mexican Japanese were not, however, passive victims of the relocation program. They attempted to carry on normal lives, taking every opportunity to improve their material conditions, and they were particularly interested in the education of their children. By January 1943, ninety children had been interned in the camp, and the Mexican government authorized them to attend the local school. The young Japanese Mexican internees who registered created a sudden increase in pupils at the local school, which did not have enough chairs for all its students. Parents of the newly arrived provided some chairs for the school, making it possible for enrolled Japanese Mexican children to sit while taking their classes.[53]

Initially the local school did not have the capacity to accept all the children from the camp. In addition, some children were not eligible to attend because of their age. Japanese Mexican parents believed that all interned children were in need of an "adequate education" and requested permission to have Seito Y. Takizawa teach at the camp. The CJAM proposed that Takizawa, a former Japanese language teacher from Navojoa, Sonora, give courses of "industria infantil" and Japanese language.[54] Officers of the Ministry of the Interior did not grant the requested permission; instead, they suggested that the CJAM hire, and pay for, the services of a teacher of Mexican nationality. They eventually authorized a Japanese teacher in the camp.[55]

All children of school age would, in the end, regularly attend the Temixco elementary school. At night, they received additional instruction from Takizawa, who was eventually allowed to teach Japanese Mexican children. During the weekends, students received their classes in Japanese. Teacher and students used to go outdoors, exercising and rehearsing for weekly performances of Japanese plays. Attending the performances of their children was the main source of entertainment for the entire community of internees. Arts and crafts, physical education, and calligraphy were the only subjects Takizawa taught at the hacienda.[56]

Despite the restrictions and poverty she endured as an internee, Minerva Yoshino is proud of the resilience of their community and their accommodation to a hostile social environment. She praises the education she received in the camp and the sense of community Japanese children developed. They shared prizes, for example, earned at the Temixco school with other children in the camp. During her interview, she remembered that colored pencils, notebooks, and other supplies came along with academic awards. A Japanese teacher was able to teach in the camp thanks to the insistence of the inmates, who wanted their children to maintain certain aspects of their culture. Minerva explained that their sensei trained children to be brave in the face of scary situations. The teacher asked his students to prove their valor by climbing the chapel stairs to the top, despite the frightening darkness and the presence of bats. Minerva cherished the parental guidance prevalent in the camp. She states that Japanese men in the camp committed no acts of physical abuse against their offspring. When children misbehaved, their parents used to hug them and hold long conversations to ensure that they would not repeat this misconduct. The children's uprooting, financial destitution, and internment in the camp, however, were abuses themselves.[57]

While trying to create a healthy environment for their children, most adults in the camp had few resources at their disposal, and their lives were organized around the hacienda's production. The Ministry of the Interior often received reports from the CJAM on the efficiency of the hacienda. Alberto Yoshida and Takugoro Shibayama informed the DIPS inspector in February 1943 that eighty Japanese men worked in the fields, while thirty others did not due to sickness, age, or refusal to work.[58]

In the CJAM report to the Ministry of the Interior, the leaders failed to mention that certain inmates were refusing to work without receiving any money in exchange for their labor. The CJAM had promised internees a salary, but inmates usually did not receive wages. Men who were able to work had to pay for the soap, food, and other items they and their families consumed. Their salary could be lower than the amount owed for the products provided by the CJAM. This situation was an incentive for internees to accept employment as live-in workers at high-ranking military officers' households in the same area or back in Mexico City.[59]

The growing tensions in Temixco finally compelled the CJAM leaders to request the intervention of the Ministry of the Interior. Luis T. Tsuji, representing the CJAM, informed minister of the interior Miguel Alemán that a group of Japanese Mexicans, "under the control of this Committee, . . . have always misbehaved affecting other colonizers." Tsuji asked the Ministry of the Interior to relocate the rebellious inmates so that they could "look for employment at other places."[60] Alemán, three years later the president of Mexico, ordered the removal of the internees from the hacienda in accordance with the CJAM request. The blacklisted men were transferred to the detention facilities in Perote, located in an extremely cold area in the coastal state of Veracruz.[61] The Estación Migratoria Perote was in fact a jail famous for the terrible conditions under which internees lived. Perote officers received these and other Japanese Mexican men whose only crime was having protested the terms of the compensation for their labor in Temixco.[62]

The Ministry of the Interior investigated the charges filed by the CJAM against the rebellious internees. Once Zintaro Matsu Nakagawa was in Perote, immigration officials took his report and wrote that he did not

> have contact with any relatives in Japan; . . . that he never assisted [the Japanese government] in any way . . . not having enough money for his own basic needs; that he does not belong to any secret Japanese association; that he professes the Buddhist religion but does not have any contact with the government of Emperor Irohito [*sic*] since he has been living in the country for approximately fifty years. That the bad behavior he was accused of consisted in his claiming that the labor or compensation received at the Temixco hacienda in the state of Morelos was not appropriate; $2.00 [two pesos] each week plus meals . . . but this arrangement changed to the benefit of the owner [of the hacienda] who determined that the owner [of the hacienda] would take fifty percent of the product, and the other fifty percent would belong to the laborers . . . that approximately sixty three Japanese persons worked the land receiving an insignificant amount . . . from which the meals were deducted, not only their own meals but everybody's food [was deducted from each working man's salary for which] he suffered serious damages since he did not have relatives [in the hacienda] but had to support the relatives of his coworkers; that most of the time, better said always, he ended up owing money [to the owner of the hacienda] instead of obtaining compensation for his labor. That this was the reason for his discontent and the bad behavior the [CJAM] accused him of, but that he thought an injustice was done against him and his coworkers.[63]

Zintaro Nakagawa had arrived in Mexico in 1906 to work on a plantation in the state of Oaxaca, and later as a miner in the state of Coahuila. Although his exact age was not documented in his file, we can infer that in 1942, he was not a young person at the peak of his productive life. Nevertheless, the Mexican government and the CJAM forced him and other men and women in the same circumstances to work in the fields in exchange for a roof and meals. His declaration reveals that a degree of demoralization was setting in as Zintaro, and probably other men in his group at Perote, did not feel they should contribute to cover the expenses of the sick, elderly, disabled, or children interned at Temixco, particularly if their own children and wives remained without income at their places of origin.[64] In addition, CJAM leaders and male internees did not consider women's labor at the hacienda payable at all. Zintaro felt that the women in the camp were an additional "nonproductive" burden; he counted men in the fields as the only laborers deserving a salary or a share of the profit resulting from the sales of the harvested products.[65]

A report from an unknown officer from the legal department at the Ministry of the Interior determined that Zintaro Nakagawa's complaints were justified, because the Japanese Mexican man was not a spy or saboteur, and thus he should not be incarcerated at the Perote jail.[66] The same resolution applied to Kato Kiyomatsu, Sanemón Yamamoto, Kei Hito Misida, and Santiago Shiguezo Kobayashi, all of whom the CJAM had ordered transferred to Veracruz in the company of Zintaro.[67] Although the minister of the interior did not keep this group imprisoned in Perote, he ordered their return to the hacienda in Temixco to be placed again under the control of the CJAM, even though the Japanese Mexicans had expressed their desire not to go back there. On September 14, 1944, Adolfo Nobuo Yoshioka, CJAM secretary, informed the DIPS that the CJAM was still in charge of the "surveillance and care" of the dissatisfied laborers.[68]

Temixco inmates had other complaints besides labor conditions, as the CJAM orders to incarcerate Dr. Manuel Hiromoto in the Perote jail indicate. Years later a revered medical practitioner in the town of Temixco, during World War II Dr. Hiromoto was separated from his wife, who was pregnant at the time. While at Perote, Dr. Hiromoto wrote a report to the DIPS, accusing the CJAM officers of abusing their power. He denounced the lack of religious freedom in the camp, expressing a feeling of isolation due to his Christian beliefs and stating that the CJAM administrators limited the practice of Catholic rites among internees of Temixco. In addition to religious conflicts, Dr. Hiromoto reported class-based clashes in the concentration camp. According to him, there was a hierarchy within the camp following traditional Japanese class divisions and strictly enforced by the Japanese administrators in Temixco. Dr. Hiromoto made clear that power in the hands of the CJAM contributed to a climate of oppression. He stated that the administrators threatened the internees with incarceration in Perote when they refused to work without compensation for their labor.[69]

Despite the harsh conditions inmates endured in Temixco, after a long separation from their families, the possibility to reunite in the camp was a powerful reason for Japanese Mexicans to look forward to their internment.

This was the case of several Japanese men detained at the Estación Migratoria Perote, who begged CJAM director Luis Tsuji in April 1943

> to take us to a labor camp [to have] the opportunity to work the land, we promise and give our word that we will behave well and that we will not complain or refuse [to do any task] even when the labor is harsher than ordinary, under surveillance, and without compensation. We only ask to be allowed to live with our family, since almost all of us used to support ourselves [and our family] from our labor [for which] since our incarceration, all our relatives are suffering in a state of horrendous misery . . . Our future is in your hands and we manifest our desire to collaborate with our second patria. We sign with our own blood [this letter].[70]

Desperate to see their wives and children, and to save them from hunger, these inmates of Perote were willing to accept the camp conditions, which did not differ a great deal from the description they had provided in their request. Keeping all members of the family together, however, did not shield children from witnessing the most devastating effects of the relocation program. Although silence surrounds the experience of Japanese Mexican children during World War II, they were undeniably exposed to painful events. During her interview, Minerva Yoshino remembered with pain two deaths that she believes could have been avoided. One of them was an elderly man with chronic diarrhea. She remembers asking him how he felt. Sensing that he needed tea, she returned with the beverage only to find him dead. The other death she laments is that of a young child who, in her view, also died from lack of medical care.[71]

Several internees died while away from their families, without proper health care in Temixco. Elderly men in particular found it difficult to survive the relocation program. According to article 14 of the 1929 Geneva Convention, "every camp [had to have] an infirmary, where prisoners of war [must] receive every kind of attention they need." If necessary, isolated quarters had to be "reserved for the sick affected with contagious diseases." Yoshino stated that such measures were not taken at the Temixco camp. In retaliation for Manuel Hiromoto addressing what he thought was an uneven distribution of resources among the Japanese Mexicans in the camp, Shibayama, the hacienda's administrator, did not allow him to take care of the health of Temixco's sick inmates.[72] Instead, internees received insufficient medical care from Dr. Tsunesaburo Hasegawa, who had been arrested in Juárez by U.S. and Mexican army platoons in March 1942 and evicted from the borderlands in the same year.[73]

The CJAM, through Dr. Hasegawa's services, took care of a number of uprooted Japanese Mexicans in the federal district and at Temixco who could not afford to pay for medical treatment for their illnesses. The CJAM hired him and paid him a monthly salary of five hundred pesos, with funds partially provided by the Red Cross to provide treatment to an excessive number of patients in too large an area to cover. Compared to the two pesos the CJAM promised to Temixco's laborers, which they stopped receiving eventually, Dr. Hasegawa's salary was a handsome sum in times of crisis. The physician nevertheless had the additional responsibility of making sure that internees in Temixco had their immunizations up to date.[74] Despite Dr. Hasegawa's efforts, and the palliative care provided by the community, several internees died from various sicknesses.[75] Summer temperatures in the area were a contributing factor, and to aggravate conditions in the hacienda, overcrowding in the dormitories eased the spread of malaria among inmates.[76]

While internees lacked medical care, appropriate shelter, and sanitary facilities, the hacienda operated from a business perspective and generated profits. The CJAM managers applied the technology available at the moment to raise productivity in Temixco, hiring technicians to oversee the operation of their agricultural businesses.[77] Thanks to the intervention of Japanese Mexican experts, 1943 was highly productive: twenty-three hectares of rice gave a harvest of ninety-five tons, plus two hectares of tomato, and five more of cucumber, eggplant, cabbage, and cantaloupe.[78]

In the eyes of Minerva Yoshino, the results of the communal labor were admirable, for she remembers a copious crop of rice sold immediately because of its quality. She laments the lack of accountability among the persons who administered the hacienda, since she believes there must have been a profit and that it had to be enough to provide a better quality of life for all inmates. Instead, the now-retired chemical biologist feels her father suffered "for nothing."[79] The scarcity of material resources showed in the clothes children wore, as both Minerva Yoshino and Dr. Raúl Hiromoto described. Dr. Hiromoto—who was born in the camp—reported to me that most internees used to wear "ropa en jirones" (ragged clothes) donated by better-off Japanese families and distributed among the families living in the camp. They also remember that the administrator's family would dress and eat better than the rest of the internees.[80]

Notwithstanding privileges and advantages that some wealthy Japanese entrepreneurs may have enjoyed and augmented through the use of their compatriots as cheap labor or their role in controlling them, there must have been other expenses in the administration of the camp that were not officially accounted for. Stephen Niblo's research on corruption in Mexico during World War II assists our understanding of the investment of at least part of the profits Japanese Mexicans earned in their businesses. In the case of Temixco, bribes to all levels of authorities to avoid harassment of Japanese Mexicans, and thus harsher living conditions, is a plausible explanation for the limited resources poor internees had access to.[81] The covert nature of bribes have made it difficult to find accurate records reflecting the flow of money from the CJAM or individual Japanese Mexicans to members of the Mexican government. Aside from bribes, money received by the CJAM was distributed in the form of food or medical care among all Japanese Mexicans in need, productive or not, interned or living in Guadalajara, Mexico City, or other areas of confinement. In consequence, productive Japanese Mexicans in Temixco carried on their shoulders the burden of supporting other evacuees with their labor.[82]

The living conditions of internees in Temixco did not get better with time. The poor state of the hacienda deplored by Dr. Felipe García Sánchez in 1942 was still lamentable two years later. Three health inspectors witnessed and reported the environment endured by the inmates of Temixco in January 1944, recommending again to improve sanitary facilities and sleeping quarters for the internees.[83]

La Tierra es de Quien la Trabaja: Zapatista Claim to Temixco

In addition to the complaints raised by exasperated inmates and the recommendations from the Health Department to introduce better sanitation facilities, the administrator of the hacienda faced other issues in February 1944. The communal landholders (ejidos) of Palmira and Temixco were the owners of an area of the hacienda, according to a 1938 presidential edict, and they advised the camp residents not to plant any new crops. The CJAM leaders realized then that the title of the property they had bought from Alejandro Lacy Orci was not cleared and that the ejidos were demanding the use and occupation of the land that legally belonged to the indigenous members of the community.[84]

To solve the matter of establishing rights to Temixco land, the Ministry of the Interior charged DIPS inspectors Donaciano Ceballos and Óscar Olvera Villafaña with the task of investigating the situation in Temixco. After a field trip, the inspectors stated that "local agrarian officers, represented by the Comisariado Ejidal, based on the ordinance published on February

7 in the Diario Oficial, notified the Japanese residing there to suspend the preparation of land for new crops. . . . The Japanese acquired said land by presidential authorization, for which the agraristas requested the extension of [the property of] the ejidos to integrate [into the same ejidos some of the] land that was already owned by the Japanese."[85]

Ceballos and Villafaña tried to explain a situation that was very complex and that directly involved Ávila Camacho and two other former presidents. Plutarco Elías Calles had "auctioned" the hacienda and his relative had acquired it when, according to the principles of the Mexican Revolution, the hacienda had to be granted to the ejidos; Lázaro Cárdenas had ordered its transfer to the ejidos, affecting the interests of Elías Calles's family; and Ávila Camacho had approved the sale of the hacienda to the CJAM leaders, knowing that it was claimed by the ejidos. The ejidatarios did not renounce the rights they had fought for during the Revolution and demanded the land that had been granted to them in 1938 by presidential decree.

Donaciano Ceballos was initially sympathetic to the CJAM. He expressed his opinion that the improvements made to the Hacienda de Temixco had been costly and that the new owners would, in his view, experience an unfair and great loss. He considered the intervention of the Ministry of the Interior necessary "to request from the Comisariado Ejidal de Temixco to abstain from claiming the right to the land that the Japanese have been cultivating and those that are already cleaned and plowed for new crops."[86]

In October 1944, the Comisariado Ejidal (ejidos commissariat), an institution that was also the product of the socialist changes promoted by the Mexican Revolution, intervened. The Comisariado had the authority to oversee the agreements made between the ejido and the government. Its members demanded from the Ministry of the Interior "to force the transference of the affected land [to the ejidos], avoiding the mocking of the presidential resolution that benefits our [Mexican] peasants lacking land, while the enemies of Mexico are failing to make full use of it."[87] Nationalist rhetoric had caught up with President Ávila Camacho. He had insisted that war and production were a national priority and promoted the demonization of the Japanese, but the Comisariado Ejidal now reminded the Mexican president of the division he had created between Japanese Mexicans and indigenous Mexicans and what side Ávila Camacho was supposed to be on.

Despite ejidatarios' claim to the hacienda's land, they were not demanding the entire property. According to the Revolution's core philosophy, the indigenous community was only asking to take possession of and work the land that had not been cultivated during the years the CJAM had occupied the hacienda.[88]

DIPS agent Donaciano Ceballos switched his position in the conflict after several meetings with the ejido officials, although he did not provide a reason for his new approach to the issue. Ceballos now considered that the land he had previously reported as occupied, and therefore not available for the ejido, was vacant. He went beyond his call of duty, recommending that the director of the DIPS, his own supervisor, obey

> the resolution of the President of the Republic, [thanks to which] all land that is property of the Japanese, now belongs to the ejidatarios of this area; furthermore, a great area of the land belonging to the mentioned Japanese subjects is not even cultivated. With the purpose of avoiding great problems between the ejidatarios and the subjects in my care, because of the land dispute, I beg you with all respect, to study the case, . . . taking into consideration that the ejidatarios are willing to take the land with the intervention of the agrarian officers as soon as the current rice crop is harvested.[89]

On February 19, 1944, General Manuel Ávila Camacho made public his decision to confirm the ownership of the land by the Palmira and Temixco ejidos.[90] Yet despite the presidential resolution, and the opinion of inspector Ceballos, the DIPS had switched sides once again, confirming ownership of the landholdings by the CJAM.[91] Thus, the lower rank officials apparently defied the presidential order to deliver the tracts of land to the ejidatarios. According to Ricardo Trujillo, DIPS inspector surveying the property in dispute, "in regards to the land, property of the Japanese, supposedly uncultivated, and in application of the term that makes possible that idle land can be claimed by others who will make full use of them, that is not the case, since everything that is cultivable has been sown, or at least plowed and prepared for the next [agricultural cycle].[92]

Eduardo Ampudia, chief of the DIPS, refused to intervene to force the Japanese owners of the hacienda to evacuate the land the ejidatarios were claiming.[93] The legal or illegal methods to calm the ejidatarios remain unknown. The last presidential edict published in the *Diario Oficial* in regard to the vacant land in Temixco made it clear that at least some of the area sold by Alejandro Lacy Orci was the legal property of the ejidatarios.[94]

Silence and a lack of accurate records have made it difficult to identify how the CJAM leaders withheld the land ejidatarios had requested and obtained through presidential decree. Attributed to the good heart of Ávila Camacho and his sympathy for the Japanese Mexicans, the retention of the entire landholding by the CJAM is still in need of a more complex explanation.[95] Once again, Stephen Niblo's research on corruption in Mexico during World War II is useful in my interpretation of the development and conclusion of this issue. The DIPS officials' continuous switching of their support for the parties involved suggest that bribing was involved in handling the issue of land tenure. Ávila Camacho's presidential period was characterized by a reversal in the land distribution to peasants, but the Temixco dispute had demanded that he declare his nationalism by publicly granting the land to the ejido. In the end he allowed low-rank DIPS officials to defend the CJAM's property. Given the conditions of the sale, and their vulnerability, the CJAM leaders would have been willing to bribe authorities in order to keep the hacienda and their crops. Their paying "mordidas" to Mexican authorities would have been a regular procedure during Ávila Camacho's administration to avoid the enforcement of a law or regulation.[96]

While application of the Agrarian Reform Law in Mexico threatened the integrity of the landholdings Shibayama was administering, he continued to request small privileges at Temixco, which contributed to the class gap within the hacienda. On January 16, 1945, he described his situation to Chief Ampudia: "Because this is a very sad place, not having access to the entertainment offered by cities, and counting six persons in my family, and wishing to provide them with periods of tranquility and amusement, I beg to that superior office, if you consider it appropriate, to authorize the installation of a long wave radio in my own residence, battery powered."[97]

Ampudia authorized the use of the radio. While the Shibayama family had access to small and considerable luxuries, most Japanese Mexicans lives were filled with wants and needs that were still not solved when the Mexican government ordered their liberation in December 1945.[98]

Today, the hacienda is a tourist resort, with several luxurious swimming pools and other amenities. The exuberant vegetation, the magnificent weather, and the well-paved highway make it one of the main attractions in the Cuernavaca area.[99] The transformation of the hacienda into a tourist attraction makes it difficult to imagine the poverty endured by Japanese Mexicans. Buried under the beauty of the recreation center and the official narrative is the responsibility of the U.S. and Mexican governments for the hunger, forced labor, homelessness, family separation, and even death that Japanese Mexicans suffered.

Completa Libertad: At the End of World War II

The relocation program altered the social fabric of local communities, allowing the exploitation of working-class Japanese Mexicans and the death of the most vulnerable members of this community. Whether euphemistically termed "agricultural cooperatives," "shelters," "concentration zones," or "ranches," in the context of World War II, Japanese Mexicans who did not belong in the circle of political and economic Mexican elites were subjected in all these centers to surveillance, hunger, sickness, and forced labor.

Although Mexican camps had characteristics that set them apart from U.S. concentration camps, the United States dictated the selection of internees and their release in both countries according to the American racial system. On December 17, 1944, the U.S. government issued Public Proclamation No. 21. This proclamation restored "to all persons of Japanese ancestry . . . their full rights to enter and remain in the military areas of the Western Defense Command."[100] World War II had not come to an end, but the U.S. Army officials thought that the "military situation [made] possible [the] modification and relaxation of restriction and the termination of the system of mass exclusion of persons of Japanese ancestry." In other words, the release of Japanese Americans from concentration camps was in sight.[101]

Despite the Western Defense Command's optimistic statement, the release of internees from concentration camps in the United States was gradual, and in 1947, two years after World War II ended, a group of Latin American Japanese remained interned in the Crystal City camp.[102] In Mexico, the confinement of Japanese Mexicans continued to make them vulnerable to abuse. The idea that Japanese Mexicans were transferable and exploitable had become accepted to the extent that Rodolfo Perdomo, manager of Azucarera Veracruzana, requested in January 1945 to *"acquire 2 Japanese gardeners from those who are interned in the Hacienda de Temixco. . . . Not having predilection for any of them, their selection will remain yours* [my emphasis]."[103]

Only in June 1945, when the Ministry of the Interior received a copy of U.S. Public Proclamation No. 21, did the Mexican government begin to plan lifting the restrictions imposed on the Mexican Japanese community. Because the Mexican Ministry of the Interior followed the United States' instructions to release internees, Mexican officials investigated how the U.S. racial classifications would apply this time to Mexican candidates for release. The Mexican officials in charge of the DIPS in 1945 understood that the term "persons of Japanese ancestry" used to free internees in the

United States meant only mixed Japanese Mexicans (of Japanese and *mestizo* origin); in consequence, "pure" Japanese would not be eligible for release, according to Ministry of the Interior's interpretation of U.S. guidelines.[104]

American racial classifications became, once again, the foundation for who was eligible for freedom and who should remain in the concentration camps. General Emilio Baig Serra, DIPS chief, requested clarification in July 1945 from the Mexican minister of foreign affairs regarding the "interpretation that the North American authorities give to the words 'Japanese ancestry' in order to apply the dispositions dictated by the U.S. government, through which individuals described in those terms have been allowed to return to their homes on the Pacific Coast of the United States."[105] In response, Pablo Campos Ortiz, chief officer of the Ministry of Foreign Affairs, informed the Ministry of the Interior that the United States considered persons of Japanese ancestry both mixed and "pure" Japanese. The American racial classification of Japanese covered all individuals "with Japanese blood, regardless of their nationality or place of birth. Their policy included all persons who had Japanese ancestors in the last three generations—in other words, whose blood was Japanese in 1/8 or larger quantities."[106]

Diplomat Campos Ortiz observed that the American racial classification of Japanese had dire consequences for Japanese Mexicans who did not have any relationship with the Japanese state. Campos stated that "naturally, this interpretation [of U.S. racial categories] caused pain and difficulties to a large number of our loyal subjects." Although the Mexican government had complied with the U.S. instructions to uproot all persons of Japanese descent, Campos Ortiz acknowledged too late to avoid damages suffered by the civilian population that it had been unfair to apply systematically this racial measure of control.[107]

After the Ministry of Foreign Affairs stated that, according to U.S. government dispositions, all Japanese Mexican internees were now eligible to leave the internment camps regardless of their generation, it still took three more months to initiate the dismantling of the concentration program. The delay was coordinated with the U.S. Department of Justice, which ordered that Latin American Japanese in the United States, and by extension in Latin American countries, remain "in internment pending final review of their cases." Tom C. Clark, U.S. attorney general, expected these reviews to result in the removal of "hostile Japanese nationals," who would be deported to Japan.[108]

On October 1, Héctor Pérez Martínez, undersecretary of the Ministry of the Interior, communicated the orders to local officials to "grant complete *libertad* [full freedom] to the individuals of Japanese nationality, and their relatives . . . and to write a list of all internees and the official act" confirming their release from the camps.[109] On October 2, 1945, Roberto Guzmán Araujo, representing the Ministry of the Interior, along with other state and local officers held a strange ceremony in Temixco to make the closure official. Guzmán Araujo addressed the Japanese Mexican community to share

> the decision dictated by the President of Mexico to grant you freedom, a dictate that is inspired in the historic trajectory of Mexico in the defense of liberty and democracy, and that is undertaken because Mexico and its allies have ended the war against your nation. The Government of the Republic hopes to see that you respect the laws of our country and that, when returning to the life that you had before, you will follow and respect the institutions of our Motherland. Now you are free.[110]

Although the Mexican and U.S. governments were responsible for the uprooting of Japanese Mexicans, both nations, once again, refused to acknowledge the losses that the Japanese Mexican community suffered during World War II. In the United States, Japanese Americans received a different message, from Dillon Myer, director of the War Relocation Authority:

> Wherever individuals or families find themselves in need of public assistance after relocation, the WRA field offices will help to facilitate arrangements with the appropriate state or local agency. In view of the funds that are available and the arrangements that are being made, the War Relocation Authority feels wholly confident that no evacuee will be deprived of adequate means of subsistence by reason of the closing of the centers.[111]

Temixco internees did not receive public assistance at the closure of the camp. Moreover, they continued to be vulnerable after their "liberation." On October 8, 1945, General Eulogio Ortiz wrote a letter to Chief Baig Serra, asking to be informed if, in fact, Temixco's internees had been freed. If that was the case, General Ortiz wanted to learn the whereabouts of "these Japanese" to offer them employment on his ranch. "After all, nobody will frown upon me if I hire this kind of skunks," wrote Ortiz, convinced that the former inmates remained negligible human beings at his disposal.[112]

Approximately thirty-four children under the age of seventeen were internees of the Temixco Hacienda in October 1945. Fifty-eight of the sixty-nine persons registered in the hacienda's census and in the Act of Freedom at the time of their liberation from the camp had arrived from the U.S.-Mexico borderlands.[113] None of them received government assistance to reintegrate into their previous communities, or to start a new life in the places they had been forced to live in. Sixty-five years after the conclusion of World War II, the experiences of most of the Japanese Mexican community are not even part of the official narrative. While the Mexican state continues to celebrate the achievements of Japanese Mexican entrepreneurs, congratulating them for the "farms" they opened during World War II, in Mexico's memory, and in Japan's memory as well, Japanese Mexican concentration camps never existed.

CHAPTER EIGHT

A Transnational Family

Life in Crystal City Camp

On December 8, 1941, Denkei Gushiken drove his Chevrolet truck over the bridge from Ciudad Juárez, Chihuahua, to El Paso, Texas, to start his work as usual.[1] Denkei Gushiken was a Japanese national whose daily life was divided between the United States and Mexico. Unlike his wife and children, Denkei enjoyed a resident alien status in the United States; thus, the forty-one-year-old man crossed the border every day to support his family in Juárez. Even if he did not have a permit to reside in Mexico, Mexican immigration officials would not bother him as long as he had a U.S. residence card.[2]

Denkei Gushiken's family mirrored multiculturalism as well as the diverse national origins and legal status of immigrants in the borderlands. Denkei and his wife, Tsune Gushiken, were Japanese nationals, but their children had been born in Mexico. Tsune, about thirty-one years old in 1941, lived in Ciudad Juárez with their daughters, Keiko and Haruye, and five-year-old son, Denmei. Keiko and Haruye attended the Emilio Carranza Elementary School in their neighborhood, where they learned their subjects in Spanish. The young Mexican Japanese schoolgirls were ten and seven years old at the time of their father's arrest.[3] Children and mother endured almost two years of separation from Denkei after his arrest in El Paso. Reunification meant abandoning the family's home in Juárez to spend several years in an internment camp in Texas. Although it is possible to obtain only glimpses of their lives in Mexico as free persons, and in the United States as internees, the Gushikens' experiences on both sides of the border during World War II are undoubtedly inserted in social processes of hybridism and mestizaje that complicate notions of race and citizenship.

A Continental Project

When President Franklin D. Roosevelt ordered Japanese Americans interned in camps during World War II, the United States extended its management of the population of Japanese descent to the entire hemisphere. The transfer of thousands of Latin American Japanese to concentration camps in the United States, however, was handled by different U.S. agencies. While the War Relocation Authority (WRA) controlled Japanese Americans, the Immigration and Naturalization Service (INS) was in charge of confining persons of Japanese, German, and Italian descent who were practically kidnapped and "delivered" to U.S. military personnel in 1942 by local police officials in Latin America. Consequently, in the same year, the INS opened several detention facilities in the United States to intern Latin Americans from Peru, Costa Rica, El Salvador, Colombia, Panama, and other American republics. The INS classified Latin American Japanese as illegal immigrants, though they entered the United States against their will. The objective of the United States was to have a pool of civilians from the Axis nations available to exchange for U.S. civilians who remained in Japanese-controlled territories.[4]

The first 2,264 prisoners of Japanese descent from Latin America were men. Later, more prisoners arrived in the United States when the U.S. State Department gave Latin American Japanese interned in U.S. concentration camps the "choice" to bring their families to raise the number of persons available for exchange. Latin Americans were willing to accept their confinement if that meant joining their parents, children, or spouses, who at that time were awaiting deportation to Japan.[5] The confinement of the Gushikens at Crystal City camp illustrates the troubles of thousands of Latin American citizens during World War II.

Denkei Gushiken was on his way to open up his store in El Paso and manage its daily operations when he was arrested by military police and INS officials at the Santa Fe Bridge hours after the Japanese attack on Pearl Harbor. Denkei's downtown business, Den Produce Company, was frequently visited by customers from segregated Mexican and African American neighborhoods. Gushiken had been in the produce business for ten years, creating strong relations in an area that included providers and clientele from the states of Chihuahua, Texas, New Mexico, and Arizona.[6]

Denkei Gushiken dealt with at least two different racial systems in the two countries united by the international bridge he crossed daily. Although Mexican communities had not formulated Jim Crow–type laws, and national narratives repeatedly took pride in the idea of racial democracy, the

Gushikens confronted a complex racial system that ultimately marked Asian immigrants as nonideal elements of the Mexican nation.

President Manuel Ávila Camacho's facile compliance with and enforcement of U.S. racial policies left Japanese Mexicans without legal protection or recourse once their civil rights were suspended by presidential order. Some Japanese Mexicans and their children were forced to leave their place of birth or residence to join the Japanese Latin Americans interned in concentration camps in the United States. Although the Gushikens' confinement in Texas was atypical in the management of Japanese Mexicans, it is at the vortex of international agreements and social processes that rendered nationality, ethnicity, and citizenship notions highly unstable.

The INS detained Denkei Gushiken for more than a year at the Lordsburg Internment Camp, located in New Mexico, 160 miles northwest of El Paso.[7] His detention affected his family right away, for he was forced to leave his wife and children in Juárez without economic support for two months. Within days of his arrest, by government dispositions, his bank account was frozen, his store closed, every item he owned in the United States seized, his business partner arrested, and his father, Denhichiro Gushiken, sent to a farm in New Mexico.[8]

Conditions in the POW camp in which Denkei Gushiken was interned were deplorable. The U.S. Army considered the Lordsburg camp a temporary site of confinement. Because prisoners did not have diplomatic representation at the time of their internment, they were subjected to mistreatment without immediate access to legal defense. It was not until August 10 that a Spanish diplomat visited the Lordsburg camp and reported on the prisoners' conditions, which didn't improve until December 1942, when the U.S. army accepted that the Geneva Convention applied to the management of its internees as well as its prisoners of war. Inmates remained separated from their families, however, and their confinement contributed to deterioration of their health and emotional states.[9] Censorship of internees' letters required hiring Japanese readers, who took a long time reviewing the texts. Control over their communications was a demoralizing factor in the lives of inmates at Lordsburg camp. It delayed the news of Denkei's arrest from getting to Juárez and made it difficult for the family to make plans together to solve their financial problems and figure out how they would reunite.[10]

Several U.S. and Mexican state institutions affected the lives of the Gushikens during this period of tribulation for the Mexican Japanese in the borderlands. Some of the officials who intervened in the process of their uprooting did so as part of their assigned responsibilities (INS and FBI officials among them); others had a more positive role and went beyond their call of duty, such as when Gushiken, while being detained, requested their assistance in delivering money from his frozen bank account to his family in Juárez. Although the federal government had granted detainees permission to withdraw thirty dollars a month to pay for items not supplied by the INS, that amount was not enough to support the Gushiken family, which did not receive any financial assistance for two months after Denkei Gushiken's arrest.[11]

Despite the restrictions on withdrawing money from his bank account, Gushiken managed to obtain permission from the U.S. government to submit fifty dollars to his family.[12] Social worker Frances L. Rand, from the State Department of Public Welfare, in the course of her diligent investigation in Juárez before handing money over to Tsune Gushiken, documented a stable friendship relationship between Tsune and her neighbor Mary Romo. Rand learned that Tsune Gushiken had been "entirely dependent upon the kindness of Mrs. Romo," who "has given food to the family and has stood good for credit for them," evidencing solid collaboration between the Mexican woman and the Japanese immigrant to continue raising Keiko, Haruye, and Denmei.[13] Rand took it upon herself to continue her visits to Tsune's supportive friend. Mary Romo reported that "Mrs. Gushiken had about taken care of her obligations and that she believed that she would get along nicely from now on." Denkei Gushiken had made every effort to keep his family together.[14]

Notwithstanding the labor Denkei performed at Lordsburg camp, for which he received ten cents an hour, his income was not stable or secure enough to support his wife and children.[15] In addition, deportation to Japan was looming for all Latin American Japanese in the United States, depending on the arrangements between the Japanese and U.S. governments for the exchange of prisoners.[16] To keep his family united and make sure that their basic needs would be covered, Denkei petitioned for a transfer from the alien detention camp in Lordsburg, New Mexico, to the family detention center in Crystal City, Texas. This camp allowed unification of "enemy alien" families in order to have control "of even larger numbers of aliens" to hold as pawns in the exchange for U.S. citizens with the Axis powers.[17]

Family Reunification

Denkei Gushiken requested from the INS that his wife and children be transported across the border to join him in the camp in Crystal City. When orders arrived for his deportation to Japan, he needed to have his family with him to leave the United States. In a desperate attempt to expedite their reunion, Gushiken offered to cover at least a portion of his family's travel expenses to the camp.[18]

The INS Crystal City camp opened in December 1942 in the county of Zavala, Texas, ninety-five miles from Nuevo Laredo in the Mexican border state of Tamaulipas. Persons of Japanese and German origin from Latin America composed the majority of internees, although Latin American Italians and American Japanese from Hawaii and Alaska were also integrated into the camp, which was assigned to detain families originally residing outside the continental United States.[19] The State Department had realized that separating Latin American families would eventually stir anti-American sentiments. As Secretary of State Cordell Hull said in 1942, "we left behind for eventual repatriation their inherently non-dangerous wives and minor children. Our representatives in those countries now report that these women and children who were left behind constitute a most dangerous focus of anti-American propaganda and that they should be removed at the earliest opportunity."[20]

Thus, the U.S. State Department's decision to hold more prisoners of war in the country aimed to increase the number of civilians available for exchange, avoid anti-American propaganda by relatives of uprooted Latin Americans, and erase direct testimonies from wives and children of kidnapped Latin American Japanese, Germans, and Italians. The decision provided an opportunity for the Gushiken family to be reunited during the war, albeit in an internment camp.[21] On April 13, 1943, fourteen months after his arrest, Denkei received news from his family. Tsune let him know of the family's situation and hopes:

Beloved husband:

I have just received your letter dated March 21st in which you said you were leaving the next day for the Family Interment Camp at Crystal City, Texas. You also advise me that you are making arrangements for my reunion with you and the children, you cannot imagine the happiness that your letter has brought me and I am hoping with all my heart that this will come through after all these long months of worring [sic]. God is good to us and will unite us again.

Dear, I do not know how long the permmit [sic] will take, it will be much better if you make arrangements to send me some money because I am completely out of money, if permit comes soon we can always have that money.

The kids send you their love and hope to see you very soon, your devoted wife.

Tsune Gushiken[22]

Legal discrimination against Japanese in the United States had previously reduced the possibilities for Tsune Gushiken and her children to join her husband and their father in America. Ironically, war against Japan forced INS officers to allow the Gushikens to cross the border on August 20, 1943. INS officials wrote in the Gushikens' records that local authorities had apprehended them in Ciudad Juárez and "delivered" them to the INS. Once across the border, they were interrogated by an INS Board of Special Inquiry to determine their eligibility to enter the United States.[23]

Tsune Gushiken's signature differs in character from the rest of the letter she sent from Juárez. We can infer that the letter was written in English by another person (perhaps Frances Rand) to expedite the communication between husband and wife since censors would not allow the immediate delivery of correspondence written in Japanese or Spanish. The letter conveys the sense of urgency and despair created by the prolonged separation of the family.[24]

Once the INS approved Denkei Gushiken's request, a series of formal steps were necessary to comply with official requirements justifying the transfer of "enemy aliens" across borders. W. F. Kelly, assistant commissioner for alien control to the INS district director in El Paso, Texas, submitted instructions to the "Embassy of Mexico City to effect the transfer of the wife and three children of the above named alien enemy, now interned at Crystal City, Texas, to the United States for the purpose of joining the subject at his present location. The Consulate at Juarez will notify you when this family will be brought to El Paso and the aliens should be accorded hearings before a Board of Special Inquiry."[25]

The Gushikens were not the only persons of Japanese descent crossing the Mexican border to join family members in an internment camp. Although the number of Japanese Mexicans the U.S. State Department transferred from Mexico to internment camps in the United States is unknown, their detention was part of the aggressive U.S. campaign to seize as many Japanese persons as possible for future civilian exchanges.[26] Given the choice between Japanese American and Latin American Japanese, the U.S. general public would be more willing to accept the deportation of persons brought from any area south of the border. U.S. officials based this conclusion on the

assumption that Latin Americans lost all their rights once classified as illegal aliens in the United States.[27]

Previous seizure and transportation of Latin American Japanese to the
United States had resulted in serious health problems for the captives. Some
spent several weeks under harsh conditions in Latin American jails; then,
when the FBI ordered them to board a U.S. vessel to be interned in a Panama detention center, prisoners spent several weeks without receiving
proper meals, in enclosed environments, performing forced labor. Upon
their arrival in America, several prisoners suffered grave illnesses, as INS
officials were compelled to recognize when Ichikoku Yatomi, a Peruvian
Japanese man, died from tuberculosis.[28]

The death of Yatomi in Los Angeles while under the custody of INS
made U.S. officials realize they needed to ensure that future internees were
alive and in fit condition to travel when an exchange of prisoners occurred
between Japan and the United States. Consequently, in August 1943 a group
of thirty-three Japanese Mexican women, men, and children received a
medical examination and immunizations to comply with INS requirements
before they crossed the border into the United States.[29]

To follow international protocols in transferring residents of Mexico,
the U.S. Embassy requested permission from the Ministry of the Interior
for the Gushikens to leave the country, an authorization granted without
question. Tsune Gushiken had decided to join her husband, even if in an
internment camp, instead of accepting relocation to the interior of Mexico.
In this sense, she and her children crossed the border of their own will. INS
officials wrote in the Gushikens' records, nevertheless, that local authorities
had apprehended Tsune and her children in Ciudad Juárez and "delivered"
them to the INS. This was a common process in the transfer of Latin American Japanese to United States.

INS officials registered Latin American residents interned in U.S. concentration camps as "apprehended" persons. Whether these people were
seized by local police or U.S. soldiers, or "voluntarily" boarded the U.S.
ships or planes to reunite with their families, in the officials' logic, their
apprehension changed their status to prisoners of war. This procedure took
place to satisfy the U.S. government's desire to comply with the Geneva
Convention in some of the steps for internment in American territory. Under
the 1929 Geneva Convention, the United States was entitled to deprive prisoners of war of their freedom.[30]

Tsune Gushiken's management of her possessions is one example of how
INS restrictions affected an individual's economic stability during World
War II. She had to dispose of nearly everything she owned when she left

Juárez for the internment camp in Crystal City. At her entry into the United States across the Santa Fe Bridge, she was carrying $1,848.00 in cash and $242.65 in endorsed checks, perhaps the product of selling all her property in light of the family's impending departure to Japan. INS camp regulations did not allow internees to have large amounts of money, and thus Tsune surrendered her cash and checks to the INS officials at the bridge.[31]

Once across the border, the Gushikens endured a hearing before an INS Board of Special Inquiry. Every civilian Latin American prisoner entering the United States during World War II had the same type of hearing before his or her transfer to a Department of Justice concentration camp. The members of each INS board followed a script they knew would result inevitably in the classification of each Latin American Japanese in custody of U.S. authorities as an alien ineligible to enter the United States. The chairman of the board, Paul L. Stoops, was the Spanish-English translator between the officials and the Gushiken family. Gordon W. Bulger and Coggeshall (whose first name is omitted in the records) were the other two INS inspectors who deliberated on the Gushikens' application for admission into the United States. Coggeshall also acted as secretary of the board, stating out loud that the immediate grounds for INS detention of the family was their "race."[32]

After stating for the record that the Gushikens were members of a "race ineligible to citizenship," Coggeshall proceeded to provide biographical information pertaining to Tsune and her children, including their racial categorization. Denkei's wife was interrogated exhaustively. Her answers revealed that she had been married in Japan, traveling in 1930 to join her husband in Mexico. She had attempted on four occasions to obtain a tourist visa for the United States but had been excluded each time because of her racial classification. Members of the Board of Special Inquiry queried Tsune about her attempts to obtain a visa in an accusatory tone:

Q. You are advised that the records of this service show that one Tsune Gushiken has been excluded from admission to the United States at the port of El Paso, Texas as follows:

August 12, 1930 (Central Office File No. 55733/534)

February 6, 1932 (Central Office File No. 55813/908)

May 19, 1934 (Central Office File No. 55813/908)

November 30, 1936

As an alien found to be ineligible to citizenship and not entitled to the benefit of any of the exemptions provided in Paragraph (C), Section 13 of the Immigration Act of 1924, and as an immigrant not in possession of an unexpired Immigration Visa as required by the Immigration Act of 1924 (El Paso District Director's File No. 7001/405) To whom do these records refer?

A. They refer to me.

Q. When and where were your children, Keiko, Haruye, and Denmei, born, and of what country are they citizens?

A. They were all born in Juarez, Chihuahua, Mexico. . . . They are citizens of Mexico by birth, and citizens of Japan through my husband and myself.

Q. Of what race are your children?

A. They are of the Japanese race.[33]

The entire predetermined procedure had the objective of establishing for the record that Tsune Gushiken and her children had attempted to commit the crime of entering the United States when her "race" was legally excluded. While the white actors in this hearing enjoyed the power to prevent Tsune and her children from reuniting with her husband and their father, Tsune found herself in a vulnerable position, having already been forced to sell, give away, or abandon everything her family had in Mexico. She did not have but one hundred dollars in her possession, the largest amount INS internees were allowed to bring with them into the camps.

The inspectors continued providing details of Tsune's futile attempts to obtain U.S. visas for herself and her children during the 1930s. The board was emotionally abusive. There was no need to prove that Tsune Gushiken and her children had dared to apply for visas to enter the United States. They were still racially ineligible to enter the country since they had "admitted" to being of the "Japanese race." Yet, despite the prearranged agreement among the various departments that Tsune and her children would enter the Crystal City detention camp, the INS officers, throughout their irrelevant interrogation, tried to find inconsistencies between their records and her answers.

In reviewing the Gushiken family's files, the inspectors found that only Keiko, the oldest daughter, had been granted a temporary visa, from 1939 to 1941 to study in El Paso, and that she had been excluded on other occasions. The INS officers took several opportunities to repeat during the hearing that children of Japanese descent were ineligible to visit, live, or work in the United States due to their racial classification. Tsune's children heard from the INS authorities that their racial phenotype was linked to illegality and crime, and that the mere fact that they were of Asian descent disqualified them to be in the United States. Nevertheless, Coggeshall made sure to state for the record that the "children [were] brought before the Board, but not questioned due to their tender years."[34]

While interrogated by the INS Board of Special Inquiry, Tsune Gushiken stated that she had never been in the United States and that she intended to remain in a U.S. government camp for the "duration of hostilities." At the conclusion of the harsh interview, the board deliberated on its findings. Inspector Bulger voted to "EXCLUDE the alien, Tsune Gushiken and children, Keiko, Haruye and Denmei, as aliens found to be INELIGIBLE TO CITIZENSHIP AND NOT ENTITLED TO ANY OF THE BENEFITS OF ANY OF THE EXEMPTIONS PROVIDED IN PARAGRAPH (C), SECTION 13 OF THE IMMIGRATION ACT OF 1924."[35] In addition to their exclusion on the grounds of being racially ineligible to enter the country, the Gushikens were excluded "as persons NOT IN POSSESSION OF VALID PASSPORTS OR OTHER OFFICIAL DOCUMENTS IN THE NATURE OF PASSPORTS SHOWING THEIR ORIGIN AND IDENTITY."[36]

Asserting the lack of passports as a reason to exclude the Gushikens was part of the arbitrary INS procedures to make Latin American Japanese illegal. Historian C. Harvey Gardiner states that U.S. officials collected all documents, including passports, from Latin American Japanese after their arrest in the American republics, and before they had their INS hearings in the United States. When INS members of the hearing board asked Latin American prisoners if they had passports, "with varying degrees of suppressed bitterness, they responded firmly 'No.'" Each heard an official declare, "You must recognize the fact that your entry into the United States is illegal."[37] Although the board members determined that Tsune and her children were to be excluded from entrance to the United States, the INS officials granted a temporary permit for them to join Denkei Gushiken at an internment camp.

The entire procedure converted Latin American prisoners into "illegal aliens" committing a crime by entering the United States without visas and passports. As with many other contradictions of the relocation program, and in U.S. society generally, exclusion and temporary permits were tools to create a façade that legality prevailed in this country. U.S. immigration laws made illegal the entry of Asians; consequently, the Gushikens' presence in the United States was a crime. As illegal aliens, the Gushikens would not be entitled to the protection of U.S. laws. The board's verdict, and the immigration law, criminalized their racialized bodies, not their nationality. The INS verdict did not refer to Tsune's Japanese citizenship but emphasized her race and that of her children, who were Mexican by birth. Consequently, because of their race, Tsune and her children could be punished should they remain in the United States without a visa. But the United States needed them as war hostages; therefore, the INS board granted the Gushikens a temporary permit to make their presence "legal" in the United States for the duration of their travel from El Paso to the Crystal City camp. Once there, Tsune and her children would again be defined by their criminal status, as illegal aliens without civil rights.[38]

The INS board ordered "the four alien enemies" to take the Southern Pacific train to Uvalde, New Mexico. Tsune and her children left El Paso on the same day of their hearing. After ten years of building a life in Mexico, the family was reduced to two suitcases of possessions. Tsune Gushiken "took one suitcase in the coach with her and another suitcase was checked on her ticket for transportation in the baggage car. She also had a few personal effects consisting of one ironing board, one washboard, one small bicycle, one bundle of bed clothes, one wash tub filled with dishes and other articles, and one straw basket of miscellaneous articles," which were crated for shipment to Crystal City camp at a later date.[39] The family would try to make a home in the internment camp with the few belongings they could bring with them. They did not know whether they would be deported to Japan or to Mexico at the end of the war or how long they would remain in U.S. concentration camps, but their main objective was to remain united.[40]

Unaware of the Gushikens' transfer to Crystal City camp, in September 1943 Frances Rand knocked at the door of what had been the family's home in Juárez. The social worker was attempting to deliver a check for Tsune from Denkei's account. When Rand learned that the house was empty, she paid a visit to Mary Romo, the neighbor, who informed her of their internment in an INS camp in the United States. Mary Romo asked Frances Rand to let Tsune Gushiken know how worried she was about her friend and their children. She expected Tsune to send a card to "let her know if she arrived there safely. Mrs. Romo said that she had seen Mrs. Gushiken as far as El Paso and saw her and the children on the train, but that she had not heard of her since. She says that an Immigration official was to meet Mrs. Gushiken and her children in Uvalde and take them by car to join Mr. Gushiken in the Camp there."[41]

Thanks to Rand's reports, and the answers Tsune gave to INS authorities, we learn of the Gushikens' strong relationships in Mexico.[42] Although this is an obvious consequence of having resided for several years in the same place, social scientists have argued that an inability of Asian immigrants to develop a sense of community with the receiving societies is one of the factors in the creation of anti-Asian sentiments and activities.[43] In the course of denouncing the mistreatment of Japanese, for example, historian Donald Collins places partial responsibility for popular anti-Japanese sentiment and internment on the Japanese themselves. He argues that Japanese isolated themselves, clustering in certain residential areas and economic activities, and did not assimilate into their communities. The danger of such statements is that they render Japanese as permanently exotic and superfluous elements of their societies, ignoring the legal and social segregation of Asian immigrants in the American continents.[44] Contrary to academic arguments and traditional beliefs that Japanese immigrants and their children formed a closed community, Japanese immigrants created several kinds of networks.[45] Mary Romo, for example, was only one of the many relationships the Gushikens had. The younger members of the family had even deeper relationships within their communities than their parents did. Although their parents were torn between accepting their deportation to Japan and fighting to stay on the American continent, second- and third-generation Japanese Mexicans thought of their country of birth as home and had few ties with their parents' or grandparents' country. Keiko, Haruye, and Denmei Gushiken did not know another way of life aside from the one they had lived in Mexico. The youngsters had never been to Japan; they had been raised in Mexico, spoke Spanish, and were attached to their teachers, friends, and neighbors. Now they had to create new networks with immigrants from many other countries. And their family would face even more complex issues while in INS custody.[46]

Denkei Gushiken's struggles to support his family were not totally solved when his wife and children arrived in Crystal City. Other familial matters concerned him. He remained worried about his father's precarious situation.[47] At approximately seventy years of age, Denhichiro Gushiken had been sent by the INS to the Spence-Champion Farm in Tularosa, New Mexico. To earn money to cover his basic living expenses, Denhichiro worked on the farm "at odd jobs." Mrs. Nowell, the wife of the farm foreman, whose first name is not reported in the INS files, was worried about the health and quality of life of the elder Gushiken. She informed Fern Aument, employee at the Department of Public Welfare, that she "had been concerned about what would happen to Mr. Gushiken should he become ill enough to require nursing care. There is no hospital in this country where he could be admitted and consequently, she would feel that she should take care of him." Mrs. Nowell thought that no public facilities would admit a Japanese immigrant, and although she was worried about Denhichiro Gushiken, she reported that she would not be able to take care of him: "She really is not able to do so since she has several small children in addition to her household duties, helps with the outside work. She advanced the theory that Mr. Gushiken is lonely and a little frightened."[48]

In an attempt to take care of every member of his family, Denkei Gushiken requested the internment of his father in the Crystal City INS camp.[49] He did not want to leave behind the elderly Gushiken if he and his family were deported. In January 1945, the INS approved his petition. Denhichiro Gushiken was "assisted" by Border Patrol officers at Alamogordo, New Mexico, in boarding the train for Crystal City. "Because of subject's age and small command of English," great care was taken by the Crystal City camp officer in charge, Joseph L. O'Rourke, to make sure that the "Patrol Officers contact the dining car steward on the train at El Paso and assist in arranging for meals" for Denhichiro Gushiken.[50]

A New Life in the Internment Camp

With the arrival of Denhichiro at the INS camp, all members of the transnational family were finally together to take care of one another. Internees did not endure the same harsh conditions other Japanese Americans experienced in WRA-administered camps. Or at least, this is what the INS authorities wanted to convey to foreign officials. The Crystal City camp had become something of a showcase since its first building was erected. The supervision of the Spanish diplomats who inspected the facilities and reported to the Japanese government on the material conditions of the Japanese internees guaranteed better facilities than in camps run by the WRA.[51]

The internees' section included housing facilities, schools, a grocery store, a meat market, a hospital, and a library. Families lived in three-room cottages and in apartments of one to two rooms and shared bathrooms. Internees were in charge of their own cooking, and they had a voucher system to buy food. They operated a canteen, a beauty parlor, and a barbershop in the camp. In addition to running these businesses, Latin American Japanese had a Spanish-language newspaper. Yet, despite the apparent comfort and independence internees enjoyed in the camp, they were still hostages of the U.S. government, and the officials handling the camp treated them as such.[52]

INS public relations director Jerre Mangione described the camp as a happy "town behind barbed wires," and reported after his visit that children thought camp administrator Joseph O'Rourke was the "Pied Piper reincarnated." Yet, conditions were not satisfactory from the prisoners' point of view. O'Rourke, a former Border Patrol officer "with no college education, or special training," insisted on making children believe that "the fence around them was intended for the people on the other side of it." Obviously, only the youngest did not know the truth, but O'Rourke worried that the older children's "bitterness and resentment . . . might affect the younger children."[53] Although O'Rourke did not provide details on how children expressed their bitterness and resentment, his was an official recognition that they were unhappy within the camp. The experience inevitably traumatized children.[54]

Heidi Gurcke Donald, a Latin American German child interned in the camp, regrets the time her family spent in Crystal City. As an adult, she recalls the permanent surveillance she and her family were subjected to. The last image she had before going to sleep symbolized their imprisonment: "At night, there were stars, though the floodlights along the fence hampered our view." Heidi has a strong memory of "the shadows those lights cast through the curtain" in their bedroom.[55]

The children's bitterness, reported by O'Rourke, did not come exclusively from the threatening sentries and the barbed wire surrounding their living quarters. They missed home, despite O'Rourke's paternalistic administration of the camp or Mangione's claims that the camp had a "lively . . . almost cheerful atmosphere."[56] Adults also had reasons to feel depressed, and material conditions added to their emotional distress. Housing was not designed for families who had more than four children. The tin-and-plywood barracks built in the desert left the internees exposed to the 120-degree summer temperature. Former internee Seiichi Higashide reported that the desert temperature "became so hot that we blistered if we touched metal parts of beds. . . . Every evening we hosed down the roof of our barracks and cooled its floor by washing it with water. We then spread our thin straw mats on which to sleep, because the beds were too hot to sleep in." Whatever comfort they managed, it did not erase the fact that they had been uprooted and awaited deportation.[57]

Latin American Japanese and other prisoners in the camp proved their resilience by facing uncertainty and altering their environment to fit their needs. The cold winter was harsh in the noninsulated barracks, whose exterior and interior walls were covered with tarpaper, but prisoners adjusted to their facilities. They beautified them, created gardens, made furniture for their rooms, and built additional rooms and porches. From 1943 to 1945 internees paid $50,000 out of their own pockets, earned through their labor, to make these improvements. Administrator Joseph L. O'Rourke boasted about the investment internees made to improve the concentration camp. Yet, former internee Heidi Gurcke Donald reminds us that O'Rourke wrote his report in 1945, glossing over previous years. She recalls that "while we were there, the area within the fences was bleak, with raw, new construction and dirt roads." In her view, embellishment of the camp would not be enough to make internees happy, and INS officials manipulated images and information to render the camp more amenable than it actually was for children and adults.[58]

Heidi argues that all inmates were conscious of their status as prisoners despite O'Rourke's claims that this was a happy town: walking around the camp was depressing when the view was blocked by the guards, and behind them, the desert reminded internees of their isolation and helplessness. Prisoners from Latin America who were used to a different climate and landscape did not enjoy the dusty roads in summer or the mud that covered them in the winter once the snow had melted. Heidi Gurcke Donald remembers that "grit seeped into the buildings, and the furniture of even the most dedicated housewives was filmed with dust. Scorpions, cockroaches, spiders, and biting red ants were frequent houseguests; outdoors rattlesnakes were not uncommon." The camp was an unsafe, bleak environment.[59]

Publishing a beautified image of the camp, INS administrators emphasized its high level of activity, both economic and recreational. INS public relations director Mangione, based on his visits to numerous internment camps, wrote a report claiming that there was no evidence of emotional stress among the internees at Crystal City. Despite Mangione's opinion that internees did not experience stress, racial categories defined many of the activities in the camp and generated tensions. Although today the justification for such racial divisions is that the Geneva Convention dictated separation by nationalities, Italians and Germans shared living quarters in which the division was racial, not national. Elsewhere, WRA camps and U.S. military quarters were racially segregating American citizens, just to mention some of the institutions in the United States that compelled separation among races.[60] On the other hand, the Department of Justice placed in the same group Latin American Jews and Nazis, which, in addition to the presence of socialist and anti-Nazi "white" Latin Americans, caused complex internal conflicts among prisoners.[61]

Lower ranking officials did not stray from their supervisors' racial views. INS camp guards embodied popular and official racial ideas that had prevailed in most of U.S. history. Moreover, during World War II, white sentries were particularly displeased when Japanese internees received butter and other items that were rationed in the United States. Their feelings were fueled by newspaper articles with titles such as "America's Jap 'guests' Refuse to Work But Nips enslave Yankees," or "Hostile Group is Pampered at Wyoming Camp." Such hostility did not manifest itself exclusively in the camps. Outside, U.S. policies on racial relations segregated and marginalized communities of color.[62] Historian Antonia Castañeda, Crystal City native, reported the effects of racism on Mexican Americans intertwined with the fate of Japanese Americans. She narrated her family's experience in her hometown during World War II:

> The family migrated, my mother told me, because the only work my father, Jose Castaneda, could get in our native Texas was at "Mexican or peon wages." His last job in our hometown of Crystal City, as a day laborer on the Justice Department's Japanese-American internment camp, ended with the arrival of the internees. "They didn't like the Japanese either," she whispered. . . . He returned to Texas in 1946 only to find the same virulent racism, dual-wage labor system, and segregated education.[63]

Like the Mexican Americans the Latin American Japanese displaced in Crystal City, and against newspaper allegations that Japanese internees refused to work, they contributed to war production by working in farms surrounding the camps. They received reduced wages and had to pay the wages of the sentries who ensured they would not escape. Latin American Japanese worked in the construction of roads under the Public Roads Administration, filling the same roles Chinese contract laborers had in the nineteenth century. Their duties included digging three-foot holes, inserting charges of dynamite to expedite the excavation of the terrain over which roads were constructed, and hanging from a rope to drill on difficult-to-reach slopes.[64]

Internees had several reasons to work in the concentration camps. Knowing that they could be deported at any moment, and that they would need as much money as possible to start their lives anew, most internees accepted employment in and out of the camps. In spite of the INS praise of these communal economic activities, they did not have the entrepreneurial character the INS public relations office advertised. Historian Richard Drinnon states that in some of the U.S. concentration camps, shops did not operate to make profits for the internees, but rather catered to Caucasian employees. In any case, the operations of shops followed article 12 of the Geneva Convention, which stated that "canteens shall be installed in all camps where prisoners may obtain, at the local market price, food products and ordinary objects" and that profits were to be "used for the benefit of prisoners."[65] Internees working in the "self-administered" shops received a fixed salary in cash, ten cents an hour, or vouchers and tokens. They received a maximum of sixteen dollars per month, which helped them pay for the items they did not receive from the INS.[66]

The INS Crystal City camp dealt with internees classified as illegal aliens; they endured an oppressive atmosphere that beauty parlors and barbershops could not diffuse. Searchlights and guard dogs helped to heighten security, while identification numbers were stenciled on inmates' shirts and jackets. When internees first arrived, the INS administrators threatened them with dividing their families again if their members did not behave according to the camp's rules.[67]

Indeed, reunification of Latin American families was a privilege. Although the United States desired to have as many prisoners as possible, INS officials were counting on a continual exchange to leave room for subsequent internees. Thus, some Latin American Japanese were denied their applications to reunite with their relatives in the Crystal City camp when there was no space available to intern them.[68]

War strategies made the exchange of prisoners with Japan difficult, and the Department of Justice had had canceled the import of family members of Latin American prisoners by October 1944.[69] The INS, nonetheless, continued to take measures to keep Latin Americans confined.[70] To ensure the inmates would not escape, armed guards patrolled the area, and they would shoot internees attempting to leave the camp: camp guards had killed four internees at other concentration camps and wounded others.[71] As historian Richard Drinnon notes, the murders of internees made the "euphemisms 'temporary havens' or 'wayside stations' grotesqueries. That such killings were relatively infrequent made them no less exemplary. The possibility was always no farther away than the nearest armed sentry."[72] Because the Department of Justice and the State Department transferred their prisoners to various camps, news of extreme disciplinary actions and deaths spread with the arrival of new internees.

Impending Deportation

In spite of the oppressive environment in the camp, inmates had certain protections and the possibility to defer their deportation thanks to the provisions of the Geneva Convention. The Spanish Embassy was officially designated by the Japanese state to serve as the liaison between the Japanese in the exterior and the U.S. government. Spanish diplomats visited the facilities on several occasions to make sure internees were treated according to the Geneva Convention. The diplomats requested that INS officials document express consent for repatriation from internees. The U.S. State Department assured the Spanish Embassy that they would ask the internees if they wished to be repatriated, although the department had received the prisoners for the purpose of their repatriation.[73] For that reason, in February 1944, Crystal City managers required Denkei and Tsune Gushiken to express their will in relation to their possible deportation.[74]

Husband and wife initially refused repatriation. They wished to stay on the North American continent, but the reunion of Denkei's father with his family in Crystal City made their decision very difficult to carry out. The elder Gushiken desired to return to his country, while his children and grandchildren elected to remain in the concentration camp for the duration of the war.[75]

The decision to stay or to accept deportation to Japan created tensions among internees over the years, reaching its climax at the conclusion of the war. Some internees thought that censors had not allowed news of the Japanese victory and were willing to accept deportation to join a triumphant nation. Many patriotic internees felt that, even if Japan had been defeated, they had the duty to return to their country to help in its reconstruction. Others felt a deeper attachment to the Latin American country from which they had been seized. Some elderly internees wanted to spend their last years in Japan, but others did not have anyone to take care of them in their place of birth. Some parents believed that the camp school had taught their children to disdain the Japanese culture and to diminish the value of family union; thus, among other reasons, they made the decision to raise their children in Japan. Discussions among internees of their feelings created resentment, accusations, and changes of mind.[76]

With the passage of time, the conflicting desires of the various generations confined in Crystal City camp fluctuated according to international events affecting the lives of transnational families. On February 25, 1946, months after the United States dropped two atomic bombs on Japan, Tsune Gushiken confirmed her decision to stay in the United States:

It is a well known fact that my native province, Okinawa, had been a battle field. Consequently, a number of towns and villages, including my native town of Motobu, had been demolished and ruined and many natives are now homeless. For the welfare and happiness of my family, I do not wish to repatriate. Furthermore, my father-in-law is in an advanced age of 72, and though he had at one time desired to return, [he] has now changed his mind after giving careful consideration as to the family welfare. It is my earnest desire and hope that you will kindly grant me and my family our wish to remain in the United States.[77]

Denhichiro Gushiken gave a similar explanation for his desire to remain in the United States, suggesting that his and Tsune's statement were written in English by the same person. In all probability, the writer used the same format to express the desire of other internees to avoid repatriation to a devastated country:

> Because of the fact that my wife is in Okinawa and her well-being being unknown, I had applied for the repatriation. However, I have absolute confidence in the American Occupation Forces that she will be well cared for and after giving careful consideration to the happiness and well-being of the family here, I have decided to remain in the United States. I will greatly appreciate your kind consideration given my request and that it be granted.[78]

At the end of World War II, the camp continued operating, with its inmates being mainly Latin American Japanese. Denkei Gushiken and his family planned to return to El Paso, hoping they would be allowed to remain together in the United States.[79] On June 11, 1946, however, they received a statement from the INS advising the family that only Denkei Gushiken would be allowed to reside in the United States. He was the only member of their nuclear family to have the status of "United States legal resident." Tsune and their children would be deported.[80]

Latin American Japanese did not have the option to return to their homelands in the American republics. Many nations, among them Mexico, considered minor children of Japanese subjects as Japanese nationals. This meant that not only Tsune and Denkei would have great difficulty re-entering Mexico, but Keiko, Haruye, and Denmei could be also rejected by the Ministry of the Interior, in charge of immigration matters in Mexico, despite having Mexican birth certificates. Confronting their family's separation once more, Tsune and Denkei Gushiken requested their repatriation to Japan in the company of their children and Denkei's father.[81] Their situation was made even more stressful as Tsune was carrying a baby and enduring a complicated pregnancy. In June, Denkei confirmed his desire to return to Japan in the company of his entire family: "I have been informed that I am released, but I refuse to accept [the option granted by the INS to stay in the United States]. I desire repatriation to Japan together with my family at the earliest possible moment. This is my final decision and I am fully aware that under no circumstances will I be permitted to change my mind."[82]

Almost one year had passed since two American atomic bombs had destroyed Nagasaki and Hiroshima, ensuring victory for the United States. Yet, Latin American Japanese prisoners remained at the Crystal City camp. Unlike German prisoners, whom many Latin American republics accepted back or who were released by the INS under a "relaxed parole" to live in freedom in the United States, Latin American Japanese faced uncertainty and rejection.[83]

"We were, without question, 'birds in a cage,'" stated Japanese Peruvian Seiichi Higashide, describing how Latin American internees felt while detained in the Crystal City camp.[84] The stress did not help Tsune's health; she lost her baby on July 14, 1946, in the Crystal City camp. In the meantime, the Gushikens continued to provide the best care they could for their children.[85]

In January 1947, Denkei and Tsune made a request to the financial officer at Crystal City camp to buy a portable typewriter, deducting seventy dollars from their own funds held by the INS to pay for it (most likely ordered through a catalog). "My daughter, Keiko Gushiken, is now learning typing at this camp school and wish [*sic*] to purchase the typewriter for the purpose," wrote one of the parents or a translator to justify the purchase. Signing this petition, they probably recognized one of the multiple ironies that informed their lives at the camp: a portable typewriter had been seized from Denkei's store by federal officers in 1941, lost among other essential items during the relocation program.[86]

In preparation for the repatriation of the entire family, and aware that starting a new life in a destroyed Japan would require every cent he could collect, Denkei Gushiken tried to obtain information from the U.S. Treasury Department in March 1947 about the property he had owned at the time of his detention.[87] Despite Gushiken's previous refusal to authorize the sale of his belongings to pay for the storage of articles seized by federal authorities, Mike Dipp, owner of the City Market, adjacent to Gushiken's shop in El Paso, had received the items from federal officers, perhaps gratis. Dipp had auctioned some of the items, keeping the money collected as payment for storage of Gushiken's remaining property.[88] In addition to the loss of his store and its inventory, Gushiken was informed that one of his trucks was deemed an "abandoned worthless chassis" and was turned over to the "scrap drive committee" in El Paso. Denkei's other truck was sold to Price's Diary-Creamery in El Paso for $770, a sum that was deposited in his blocked account at El Paso National Bank in August 1942.[89]

Leaving behind debts, property, and friends, the Gushiken family traveled under escort to San Francisco for repatriation to Japan on April 15, 1947.[90] Tsune Gushiken, thirty-six years old at the time, was expecting a baby again. She was about six months pregnant and risked her health and that of her baby while enduring a long trip to a destroyed country. L. T. McCollister, acting officer in charge of Crystal City Internment Camp, informed Central Office that if deportation did not take effect soon, Tsune's pregnancy would impede it later. Her previous miscarriage made "doubtful whether she would be able to travel at a later date." Once in Japan, Denkei notified McCollister of their most recent trouble: "Although we arrived safely in Yokohama we were a little disappointed for we haven't received our four handbags and a suitcase that belongs to Mr. Hayashi." The Gushikens could not even make sure that the few possessions they had salvaged from their displacement would arrive with them at their final destination. And so, the youngest members of the family, who had faint ties with the country of their parents, landed in a war-ravaged place to start a new life with serious material wants.[91]

The losses the Gushikens experienced, including their freedom and the right of the youngest members of the family to remain in their country of birth, were a result of nationalist policies, racist ideologies, and international economic imbalance. Citizenship rights, already so closely linked to racial classification in the United States and Mexico, totally disappeared with the urgencies of World War II and the implementation of the relocation program on both sides of the border. Along with the Gushiken family, Mexican and other Latin American Japanese remained under tight control even after the end of World War II in 1945, remaining either interned in camps or banned from the U.S.-Mexico borderland area.[92]

To this day, the Mexican government denies having deported any person of Japanese descent to the United States during World War II.[93] The language and the procedures used to uproot Japanese Mexicans have only masked the fact that the Mexican government, led by Ávila Camacho, was complicit in the United States' plans to use Latin American Japanese as pawns. The transference of Japanese Mexican civilians to the control of the U.S. government was coordinated with the assistance of the Portuguese Embassy, the liaison between the Japanese and the Mexican governments.[94]

Although the relocation program took a different character in each nation, the United States and Mexico declared those persons of Japanese descent "enemy aliens," without consideration of their age, personal values, religious affiliation, financial status, prior citizenship, or nationality. No resident of the borderlands area was ever tried or condemned for espionage or conspiracy in Mexico or in the United States during World War II. On the contrary, persons like the Gushikens had been valued members of their communities, as several written testimonies confirm. Some were Mexican citizens by birth, others had acquired their Mexican citizenship through naturalization, while the rest were relatives of Mexican citizens. Most refused to be passive victims and made use of every legal recourse to nullify the effects of the relocation program on their lives. None proved to be a danger to the national security of Mexico or the United States, but their value as pawns of economic and political interests placed them in harm's way.

Conclusion

The crime remains the same. Injustice can only be judged from within
itself; it cannot be lessened or mitigated by comparison.
　　　　　—WOLFGANG SOFSKY, *THE ORDER OF TERROR*

Japanese Mexican communities were of critical significance during World
War II within the larger scope of Mexican, U.S., and world history. The
development of international relations and the global organization of the
economy directly informed the management of Japanese immigrants and
their descendants in the U.S.-Mexico borderlands. Such social-political processes began at end of the nineteenth century, when American corporations expanded their operations beyond national borders and participated
in the organization of an economy of transnational communities. U.S. enterprises exploited Mexican natural resources and imported Asian contract
laborers to work mainly in the U.S.-Mexico borderlands. The exploitation of
immigrant labor and racist laws marginalized Japanese workers and their
descendants in both countries. Racialization and marginalization processes,
however, occurred differently in Mexico than in the United States. For
example, Mexican society allowed Japanese immigrants to marry Mexican women, while Jim Crow laws in the United States strictly prohibited
the integration of Japanese immigrants and their descendants into U.S.
society.

World War II brought an opportunity for the United States to initiate a
series of economic negotiations with Latin American states. During the
Third Meeting of Ministers of Foreign Affairs of the American Republics
of January 1942, U.S. diplomats extracted the promise from Latin American governments to deliver raw materials necessary for the war effort. In
exchange, the United States promised economic and military assistance to
Latin American elites in need of controlling their local opponents, including

a working class demanding a higher standard of life. The consolidation of this hemispheric front informed the management of citizens of the Axis nations at war against the United States as well as their descendants.

The creation of a hemispheric alliance in the Americas, in addition to previous exploitation of Asian laborers and orientalization, led to the uprooting and isolation of Japanese immigrants and their descendants across both continents. Consequently, the government in the United States and governments in Latin American countries collaborated in seizing citizens of Japanese, German, and Italian descent to confine them in American camps. The internment of Latin American Japanese men, women, and children followed national policies of segregation and racial exclusion in the United States. INS inspectors documented their arrival, and following federal immigration racial policies, the U.S. officials in charge of registering the uprooted residents of various American republics declared Latin American Japanese individuals as "racially ineligible" to enter the country and thus not entitled to civil rights. Inside the U.S. camps, Latin American Japanese, including those born in Mexico, were subjected to national policies of segregation, occupying separate quarters from white internees. Whether in the United States or Mexico, Japanese Mexicans endured material losses, separation from family members, and restriction of their mobility well beyond the end of World War II.

The organization of a war economy in the Americas determined the eviction of Japanese Mexicans from the U.S.-Mexico borderlands during World War II and the expansion of U.S. racial segregation into Mexico. In compliance with the United States' request to control Japanese Mexicans, President Manuel Ávila Camacho ordered the dislocation of the entire Japanese Mexican community and approved the creation of concentration camps and zones of confinement. During Ávila Camacho's administration, a new pro-American nationalism developed, which positioned Japanese Mexicans as an internal racial enemy during World War II.

Japanese immigrants in Mexico's borderlands had contributed to the creation of a hybrid culture during the first forty years of the twentieth century. They created deep ties in their communities through interracial marriages, businesses, participation in labor struggles, and simple residence among Mexican neighbors. The Mexican state, however, made them racial targets during World War II, reversing the assimilation process that had steadily taken place in the Mexican borderlands in previous years. When Japanese immigrants, their spouses, children, and grandchildren were forced to abandon their homes, the borderlands lost an important cultural and economic element of its transnational community.

Facing the possibility of strong anti-imperialist protests, the Mexican government demonized Japanese Mexicans and suspended the civil rights of all citizens, claiming a state of emergency. President Ávila Camacho thus acquired a large degree of control over the entire Mexican citizenry in the course of handling Japanese Mexicans as an internal enemy. Because the president exercised his power against an already vulnerable racialized target and sustained the privileges of national elites, his antidemocratic rule went unchallenged. The experiences of the Japanese Mexican community during World War II demand a critique of the judicial frame of modern states that allow presidents to cancel the citizenship status of certain denizens of the nation and the civil rights of all citizens during alleged states of emergency. Furthermore, the handling of Japanese Mexicans went against principles of the 1929 Geneva Convention relative to the treatment of prisoners of war, a convention to which both the United States and Mexico subscribed.

Lacking legal recourse to challenge the relocation program in view of the cancelation of constitutional rights, Japanese Mexicans and their allies still protested the uprooting. Entire communities wrote and submitted petitions on behalf of Japanese Mexicans, who were considered valuable members of ejidos and pueblos. Although their efforts proved futile in most cases, they were evidence of the bond developed between Japanese immigrants and their Mexican communities.

Ultimately, Japanese Mexican, Mexican, and U.S. elites agreed to leave the uprooted Japanese Mexicans responsible for their own sustenance despite the provisions of the 1929 Geneva Convention, which mandated the housing, employment, and medical care of displaced civilians and prisoners of war in zones of conflict. The operation of several concentration camps exploited the labor of destitute Japanese Mexicans; however, experiences varied among them. Gender, class, age, and religion determined the degree of marginalization and isolation Japanese Mexicans endured in concentration camps and zones of confinement. Members of the Japanese elite controlled common funds and mediated between Japanese Mexican individuals and the government during World War II. The elite's financial and political capital allowed them to support a certain degree of mobility in sharp contrast with the restrictions the Mexican government imposed on most Japanese Mexicans.

Until recently, narratives of the relocation program in Mexico have depended largely on the perspective of the government and other institutions. They have focused mainly on the experience of the Japanese Mexican elite and their friendly relationship with the administration of President Manuel

Ávila Camacho, obliterating the role of race, gender, and class in the destitution of Japanese Mexicans. Examining the relocation program from the perspective of subjects of the relocation program allow us to identify characteristics of the criminalization of Japanese Mexicans during World War II. While men were considered dangerous and suffered arrest and incarceration, the Mexican government regarded women of the Japanese Mexican community as inoffensive. Yet, the state forced destitute women to take on a double load of work, outside and at home, to provide for their families. In addition, while Japanese Mexicans were uprooted en masse regardless of their nationality or citizenship status, the Mexican government treated German Mexicans and Italian Mexicans on an individual basis.

The extent of the damage inflicted by the governments of Mexico and the United States against Japanese Mexicans surpassed material losses. The health of many Japanese Mexicans was deeply affected, and several uprooted men and women died from causes related to their eviction from the U.S.-Mexico borderlands. In the course of my research, it was impossible to measure the pain families experienced when parents and children scattered or died as a result of the relocation program. Because the loss of memory has contributed to the psychological trauma that entire generations have experienced during and since World War II, it is necessary to insist on the recollection and writing of the history of the victimization and resilience of Japanese Mexican communities. Although reparations will never recover the property, soften the emotional pain suffered, or restore the lives of uprooted Japanese Mexicans, this book has established accountability for such losses, which warrant state apologies and financial reparations. It is the obligation of the Mexican and U.S. governments to acknowledge their responsibility in the dislocation of the Japanese Mexican community as an integral part of the history of the U.S.-Mexico borderlands.

Notes

Works frequently cited in these notes have been identified by the following abbreviations:

CJAM	Comité Japonés ·le Ayuda Mutua (Japanese Mutual Aid Committee)
CTM	Confederación de Trabajadores Mexicanos
DIPS	Departamento de Investigación Política y Social (Department of Social and Political Investigation)
FBI	Federal Bureau of Investigation
INS	Immigration and Naturalization Service
IPS	Investigaciones Políticas y Sociales (the Archivo General de la Nación does not use the complete name of this department and omits the initial letter of Dirección de Investigación Política y Social).
NARA	National Archives and Records Administration
PRI	Partido Revolucionario Institucional
PRN	Partido Nacional Revolucionario

Introduction

1. Sovereignty principles during my generation were related to self-determination and independence, or the right of a country's inhabitants to decide how to rule their nation without the interference of other nations. In spite of Mexican supporters of

foreign intervention, territoriality was very important, as the French and the United States armies had entered Mexico, showing their power against the desires of the Mexican government and population.

2. Edward R. Slack, Jr., "Sinifying New Spain: Cathay's Influence on Colonial Mexico via the *Nao de China*," in *The Chinese in Latin America and the Caribbean*, ed. Walton Look Lai and Tan Chee-Beng (Leiden, Netherlands: Brill Academic Publishers, 2010), 7–34; Tatiana Seijas, *Asian Slaves in Colonial Mexico: From Chinos to Indians* (New York: Cambridge University Press, 2014); Javier Amado Corona Baeza, "La inmigración coreana/The Korean Immigration," in *Henequén: Leyenda, historia y cultura/Its Legend, History and Culture*, ed. Maureen Ransom Carty (Mérida: Instituto de Cultura de Yucatán, 2006), 168–73.

3. Laura J. Torres-Rodríguez, "Diseños asiáticos: Orientalismo y modernidad en México" (PhD diss., University of Pennsylvania, 2012).

4. John D. Márquez, *Black and Brown Solidarity: Racial Politics in the New Gulf South* (Austin: University of Texas Press, 2013).

5. Sinification is the perception of a person or community as Chinese, or the adoption of some Chinese cultural practices.

6. Ian Haney-López, *White by Law: The Legal Construction of Race* (New York: New York University Press, 1997), 54–60, 106–7; Eiichiro Azuma, *Between Two Empires: Race, History, and Transnationalism in Japanese America* (New York: Oxford University Press, 2005).

7. Eiichiro Azuma, "Japanese Immigrant Settler Colonialism in the U.S.-Mexican Borderlands and the U.S. Racial-Imperialist Politics of the Hemispheric 'Yellow Peril,'" *Pacific Historical Review* 83, no. 2 (2014): 263–64; Sergio Hernández Galindo, *La guerra contra los japoneses en México durante la Segunda Guerra Mundial: Kiso Tsuru y Masao Imuro, migrantes vigilados* (México, DF: Itaca, 2011).

8. Azuma, *Between Two Empires*; Emily Anderson, "Containing Voices in the Wilderness: Censorship and Religious Dissent in the Japanese Countryside," *Church History* 83 (2014): 398–421; Raymond A. Mohl, "Asian Immigration to Florida," *Florida Historical Quarterly* 74, no. 3 (Winter 1996): 269–70; Michiko Tanaka, "Seki Sano and Popular Political and Social Theatre in Latin America," *Latin American Theatre Review* 27, no. 2 (Spring 1994): 53–69. Rodolfo Nakamura also reported his father's dissension. Rodolfo Nakamura Ortiz interview, Mexico City, July 25, 2006.

9. Thomas Calvo, "Japoneses en Guadalajara: 'Blancos de honor' durante el seiscientos mexicano," *Revista de Indias* 43, no. 172 (1983): 531–47; Jerry Garcia, *Looking Like the Enemy: Japanese Mexicans, the Mexican State, and U.S. Hegemony, 1897–1945* (Tucson: University of Arizona Press, 2014).

10. Melba Falck Reyes and Héctor Palacios, *El japonés que conquistó Guadalajara: La historia de Juan de Páez en la Guadalajara del siglo XVII* (Guadalajara: Universidad de Guadalajara, 2010).

11. Slack, "Sinifying New Spain"; Fortino Corral Rodríguez, "Génesis del relato fantástico en México," in *Ruta crítica: Estudios sobre literatura hispanoamericana*, ed. Fortino Corral Rodríguez (Hermosillo: Universidad de Sonora, 2007); Rubén Medina, "El mestizaje a través de la frontera: Vasconcelos y Anzaldúa," *Mexican Studies/Estudios Mexicanos* 25, no. 1 (2009): 101–23; Seijas, *Asian Slaves*.

12. Taunya Lovell Banks, "Mestizaje and the Mexican Mestizo Self: No Hay Sangre Negra, So There Is No Blackness," *Southern California Interdisciplinary Law Journal* 15, no. 199 (2006): 215–18.

13. Avital Bloch and Servando Ortoll, "The Anti-Chinese and Anti-Japanese Movements in Cananea, Sonora, and Salt Lake River, Arizona, during the 1920 and 1930s," *Americana: E-journal of American Studies in Hungary* 6, no. 1 (2010), http://americanaejournal.hu/vol6no1/bloch-ortoll.

14. Torres-Rodríguez, "Diseños asiáticos"; Azuma, *Between Two Empires*; Hernández Galindo, *La guerra contra los japoneses en México*, 26–28.

15. Akemi Kikumura-Yano, ed., *Encyclopedia of Japanese Descendants in the Americas: An Illustrated History of the Nikkei* (Walnut Creek: AltaMira Press, 2002), 210–11; Daniel M. Masterson and Sayaka Funada-Classen, *The Japanese in Latin America* (Urbana: University of Illinois Press, 2004), 31, 59–61, 109; Roger Daniels, *Asian America: Chinese and Japanese in the United States since 1850* (Seattle: University of Washington Press, 1988), 115; Charles H. Harris III and Louis R. Sadler, *The Texas Rangers and the Mexican Revolution: The Bloodiest Decade, 1910–1920* (Albuquerque: University of New Mexico Press, 2007), 613; Garcia, *Looking Like the Enemy*, 103. Alberto Violante Pérez to C. Secretario de Gobernación regarding Luis So, March 21, 1944, 2-1/362.4(52)1208, Dirección General de Investigaciones Políticas y Sociales Archives (hereafter IPS).

16. "Chinese chink Japanese eat shit and do not give it to me."

17. "Japs May Colonize in State of Chihuahua," *El Paso Herald*, November 11, 1907, 5; Gerald Horne, *Black and Brown: African Americans and the Mexican Revolution, 1910–1920* (New York: New York University Press, 2005), 6, 52–54.

18. Julian Lim, "Chinos and Paisanos: Chinese Mexican Relations in the Borderlands," *Pacific Historical Review* 79, no. 1 (2010): 66; Evelyn Hu-DeHart, "Indispensable Enemy or Convenient Scapegoat? A Critical Examination of Sinophonia in Latin America and the Caribbean, 1870s to 1930s," in *The Chinese in Latin America and the Caribbean*, ed. Walton Look Lai and Tan Chee-Beng (Leiden, Netherlands: Brill Academic Publishers, 2010), 83–87.

19. Azuma, *Between Two Empires*; Bloch and Ortoll, "Anti-Chinese and Anti-Japanese Movements"; Azuma, "Japanese Immigrant Settler Colonialism"; Andrea Geiger, *Subverting Exclusion: Transpacific Encounters with Race, Caste, and Borders, 1885–1928* (New Haven, CT: Yale University Press, 2011); Gabriel Trujillo Muñoz, *Entrecruzamientos: La cultura bajacaliforniana, sus autores y sus obras* (Mexicali: Universidad Autónoma de Baja California, 2002), 63.

20. Geiger, *Subverting Exclusion*, 36, 173, 262; Erika Lee, "Orientalisms in the Americas: A Hemispheric Approach to Asian American History," *Journal of Asian American Studies* 8, no. 3 (2005): 235–56.

21. Nayan Shah, *Contagious Divides: Epidemics and Race in San Francisco's Chinatown* (Berkeley: University of California Press, 2001); Hernández Galindo, *La guerra contra los japoneses en México*; Alexandra Minna Stern, *Eugenic Nation: Faults and Frontiers of Better Breeding in Modern America* (Berkeley: University of California Press, 2005).

22. P. Scott Corbett, *Quiet Passages: The Exchange of Civilians between the United States and Japan during the Second World War* (Kent, OH: Kent State University Press, 1987), 142.

23. After World War II, Latin American Japanese interned in U.S. concentration camps were excluded from legal existence in the United States because immigration laws of the period prohibited the entrance of persons of Asian origin, and the internees had not been granted visas when they had been removed from their countries to be interned in U.S. concentration camps. Thus, according to the U.S. State Department, the abducted Latin American Japanese had committed a crime when they had been forced by U.S. government officials to enter the United States. Ibid., 139–66.

24. Ibid., 142.

25. For militarization processes in the borderlands, consult Kelly Lytle Hernández, *Migra!: A History of the U.S. Border Patrol* (Berkeley: University of California Press, 2010); Gary Clayton Anderson, *The Conquest of Texas: Ethnic Cleansing in the Promised Land, 1820–1875* (Norman: University of Oklahoma Press, 2005); Miguel Antonio Levario, *Militarizing the Border: When Mexicans Became the Enemy* (College Station: Texas A&M University Press, 2012).

26. The U.S. government created the Border Patrol in 1915 to arrest undocumented Chinese immigrants. Erika Lee, *At America's Gates: Chinese Immigration during the Exclusion Era, 1882–1943* (Chapel Hill: University of North Carolina Press, 2003).

27. Ibid.

28. Halbert Jones, *The War Has Brought Peace to Mexico: World War II and the Consolidation of the Post-Revolutionary State* (Albuquerque: University of New Mexico Press, 2014).

29. Stephen R. Niblo, *War, Diplomacy, and Development: The United States and Mexico, 1938–1954* (Wilmington, DE: Scholarly Resources, 1995), 123.

30. Jones, *War Has Brought Peace*, 2, 37–42.

31. Manuel Ávila Camacho, *Informes presidenciales* (Mexico City: Cámara de Diputados LX Legislatura, 1942), 101. http://www.diputados.gob.mx/sedia/sia/re /RE-ISS-09-06-09.pdf.

32. See Giorgio Agamben, *Homo Sacer: Sovereign Power and Bare Life* (Stanford, CA: Stanford University Press, 1998) and *State of Exception* (Chicago: University of Chicago Press, 2005); Nicholas P. De Genova, "Migrant 'Illegality' and Deportability in Everyday Life," *Annual Review of Anthropology* 31 (2002): 419–47.

33. Michael Omi and Howard Winant, *Racial Formation in the United States: From the 1960s to the 1980s* (New York: Routledge, 1986), 37.

34. Ibid.

35. Ibid., 61–62.

36. R. Nakamura Ortiz interview.

37. My translation. Asociación México Japonesa A.C., "Las migraciones de japoneses a México," *Asociación México Japonesa A.C.* (2009), http://www.kaikan .com.mx/kaikan/aportaciones_Migraciones.php?id=302. The Asociación México Japonesa was formed in 1957; it is the successor of the Comité Japonés de Ayuda Mutua, which was created in 1942. This organization is described in detail in chapter 7.

38. The Mexican government has kept this information in the archives of the department in charge of the control of Japanese Mexicans, Departamento de Investigación Política y Social (DIPS), whose records are identified in this book under the letters IPS.

Chapter 1

1. A substantial portion of this chapter was originally published in "Mexicani-dades de la Diáspora Asiática: Considerations of Gender, Race and Class," *Chicana/ Latina Studies: The Journal of Mujeres Activas en Letras y Cambio Social* 14, no. 1 (Fall 2014): 56–87.

2. F. Kikutake Y. to Sr. D. Julio Novoa, December 1, 1943, IPS 2-1/362.4(52)/1620.

3. Stephen R. Niblo, *Mexico in the 1940s: Modernity, Politics, and Corruption* (Wilmington, DE: Scholarly Resources Books, 1999); Masterson and Funada-Classen, *Japanese in Latin America*; María Elena Ota Mishima, *Siete migraciones japonesas en México, 1890–1978* (México, DF: El Colegio de México, 1982); Ste-phen R. Niblo, "Allied Policy toward Germans, Italians and Japanese in Mexico Dur-ing World War II," paper presented at the Latin American Studies Association Confer-ence, Chicago, 1998.

4. María Elena Paz, *Strategy, Security, and Spies: Mexico and the U.S. as Allies in World War II* (University Park: Pennsylvania State University, 1997).

5. Emma Pérez, *The Decolonial Imaginary: Writing Chicanas into History* (Bloomington: Indiana University Press, 1999); Chela Sandoval, "U.S. Third World Feminism: The Theory and Method of Oppositional Consciousness in the Post-modern World," *Genders* 10 (spring 1991): 2–24.

6. Patricia Fernández-Kelly and Douglas S. Massey, "Borders for Whom? The Role of NAFTA in Mexico-U.S. Migration," *Annals of the American Academy of Po-litical and Social Science*, vol. 610, *NAFTA and Beyond: Alternative Perspectives in the Study of Global Trade and Development* (March 2007): 98–118.

7. Among the various examples of this type of scholarship are Deena González, Vicki Ruiz, Antonia Castañeda, Emma Pérez, and Yolanda Leyva. Antonia Castañeda, "Women of Color and the Rewriting of Western History: The Discourse, Politics, and Decolonization of History," *Pacific Historical Review* 61, no. 4 (1992): 501–33; Deena J. González, *Refusing the Favor: The Spanish-Mexican Women of Santa Fe, 1820–1880* (Oxford: Oxford University Press, 1999); Vicki L. Ruiz, *From Out of the Shadows: Mexican Women in Twentieth-Century America* (New York: Oxford University Press, 1999); Yolanda Chávez Leyva, "'There Is Great Good in Returning': A Testimonio from the Borderlands," *Frontiers: A Journal of Women's Studies* 24, no. 2/3 (2003): 1–9; Pérez, *Decolonial Imaginary*.

8. Medina, "El mestizaje"; Susan Kellogg, "Depicting Mestizaje: Gendered Im-ages of Ethnorace in Colonial Mexican Texts," *Journal of Women's History* 12, no. 3 (2000): 69–92; Magali Marie Carrera, *Imagining Identity in New Spain: Race, Lineage, and the Colonial Body in Portraiture and Casta Paintings* (Austin: University of Texas, 2003); Slack, "Sinifying New Spain."

9. Medina, "El mestizaje"; Lovell Banks, "Mestizaje and the Mexican Mestizo Self."

10. Medina, "El mestizaje"; Lovell Banks, "Mestizaje and the Mexican Mestizo Self." Gloria Anzaldúa, *Borderlands/La Frontera: The New Mestiza* (San Francisco: Spinsters/Aunt Lute, 1987), 38.

11. Kikumura-Yano, *Encyclopedia of Japanese Descendants*; Masterson and Funada-Classen, *Japanese in Latin America*; Daniels, *Asian America*; Harris and Sadler, *Texas Rangers*.

12. Agamben, *Homo Sacer*; De Genova, "Migrant 'Illegality.'"

13. Kikutake to Novoa, December 1, 1943. The *Gripsholm* was the American/Swedish vessel that transported civilians between Japan and the United States during World War II.

14. She had already worked at clerical jobs for two other companies, earning between $200 and $280 (pesos) a month. That amount seemed sufficient to pay the $75 rent for the apartment she shared with her mother. Application for employment at the Banco General de Capitalización, S. A., October 1, 1941, IPS 2-1/362.4(52)1620.

15. "Juarez Japs Put on U.S. Blacklist," *El Paso Herald Post*, December 26, 1941.

16. Application for employment at the Banco General de Capitalización.

17. Ing. Eugenio Riquelme to C. Secretario de Gobernación, March 15, 1944, IPS 2-1/362.4(52)1637.

18. J. Lelo de Larrea to Banco General de Capitalización, November 30, 1942, IPS 2-1/362.4(52)/1620. My translation: "charges against the *expresada señorita*, for which [the] Department has no objection against her continuing rendering her services at that institution."

19. Kikutake to Novoa, December 1, 1943. My translation.

20. Ibid.

21. My translation. Mercedes Ramírez Mendoza to Lic. Eduardo Ampudia Valle, September 18, 1944, IPS 2-1/362.4(52)/1620.

22. My translation. Ibid.

23. Ibid.

24. "Aun conserva(ba) su aspecto oriental." (She kept her oriental aspect.) Ibid.

25. Edward Said argues that Western imperialists created nontemporal fragmented or distorted views of Asians, which were useful "for dominating, restructuring, and having authority over the Orient"; *Orientalism* (New York: Vintage Books, 1979), 3.

26. Ramírez Mendoza to Ampudia Valle, September 18, 1944.

27. Ibid.

28. Report signed by Alejandro Ortega in reference to Santiago Cobayasi, August 21, 1942, IPS 2-1/362.4(52)1446.

29. R. Candiani to C. Jefe del Departamento de Investigación Política y Social, September 30, 1942, IPS 2-1/362.4(52)/1442.

30. Ibid. Salikoko S. Mufwene, "Race, Racialism, and the Study of Language Evolution in America," in *Lavis III—Language Variety in the South: Historical and Contemporary Perspectives*, edited by Michael D. Picone and Catherine Evans Davies (Tuscaloosa: University of Alabama Press, 2006), 449–74.

31. Unsigned resolution in regard to Dr. Manuel Seichi Hiromoto, with a seal stating "Secretaría de Gobernación," January 10, 1944, IPS 2-1/362.4(52)/1444.

32. Jorge Sato to Lic. Miguel Alemán, August 27, 1942, IPS 2-1/362.4(52)995. My translation.

33. For a discussion of unpaid domestic labor, see Carmen Diana Deere, "Rural Women's Subsistence Production in the Capitalist Periphery," in *Peasants and Proletarians: The Struggles of Third World Workers*, ed. Robin Cohen, Peter C. W. Gutkind, and Phyllis Brazier (New York: Monthly Review Press, 1979), 133–48; Lourdes Benería and Shelley Feldman, eds., *Unequal Burden: Economic Crises, Persistent Poverty,*

and Women's Work (Boulder, CO: Westview, 1992). Shizutuo Matzumoto Mouaque (Pedro Matzumoto) to C. Secretario de Gobernación, June 9, 1943, IPS 2-1/362.4(52)1315.

34. Jorge Sato to Lic. Miguel Alemán, August 27, 1942, IPS 2-1/362.4(52)995. "I and my sons, even when they are not yet qualified to enter the military because of their age, are willing to take the arms at any time our motherland calls us."

35. See file of Alfonso Ayshikawa, IPS 2-1/362.4(52)/1582. Lisa Lowe, *Immigrant Acts: On Asian American Cultural Politics* (Durham, NC: Duke University Press, 1996); Yen Le Espiritu, *Asian American Women and Men: Labor, Laws, and Love*, the Gender Lens, ed. Judith Howard, Barbara Risman, and Joey Sprague (Thousand Oaks, CA: Sage, 1997).

36. Lic. Rafael Murillo Vidal to C. Jefe del Departamento de Investigación Política y Social, June 26, 1942, IPS 2-1/362.4(52)/591.

37. File including the transcription of the article published by *Tiempo* annexed to ibid.

38. Crispín Ayala and J. Asunción Alba Anguiano to C. Director General de Población, October 26, 1940, IPS 2-1/362.4(52)/1582.

39. Ibid.

40. Enrique González Chao, August 17, 1942, Inspector PS-5, to Jefe del Departamento de Investigación Política y Social, IPS 2-1/362.4(52)1582.

41. Pedro Garcia to Whom It May Concern, May 2, 1942, and Maria Tomasa Castro de Yamaguchi to C. Secretario de Gobernación, May 19, 1942, IPS 2-1/362.4(52)1224. Crispin Cobayashi Sacay to C. Secretario de Gobernación, June 19, 1944, IPS 2-1/362.4(52)1224.

42. Gender, race, and labor in both Mexico and the United States were intertwined in the beliefs that Asian men were effeminate. Yen Le Espiritu argues that the displacement of Chinese laborers from the mines and railroads of California forced them to take feminized jobs. Asian men were not employed in feminine jobs because they were effeminate; they were corralled into jobs that emasculated them and had to train themselves to perform them. See Espiritu, *Asian American Women and Men*.

43. Francisca Montoya de Shinagawa to Lic. Lelo de Larrea, September 6, 1943; Lic. Alberto de la Peña Borja to C. Secretario de Gobernación, May 14, 1943, IPS 2-1/362.4(52)/1321.

44. Camilo Marín Talavera to Sr. J. Lelo de Larrea, July 26, 1943, IPS 2-1/362.4(52)/1321.

45. Naturalization certificate signed by Jaime Torres Bodet in reference to Tosita Masato Kawano, October 21, 1941, IPS 2-1/362.4(52)/883.

46. Margarita F. de Kawano to Ciudadano Secretario de Gobernación, November 19, 1942, IPS 2-1/362.4(52)/883.

47. From 175 signatories to C. Coronel Rodolfo T. Loaiza, July 18, 1942, IPS 2-1/362.4(52)/883.

48. Capitalization in the original. Ibid. Every post-Revolution Mexican president, including leftist Lázaro Cárdenas, proposed industrialization of the nation as a solution to poverty. Manuel Ávila Camacho emphasized during his presidential period the link between production and war in every report to the nation, requesting from the Mexican workers their application to increase production. The following are examples of his production discourse: "Because the entire nation has demonstrated with its attitude that, when the time arrives, each Mexican knows how to be a soldier willing

to defend the motherland, both in the armed struggle and at work, in the production or in the sacrifice." And "when addressing my compatriots during these last months I have repeatedly exhorted them to work and to achieve harmony (applause). A nation with deficient or no production, or which superfluously spends on what does not manufacture, is a defeated nation from the start." Manuel Ávila Camacho quoted in "Sesión de la Cámara de Diputados Efectuada el Dia 1o. de Septiembre de 1942," in *Diario de los Debates de la Cámara de Diputados del Congreso de los Estados Unidos Mexicanos* (México, DF: Cámara de Diputados del Congreso de los Estados Unidos Mexicanos, 1942). http://cronica.diputados.gob.mx/DDebates/38/3er /Ord/19420901.html.

49. My translation; 175 signatories to Loaiza, July 18, 1942.

50. Lamberto Ortega Peregrina to C. Presidente Municipal at Navojoa, Son., November 23, 1942; Kawano to Ciudadano Secretario de Gobernación, November 19, 1942, IPS 2-1/362.4(52)/883.

51. Lic. J. Lelo de Larrea to Sra. Margarita F. de Kawano, December 30, 1942; Death Certificate 21241, March 4, 1943, IPS 2-1/362.4(52)/883.

52. Lelo de Larrea to Kawano, December 30, 1942. My translation.

53. See file of Alfonso Ayshikawa. As Lisa Lowe discusses in *Immigrant Acts*, damaging stereotypes of Asian men in the United States were also part of the orientalist imaginary prevailing in Mexico during World War II, IPS 2-1/362.4(52)/1582.

54. List signed by Lic. R. Guzmán Araujo, October 2, 1945, IPS 2-1/362.4(52)/1141.

55. Herlinda Cruz de Yanagui to Secretario de Gobernación, August 4, 1943, IPS 2-1/362.4(52)1061. My translation.

56. Ibid. My translation.

57. Enedina López de Kihara, Carmen L. de Komori, Carmen Fukumoto, Beatriz Harada, Emilia Tamura, and Ema Ogawa to C. Secretario de Gobernación, December 31, 1942, IPS 2-1/362.4(52)1179.

58. Gral. De Div. Benecio López Padilla in Saltillo, Coah., to Secretaría de Gobernación, Depto. de Investigación Política y Social, May 30, 1944, IPS 2-1/362.4(52)891. My translation.

59. Ibid.

60. Sucheng Chan, "Against All Odds: Chinese Female Migration and Family Formation on American Soil During the Exclusion Era," in *Chinese American Transnationalism: The Flow of People, Resources and Ideas between China and America during the Exclusion Era*, ed. Sucheng Chan (Philadelphia: Temple University Press, 2005), 34–135; Azuma, *Between Two Empires*.

61. Anzaldúa, *Borderlands/La Frontera*, 4–6.

Chapter 2

1. Slack, "Sinifying New Spain," 9.

2. Between 1624 and 1631 five Japanese persons resided in Guadalajara, according to Eikichi Hayashiya, "Los japoneses que se quedaron en México en el siglo XVII: Acerca de un samurai en Guadalajara," *México y la Cuenca del Pacífico* 6, no. 18 (2003): 10–17. See also Falck Reyes and Palacios, *El japonés que conquistó Guadalajara*;

Escipión Amati, *Historia de La Embajada de Idate Masamune Al Papa Paulo V (1613–1615)* (Madrid: Doce Calles, 2011); Calvo, "Japoneses en Guadalajara."

3. Pierre Chaunu, "Le galion de Manille. Grandeur et décadence d'une route de la soie," *Annales: Economies, Sociétiés, Civilisations* 4 (1951): 447–62; Pierre Chaunu, *Les Philippines et le Pacifique des Ibériques (XVIe, XVIIe, XVIIIe siècles)* (Paris: SEVPEN, 1960); Federico Sánchez Aguilar, *El lago español: Hispanoasia* (Madrid, MA: Fuenlabrada, 2003), cited in Serge Gruzinski, *The Eagle and the Dragon: Globalization and European Dreams of Conquest in China and America in the Sixteenth Century* (Malden, MA: Polity, 2014).

4. Slack, "Sinifying New Spain," 9–27.

5. Calvo, "Japoneses en Guadalajara"; Garcia, *Looking Like the Enemy*.

6. Falck Reyes and Palacios, *El japonés que conquistó Guadalajara*.

7. Chitoshi Yanaga, *Japan since Perry* (New York: McGraw Hill, 1949); Peter Booth Wiley, *Yankees in the Land of the Gods: Commodore Perry and the Opening of Japan* (New York: Viking, 1990).

8. Espiritu, *Asian American Women and Men*, 16–30; Azuma, *Between Two Empires*, 18–19.

9. Gary Y. Okihiro, *Cane Fires: The Anti-Japanese Movement in Hawaii, 1865–1945* (Philadelphia: Temple University Press, 1991), 16–20.

10. Espiritu, *Asian American Women and Men*, 16–30.

11. The Sociedad signed a contract with the Mexican government to acquire 160,550 acres in Chiapas, at $1.50 (pesos) per hectare in installments. Azuma, *Between Two Empires*, 18–20; Masterson and Funada-Classen, *Japanese in Latin America*, 27; Kiyoshi Karl Kawakami, *Japan in World Politics* (New York: MacMillan, 1919), 224.

12. Azuma, *Between Two Empires*, 18–20; Masterson and Funada-Classen, *Japanese in Latin America*, 27; Kawakami, *Japan in World Politics*, 224.

13. In spite of their good relations with their host communities, the cooperative's relative prosperity was interrupted during the Mexican Revolution, when several factions and individuals attacked Japanese immigrants' homes and property. The economic disruption of the period caused the cooperative to stop its operations, but its members continued residing in the area and were later joined by other immigrants. Kikumura-Yano, *Encyclopedia of Japanese Descendants*, 204; Kawakami, *Japan in World Politics*, 225–26.

14. Geiger, *Subverting Exclusion*, 127–33.

15. Daniels, *Asian America*, 107–10; Eithne Luibhéid, *Entry Denied: Controlling Sexuality at the Border* (Minneapolis: University of Minnesota Press, 2002), 56–58.

16. Daniels, *Asian America*, 107–10; Luibhéid, *Entry Denied*, 56–58; Grace Peña Delgado, *Making the Chinese Mexican: Global Migration, Localism, and Exclusion in the U.S.-Mexico Borderlands* (Stanford, CA: Stanford University Press, 2012). For a discussion on racial relations in the United States and their implications on the cultural and legal spheres, see also Espiritu, *Asian American Women and Men*; and Lowe, *Immigrant Acts*.

17. John Mason Hart, *Revolutionary Mexico: The Coming and Process of the Mexican Revolution* (Berkeley: University of California Press, 1997), 156–60; Kawakami, *Japan in World Politics*, 226; Masterson and Funada-Classen, *Japanese in Latin America*, 29; Peña Delgado, *Making the Chinese Mexican*, 15; Lim, "Chinos and Paisanos," 62.

18. Cargill, the Corallitos, Hearst, Huller, International Lumber, the MacManus Land Company, Southwestern Land and Cattle, Rio Bravo Land and Cattle, and the Riverside Ranch became owners of a vast territory of Chihuahua and Durango, which Porfirio Díaz expropriated from Mexican peasants. In Coahuila, the Seminole black mestizo and Kickapoo pueblos lost their landholdings to Eagle Pass Lumber, Jennings-Blocker, Magnum, and Ord, while at La Laguna, Mexican peasants and farmers were displaced by Noble and McClellan, Potter, Rockefeller, and Brown Brothers interests. In Sonora the Mexican government expelled Yaqui and Mayo Indians from their river valley farming landholdings as the Compañía Constructora Richardson acquired 993,650 acres, extending from south of Guaymas to the Mayo River. The railroad holdings of E. H. Harriman and his associates, James Stillman and William Rockefeller of the National City Bank and Southern Pacific Railroad, extended across the state. Other holdings in Sonora included R. H. Vick's Compañia de Terrenos y Ganados, with 1,500,000 acres; Phelps Dodge's 350,000 acres; and the Wheeler Land Company, owned by Chicago and Rockport capitalists, which held 1,450,000 acres, contiguous to William Randolph Hearst and other American landholdings in Chihuahua. The Cananea Copper Company held 346,000 acres. See John Mason Hart, "Social Unrest, Nationalism, and American Capital in the Mexican Countryside, 1876–1920," in *Rural Revolt in Mexico: U.S. Intervention and the Domain of Subaltern Politics*, ed. Daniel Nugent (Durham, NC: Duke University Press, 1998), 72–88. See also "Real Estate in Mexico," *Dunn's International Review* 11 (1907): 25.

19. Espiritu, *Asian American Women and Men*, 16–30; Yamato Ichihashi, *Japanese Immigration: Its Status in California* (San Francisco: Marshall Press, 1915), 3; Peña Delgado, *Making the Chinese Mexican*, 15.

20. Corona Baeza, "La inmigración coreana."

21. Masterson and Funada-Classen, *Japanese in Latin America*, 29; Gary Y. Okihiro, *The Columbia Guide to Asian American History* (New York: Columbia University Press, 2005), 96–97; Daniels, *Asian America*, 110–12.

22. Masterson and Funada-Classen, *Japanese in Latin America*, 29; Okihiro, *Columbia Guide*, 96–97; Daniels, *Asian America*, 110–12.

23. Kikumura-Yano, *Encyclopedia of Japanese Descendants*, 206. Masterson and Funada-Classen, *Japanese in Latin America*, 29; Kawakami, *Japan in World Politics*, 226.

24. The 1910 census reported only ten Japanese people living in the state of Oaxaca, revealing that most Japanese immigrants in Oaxaca's sugar mills had broken their contract and migrated to northern Mexico or beyond; Kikumura-Yano, *Encyclopedia of Japanese Descendants*, 102; Patrick Ettinger, *Imaginary Lines: Border Enforcement and the Origins of Undocumented, 1882–1930* (Austin: University of Texas Press, 2009); Francie R. Chassen de López, *From Liberal to Revolutionary Oaxaca: The View from the South, Mexico, 1867–1911* (University Park: Pennsylvania State University Press, 2005), 253; Geiger, *Subverting Exclusion*, 124–34.

25. Samuel L. Baily and Eduardo José Míguez, *Mass Migration to Modern Latin America* (Wilmington, DE: Scholarly Resources, 2003), 117.

26. Masterson and Funada-Classen, *Japanese in Latin America*, 31.

27. When the JMLA requested its incorporation to the American Federation of Labor, the president of the American Federation of Labor, Samuel Gompers, attempted to negotiate with the Mexican union leader, J. M. Lizarras, the acceptance of a charter on the condition of withholding union membership of Japanese and Chinese. The

Japanese Mexican alliance prevailed with Lizarras's refusal to exclude Japanese or Chinese laborers from the union. Tomás Almaguer, "Racial Domination and Class Conflict in Capitalist Agriculture: The Oxnard Sugar Beet Workers Strike of 1903," *Labor History* 23, no. 3 (1984): 325–50; Xiaojian Zhao, *Asian American Chronology: Chronologies of the American Mosaic* (Santa Barbara, CA: Greenwood Press/ABC-CLIO, 2009), 28–29.

28. Daniels, *Asian America*, 107–10; Luibhéid, *Entry Denied*, 56–58.

29. Hyung-chan Kim, ed., *Asian Americans and the Supreme Court: A Documentary History* (Westport, CT: Greenwood Press, 1992), 513; Roger Daniels, *The Politics of Prejudice: The Anti-Japanese Movement in California and the Struggle for Japanese Exclusion* (Berkeley: University of California Press, 1978), 39, 46, 59; Haney-López, *White by Law*, 44.

30. Lee, *At America's Gates*, 30–31; Luibhéid, *Entry Denied*, 2–7, 31–53; Peggy Pascoe, *What Comes Naturally: Miscegenation Law and the Making of Race in America* (Oxford: Oxford University Press, 2009), 15–30; Huping Ling, *Surviving on the Gold Mountain: A History of Chinese Women and Their Lives* (Albany: State University of New York Press, 1998), 57–59.

31. Daniels, *Asian America*, 107–10; Luibhéid, *Entry Denied*, 56–58.

32. Lee, *At America's Gates*, 30–31; Luibhéid, *Entry Denied*, 2–7, 31–53; Pascoe, *What Comes Naturally*, 15–30.

33. Geiger, *Subverting Exclusion*, 106; Bloch and Ortoll, "Anti-Chinese and Anti-Japanese Movements."

34. Masterson and Funada-Classen, *Japanese in Latin America*, 34; Payson Jackson Treat, "Immigration and the 'Gentlemen's Agreement,'" in *A League of Nations* (Boston: World Peace Foundation, 1917–1918), 449; Daniels, *Asian America*, 112–14.

35. Masterson and Funada-Classen, *Japanese in Latin America*, 33.

36. Kikumura-Yano, *Encyclopedia of Japanese Descendants*, 210–11; Masterson and Funada-Classen, *Japanese in Latin America*, 31, 59–61, 109; Daniels, *Asian America*, 115; Harris and Sadler, *Texas Rangers*, 613. Alberto Violante Pérez to C. Secretario de Gobernación regarding Luis So, March 21, 1944, IPS 2-1/362.4(52)1208.

37. Gary Y. Okihiro and David Drummond, "The Concentration Camp and Japanese Economic Losses in California Agriculture, 1900–1942," in *Japanese Americans. From Relocation to Redress*, ed. Roger Daniels, Sandra C. Taylor, and Harry H. L. Kitano (Seattle: University of Washington Press, 1991), 167–69; Daniels, *Asian America*, 113.

38. William K. Meyers, *Forge of Progress, Crucible of Revolt: Origins of the Mexican Revolution in La Comarca Lagunera, 1880–1911* (Albuquerque: University of New Mexico Press, 1994), 239; Masterson and Funada-Classen, *Japanese in Latin America*, 60. Kikumura-Yano, *Encyclopedia of Japanese Descendants*, 212; Lee Stacy, "Cananea Mines," in *Mexico and the United States*, ed. Lee Stacy (Tarrytown, NY: Marshall Cavendish, 2003), 514.

39. Antonieta Kiyoko Nishikawa Aceves, "La inmigración japonesa a Ensenada durante la primera mitad del siglo XX," *Revista Meyibó/Instituto de Investigaciones Históricas* 1, no. 1–8 (2004), http://iih.tij.uabc.mx/iihDigital/Calafia/Contenido/Vol-I/Numero1-8/Lainmigracion.htm.

40. Azuma, "Japanese Immigrant Settler Colonialism," 264–67.

41. Masterson and Funada-Classen, *Japanese in Latin America*, 60; Kikumura-Yano, *Encyclopedia of Japanese Descendants*, 212.

42. Gabriel Trujillo Muñoz, *Entrecruzamientos: La cultura bajacaliforniana, sus autores y sus obras* (Mexicali: Universidad Autónoma de Baja California, 2002), 43.

43. During the Mexican Revolution, Japan and Germany were interested in creating an alliance with Mexico, never solidified due to the different factions struggling to gain power. In Baja California, expressions of anti-American sentiments, supposedly shared by Mexicans and Japanese, were highly publicized in both the United States and Latin America. See Friedrich Katz, *La guerra secreta en México* (México, DF: Ediciones Era, 2005). Also, Horne, *Black and Brown*, 177.

44. Gerardo Rénique, "Región, raza y nación en el antichinismo sonorense," in *Seis expulsiones y un adiós: Despojos y exclusiones en Sonora*, ed. Aarón Grageda Bustamante (México, DF: Universidad de Sonora/Editorial Plaza y Valdés, 2003), 284.

45. Ibid.

46. José Luis Trueba Lara, *Los chinos en Sonora: Una historia olvidada* (Hermosillo: Universidad de Sonora, 1990), 22–23.

47. Marisela Connelly and Romer Cornejo Bustamante, *China-América Latina: Génesis y desarrollo de sus relaciones* (México, DF: Colegio de México, 1992), 43; James W. Russell, *Class and Race Formation in North America* (Toronto: University of Toronto Press, 2009), 65. In October 1940 Crispín Ayala and J. Asunción Alba illustrated this encompassing view of Asian men as sexual predators. They falsely accused Alfonso Ayshikawa and Carlos Yoshikai of forcing their "beautiful Mexican" female employees to satisfy their "bestial appetites." Ayala and Alba noted that Japanese men behaved just as Chinese deviants. See chapter 1 of this book; IPS 2-1/362.4(52)/1582.

48. José Vasconcelos, *La raza cósmica*, trans. Didier Tisdel Jaén (Baltimore, MD: Johns Hopkins University Press, 1997); Medina, "El mestizaje."

49. Vasconcelos, *La raza cósmica*, 19–21, 85.

50. Trujillo Muñoz, *Entrecruzamientos*, 49.

51. Among the northern business and landowners who were political leaders in the post-Revolutionary period are Plutarco Elias Calles, Álvaro Obregón, Abelardo Rodriguez, and Alejandro Lacy. See Manuel González Oropeza, "La discriminación en México: El caso de los nacionales chinos," in *La problemática del racismo en los umbrales del siglo XXI* (México, DF: Universidad Nacional Autónoma de México, Instituto de Investigaciones Juridicas, 1997), 52; Catalina Velázquez-Morales, "Inmigrantes japoneses en Baja California, 1939–1945," *Clío* 6, no. 35 (2006): 84, 88; Enrique Krauze, *Mexico: Biography of Power—A History of Modern Mexico, 1810–1996* (New York: Harper Perennial, 1998), 342.

52. Lim, "Chinos and Paisanos," 63–64; Hu-DeHart, "Indispensable Enemy or Convenient Scapegoat?"; Bloch and Ortoll, "Anti-Chinese and Anti-Japanese Movements"; Lee, "Orientalisms."

53. Azuma, "Japanese Immigrant Settler Colonialism," 270–73.

54. "'Yellow Peril' Plot Detected," editorial, *El Paso Herald*, August 9, 1921, 8; "Mexico Agrees to Colonization by Jap Farmers," *El Paso Herald*, January 31–February 1, 1920, 7; "Japanese Buy Big Areas of Valley Lands," *El Paso Herald*, October 19, 1920, 1.

55. González Oropeza, "La Discriminación en México," 52; Trujillo Muñoz, *Entrecruzamientos*, 47.

56. Kikumura-Yano, *Encyclopedia of Japanese Descendants*, 212.

57. Masterson and Funada-Classen, *Japanese in Latin America*, 60; Azuma, "Japanese Immigrant Settler Colonialism," 270–73; Kikumura-Yano, *Encyclopedia of Japanese Descendants*, 212; Stacy, "Cananea Mines," 514.

58. Kikumura-Yano, *Encyclopedia of Japanese Descendants*, 213; Olga Shoko Doode Matsumoto, *Los claro-oscuros de la pesquería de la sardina en Sonora: Contradicciones y alternativas para un desarrollo equilibrado* (Zamora: El Colegio de Michoacán, 1999), 47.

59. Luis Yide Tamanachi and Ignacio Koba's cases were filed, as other partnerships, within one folder. See IPS 2-1/362.4(52)/1110.

60. Daniels, *Asian America*, 119, 36, 44, 47.

61. Ibid.

62. "Japanese Buy Big Areas of Valley Lands"; Bloch and Ortoll, "Anti-Chinese and Anti-Japanese Movements."

63. Kim, *Asian Americans and the Supreme Court*, 513.

64. Daniels, *Asian America*, 119, 36, 44, 47; Masterson and Funada-Classen, *Japanese in Latin America*, 61.

65. Kikumura-Yano, *Encyclopedia of Japanese Descendants*, 212.

66. Ota Mishima, *Siete migraciones*, 81; Azuma, *Between Two Empires*.

67. Kikumura-Yano, *Encyclopedia of Japanese Descendants*, 212.

68. Daniels, *Asian America*, 156–57; Espiritu, *Asian American Women and Men*, 38.

69. Daniels, *Asian America*, 157–59; Ruiz, *From Out of the Shadows*, 76; Azuma, *Between Two Empires*.

70. Masterson and Funada-Classen, *Japanese in Latin America*, 51; Pascoe, *What Comes Naturally*, 15–51; Ruiz, *From Out of the Shadows*, 76–79.

71. Instituto Nacional de Estadística, Geografía e Informática (INEGI), *Los extranjeros en México* (Aguascalientes, México: INEGI, 2007), http://www.inegi.gob.mx /prod_serv/contenidos/espanol/bvinegi/productos/estudios/sociodemografico/ext_en _mex/extraen_mex.pdf, p. 3. Nell Irvin Painter, *The History of White People* (New York: Norton, 2010), 20; Ota Mishima, *Siete migraciones*.

72. Ota Mishima, *Siete migraciones*, 20.

73. Daniels, *Asian America*, 163.

74. Stacy, "Cananea Mines," 514; Francisco E. Balderrama and Raymond Rodrí-guez, *Decade of Betrayal: Mexican Repatriation in the 1930s* (Albuquerque: University of New Mexico Press, 2006), 178.

75. Masterson and Funada-Classen, *Japanese in Latin America*, 62; Velázquez-Morales, "Inmigrantes japoneses," 92.

76. Delfino Navarrate, in charge of the Immigration Service office in Tijuana, suggested that President Lázaro Cárdenas completely halt the immigration of Japanese persons in 1935. See Velázquez-Morales, "Inmigrantes japoneses," 91.

77. Trujillo Muñoz, *Entrecruzamientos*, 50. Doode Matsumoto, *Los claro-oscuros de la pesquería*, 124.

78. Velázquez-Morales, "Inmigrantes japoneses," 92; Masterson and Funada-Classen, *Japanese in Latin America*, 62.

79. Kevin Starr, *Embattled Dreams: California in War and Peace, 1940–1950* (New York: Oxford University Press, 2003), 55.

80. Daniels, *Asian America*, 158, 59; Okihiro and Drummond, "Concentration Camp," 169–72; Jacobus tenBroek, Edward N. Barnhart, and Floyd W. Matson, *Prejudice, War, and the Constitution*, vol. 3 of *Japanese American Evacuation and Resettlement* (Berkeley: University of Los Angeles Press, 1954), 109–36.

81. Masterson and Funada-Classen, *Japanese in Latin America*, 127.

82. Ibid.

83. Ibid., 214–15; Kikumura-Yano, *Encyclopedia of Japanese Descendants*.

Chapter 3

1. Teun A. van Dijk, "Elite Discourse and the Reproduction of Racism," in *Hate Speech*, ed. Rita Kirk Whillock and David Slayden (Thousand Oaks, CA: SAGE, 1995).

2. Report taken by Lic. Alfonso García González, Chief of the Departamento de Investigación Política y Social, rendered by Dr. Tsunesaburo Hasegawa Araki in Mexico City, April 2, 1942, IPS 2-1/362.4(52)/464.

3. Ibid.

4. "Japanese Aliens Moved into Mexico," *El Paso Herald Post*, March 21, 1942, 10.

5. Kikumura-Yano, *Encyclopedia of Japanese Descendants*, 19.

6. Trujillo Muñoz, *Entrecruzamientos*, 69.

7. "Believe Japs Reported on U.S. Units," *El Paso Times*, March 22, 1942.

8. Ernesto Chávez, *The U.S. War with Mexico: A Brief History with Documents* (New York: Bedford/St. Martin's, 2007); Quintard Taylor, *In Search of the Racial Frontier: African Americans in the American West, 1528–1990* (New York: Norton), 37–56.

9. David Montejano, *Anglos and Mexicans in the Making of Texas, 1836–1986* (Austin: University of Texas Press, 1987), 24.

10. William D. Carrigan, "The Lynching of Persons of Mexican Origin or Descent in the United States, 1848 to 1928," *Journal of Social History* 37, no. 2 (2003): 411–38; Mark Wasserman, *Capitalists, Caciques, and Revolution: The Native Elite and Foreign Enterprise in Chihuahua, Mexico, 1854–1911* (Chapel Hill: University of North Carolina Press, 1984), 84–94.

11. Shelley Bowen Hatfield, *Chasing Shadows: Indians Along the United States-Mexico Border, 1876–1911* (Albuquerque: University of New Mexico Press, 1998).

12. Martha K. Huggins, *Political Policing: The United States and Latin America* (Durham, NC: Duke University Press, 1998); Wasserman, *Capitalists*, 84–94.

13. González, *Refusing the Favor*, 3–4, 39–50.

14. Benjamin Johnson, "The Plan de San Diego Uprising and the Making of the Modern Texas-Mexican Borderlands," in *Continental Crossroads*, ed. Samuel Truett and Elliott Young (Durham, NC: Duke University Press, 2004), 273–98; U.S. Senate, *Investigation of Mexican Affairs: Hearing before a Subcommittee of the Committee on Foreign Relations* (testimony of Henry Lane Wilson), 66th Cong., 1st sess. (Washington, DC: Government Printing Office, 1920), 2249–57; Carrigan, "Lynching of Persons."

15. Huerta was a former official in the army of Porfirio Díaz. He betrayed Díaz first, then Madero. Ilene V. O'Malley, *The Myth of the Revolution: Hero Cults and the*

Institutionalization of the Mexican State, 1920–1940 (New York: Greenwood Press, 1986).

16. Horne, *Black and Brown*, 157–58; Óscar J. Martínez, ed., *U.S.-Mexico Borderlands: Historical and Contemporary Perspectives* (Wilmington, DE: Scholarly Resources, 1996), 141.

17. Friedrich Katz, *The Life and Times of Pancho Villa* (Stanford, CA: Stanford University Press, 1998), 570.

18. Claire F. Fox, *The Fence and the River: Culture and Politics at the U.S.-Mexico Border* (Minneapolis: University of Minnesota Press, 1999), 70. See also Brendon O'Connor, ed. *Anti-Americanism: Comparative Perspectives*, vol. 3 of *Anti-Americanism: History, Causes, Themes* (Oxford: Greenwood World Publisher, 2007), 77–102; Horne, *Black and Brown*, 158.

19. Friedrich E. Schuler, *Mexico between Hitler and Roosevelt: Mexican Foreign Relations in the Age of Lázaro Cárdenas, 1934–1940* (Albuquerque: University of New Mexico Press, 1998), 35.

20. Balderrama and Rodríguez, *Decade of Betrayal*, 63–90; Camille Guerin-Gonzales, *Mexican Workers and American Dreams: Immigration, Repatriation, and California Farm Labor, 1900–1939* (New Brunswick, NJ: Rutgers University Press, 1994).

21. Richard K. Showman and Lyman S. Judson, eds., *The Monroe Doctrine and the Growth of Western Hemisphere Solidarity* (New York: H.W. Wilson, 1941), 30.

22. Schuler, *Mexico between Hitler and Roosevelt*, 97.

23. Don M. Coerver and Linda B. Hall, *Tangled Destinies: Latin America and the United States* (Albuquerque: University of New Mexico Press, 1999), 81.

24. Joe C. Ashby, *Organized Labor and the Mexican Revolution under Lázaro Cárdenas* (Chapel Hill: University of North Carolina Press, 1967), 240.

25. Ibid.

26. Schuler, *Mexico between Hitler and Roosevelt*, 97.

27. Sumner Welles, *The World of the Four Freedoms* (New York: Columbia University Press, 1943), 4.

28. Arturo Grunstein Dickter, "In the Shadow of Oil: Francisco J. Múgica vs. Telephone Transnational Corporations in Cardenista Mexico," *Mexican Studies/Estudios Mexicanos* 21, no. 1 (2005): 1–32; Ashby, *Organized Labor*, vii, 32–48; John H. Coatsworth, "Measuring Influence: The United States and the Mexican Peasantry," in *Rural Revolt in Mexico: U.S. Intervention and the Domain of Subaltern Politics*, ed. Daniel Nugent (Durham, NC: Duke University Press, 1995), 69–71.

29. "Foreign News: Trotsky, Stalin & Cardenas," *Time*, January 25, 1937.

30. *Time* reported that "*Hombre Libre* ran on its front page an anti-British cartoon, on its last page an anti-U.S. cartoon." See "New President, Old Job," *Time*, December 9, 1940.

31. Ibid.

32. Ibid.

33. Ibid.

34. Schuler, *Mexico between Hitler and Roosevelt*, 201–02; Niblo, *Mexico in the 1940s*, 117.

35. See Seth Fein, "Myths of Cultural Imperialism and Nationalism in Golden Age Mexican Cinema," in *Fragments of a Golden Age: The Politics of Culture in Mexico*

since 1940, ed. Anne Rubenstein, Gilbert Michael Joseph, and Eric Zolov (Durham, NC: Duke University Press, 2001), 159–98.

36. Trujillo Muñoz, *Entrecruzamientos*, 71–72; Schuler, *Mexico between Hitler and Roosevelt*, 139–42.

37. Stetson Conn and Byron Fairchild, *U.S. Army in World War II—the Western Hemisphere: The Framework of Hemispheric Defense* (Washington, DC: Department of the Army, 1960), 333–36; Niblo, *Mexico in the 1940s*, 86.

38. Mexican authorities confined the sailors in Guadalajara first, and then in Perote for the duration of the war, although many of them escaped or achieved permission to reside in Mexico City. Paz, *Strategy, Security, and Spies*, 125.

39. This sort of official declaration supported the idea that the Mexican government removed the Japanese Mexicans from the West Coast in order to avoid the direct intervention of U.S. military or civil authorities in Mexico; however, the U.S. incursion in Juárez contradicts the official justification for their uprooting as a measure to preserve the national sovereignty. Velázquez-Morales, "Inmigrantes japoneses," 93; Trujillo Muñoz, *Entrecruzamientos*, 66.

40. Niblo, *War, Diplomacy, and Development*, 98–99.

41. Craig Thompson, "Fears Revolution in the Philippines: Theodore Roosevelt Deplores Independence in Talk Before the Science Academy," *New York Times*, April 3, 1938.

42. For the displacement of several Japanese populations, see Thomas Connell, *America's Japanese Hostages: The World War II Plan for a Japanese Free Latin America* (Westport, CT: Praeger, 2002); Corbett, *Quiet Passages*; John K. Emmerson, *The Japanese Thread: A Life in the U.S. Foreign Service* (New York: Holt, Rinehart and Winston, 1978); C. Harvey Gardiner, *Pawns in a Triangle of Hate: The Peruvian Japanese and the United States* (Seattle: University of Washington, 1981); Daniel Robinson, "Planning for the 'Most Serious Contingency': Alien Internment, Arbitrary Detention, and the Canadian State 1938–39," *Journal of Canadian Studies* 28, no. 2 (1993): 5–20; Stephanie D. Bangarth, "Religious Organizations and the 'Relocation' of Persons of Japanese Ancestry in North America: Evaluating Advocacy," *American Review of Canadian Studies* 34, no. 3 (2004): 511–40; John Herd Thompson and Stephen J. Randall, *Canada and the United States: Ambivalent Allies*, 4th ed. (Athens: University of Georgia Press, 2008).

43. "Consultative Meeting of Foreign Ministers of the American Republics," in "Official Documents" supplement, *American Journal of International Law* 34, no. 1 (1940): 14. This first meeting took place in Panama from September 23 to October 3, 1939.

44. Ibid.

45. "Second Meeting of Ministers of Foreign Affairs of the American Republics," in "Official Documents" supplement, *American Journal of International Law* 35, no. 1 (1941): 6.

46. See O'Connor, *Anti-Americanism*.

47. Sumner Welles, *The Time for Decision* (New York: Harper, 1944), 220.

48. Organization of American States, *Final Act of the Third Meeting of the Ministers of Foreign Affairs of the American Republics* (Rio de Janeiro: Organization of American States, 1942), 54, Resolution XXXIX.

49. J. Lloyd Mecham, *The United States and Inter-American Security, 1889–1960* (Austin: University of Texas Press, 1961).

50. "Foreign Relations: To Shoe an Achilles Heel," *Time*, January 26, 1942.

51. Niblo, *Mexico in the 1940s*, 98, 117.

52. Organization of American States, *Final Act*, 27, Resolution XVII.3.

53. James Petras, ed., *Latin America: From Dependence to Revolution* (New York: Wiley, 1973), 266.

54. Welles, *World of the Four Freedoms*, 60.

55. Organization of American States, *Final Act*, 6. The resolutions taken at the Rio de Janeiro meeting of 1942 had a large positive economic impact on the United States, providing this country with an enormous advantage not only during World War II but also during the Cold War. The United States demanded that free market practices between Latin American countries and the United States be set aside under the banner of a state of emergency.

56. Ibid.

57. Dana Markiewicz, *The Mexican Revolution and the Limits of Agrarian Reform, 1915–1946* (Boulder, CO: Lynne Rienner, 1993), 131.

58. Sandra F. Maviglia, "Mexico's Guidelines for Foreign Investment: The Selective Promotion of Necessary Industries," *American Journal of International Law* 80, no. 2 (1986): 286; Jones, *War Has Brought Peace*, 3; Niblo, *War, Diplomacy, and Development*, 89–95, 123.

59. Welles, *Time for Decision*, 216–19.

60. Niblo, *Mexico in the 1940s*, 6.

61. The U.S. Wartime Production Board rejected the application of the Legorreta family for American financing of an alkaline salt recovery and soil reclamation plant, but thanks to their links to the Mexican government, the project eventually received approval and resources to operate from the United States. Niblo, *War, Diplomacy, and Development*, 117–18.

62. Fein, "Myths of Cultural Imperialism," 159–66.

63. Ibid.

64. Carl J. Mora, *Mexican Cinema: Reflections of a Society, 1896–1980* (Berkeley: University of California Press, 1989), 73.

65. Niblo, *Mexico in the 1940s*, 171.

66. Monika A. Rankin, *¡México, La Patria!: Propaganda and Production during World War II* (Lincoln: University of Nebraska Press, 2010), 2–10; Jones, *War Has Brought Peace*, 127.

67. "Sesión de la Cámara de Diputados Efectuada el Dia 1o. de Septiembre de 1942," *Diario de los Debates de la Cámara de Diputados del Congreso de los Estados Unidos Méxicanos* (México, DF: Cámara de Diputados del Congreso de los Estados Unidos Mexicanos, 1942), http://cronica.diputados.gob.mx/DDebates/38/3er/Ord/19420901.html.

68. Ibid.

69. Ibid.; Pamela Sugiman, "Memories of Internment: Narrating Japanese Canadian Women's Life Stories," *Canadian Journal of Sociology* 29, no. 3 (2004): 359–88.

70. Rankin, *¡Mexico, La Patria!*, 2.

71. Manuel Ávila Camacho, "Tercer informe del presidente Manuel Ávila Camacho," *500 años de México en documentos* (1943), http://www.biblioteca.tv/artman2/uploads/1943.pdf.

72. Tetsuden Kashima, *Judgment without Trial: Japanese American Imprisonment during World War II* (Seattle: University of Washington Press, 2003).

73. "Japanese Aliens Moved into Mexico," *El Paso Herald Post*, March 21, 1942.

Chapter 4

1. Ota Mishima, *Siete migraciones.*

2. Leslie T. Hatamiya, *Righting a Wrong: Japanese Americans and the Passage of the Civil Liberties Act of 1988* (Stanford, CA: Stanford University Press, 1993), 14.

3. Julia María Schiavone Camacho, *Chinese Mexicans: Transpacific Migration and the Search for a Homeland, 1910–1960* (Chapel Hill: University of North Carolina Press, 2012), 26, 126.

4. Omi and Winant, *Racial Formation*; Agamben, *State of Exception.*

5. President Ávila Camacho's order to suspend individual rights was applicable to all citizens of Mexico. On June 2, the Mexican Congress not only ratified the decree but also stated that "suspension [of individual rights] will last for as long as Mexico is in war against Germany, Italy, and Japan . . . and may be extended, if deemed necessary by the President, up to thirty days after the date of the cessation of hostilities." "Sesión de La Cámara de Diputados Efectuada El Día 2 de Junio 1942," *Diario de los Debates de la Cámara de Diputados del Congreso de los Estados Unidos Mexicanos* (México, DF: Cámara de Diputados del Congreso de los Estados Unidos Mexicanos, 1942). http://cronica.diputados.gob.mx/DDebates/38/2do/Extra/19420602.html.

6. "Foreign Relations: To Shoe an Achilles Heel." Also, "Japanese Aliens Moved into Mexico."

7. Telegram, Ignacio N. Koba and L. M. Tanamachi to General Manuel Ávila Camacho, September 12, 1942, IPS 2-1/362.4(52)/1110.

8. Ibid.

9. The 1899 Hague Convention and the Geneva Convention in 1929 required that "the Government into whose hands prisoners of war have fallen is bound to maintain them." Japanese Mexicans suspected of espionage and removed from their place of residence were also entitled to protection by the same convention, as nations signing the Geneva conventions had agreed that "a spy taken in the act cannot be punished without previous trial." Furthermore, the 1934 International Convention on the Condition and Protection of Civilians determined that the Geneva Convention "concerning the treatment of Prisoners of War (was) by analogy applicable to Civilian Internees." Mexico was a signatory to the Geneva and Hague conventions. Convention relative to the Treatment of Prisoners of War, Geneva, July 27, 1929, chapter II, article 7, *International Committee of the Red Cross*, http://www.icrc.org/ihl.nsf/FULL/305?OpenDocument.

10. Anacleto F. Olmos, Presidente Municipal de Nogales, Sonora, to Luis M. Tanamachi, Oficio No. 2365, October 30, 1942, IPS 2-1/362.4(52)/1110.

11. The documents pertaining to the two Tanamachis, who shared their first and last names, were filed in the same folder, IPS 2-1/362.4(52)/1110.

12. Luis Tanamachi Yide to C. Secretario de Gobernación, June 28, 1943 (Navolato, Culiacán, Sin.), IPS 2-1/362.4(52)/1110.

13. Telegram, Luis Tanamachi [Yide] to Lic. Adolfo Ruiz Cortines, Oficial Mayor de la Secretaría de Gobernación, August 17, 1943. IPS 2-1/362.4(52)/1110.

14. Telegram, Adolfo Ruiz Cortines to Ignacio Koba and L. M. Tanamachi, October 3, 1942, IPS 2-1/362.4(52)/1110.

15. Roderic Ai Camp, *Mexican Political Biographies, 1935–1993*, 3rd ed. (Austin: University of Texas Press, 1995), 420. See also Adrian A. Bantjes, *As If Jesus Walked on Earth: Cardenismo, Sonora, and the Mexican Revolution* (Wilmington, DE: Scholarly Resources, 1998).

16. General Anselmo Macías Valenzuela to the C. Secretario de Gobernación, October 2, 1942, IPS 2-1/362.4(52)/1110.

17. Jorge Cicero, "International Law in Mexican Courts," *Journal of Transnational Law* 30, no. 5 (1997): 1035–86. An amparo is a legal recourse to remedy unfair or illegal actions by a government agency.

18. Anacleto F. Olmos to Ignacio K. [*sic*] Koba, October 30, 1942, IPS 2-1/362.4(52)/1110.

19. Ibid.

20. Adolfo Ruíz Cortines to General Anselmo Macías Valenzuela, November 3, 1942, IPS 2-1/362.4(52)/1110.

21. Inspector 135 to Secretaría de Gobernación/Migración, November 4, 1942, IPS 2-1/362.4(52)/1110.

22. Margarito T. Hayakawa to C. Secretario de Gobernación, April 9, 1942, IPS 2-1/362.4(52)1587.

23. Hiroshi Tanaka to C. Secretario de Gobernación, April 23, 1942, IPS 2-1/362.4(52)1221. See also IPS 2-1/362.4(52)994, IPS 2-1/362.4(52)995. and IPS 2-1/362.4(52)1179.

24. Hiroshi Tanaka to C. Secretario de Gobernación, April 11, 1942, IPS 2-1/362.4(52)1179; Tanaka to C. Secretario de Gobernación, April 23, 1942.

25. Hayakawa to C. Secretario de Gobernación, April 9, 1942.

26. Niblo, *War, Diplomacy, and Development*, 5–7. Antonio de P. Araujo to C. Subjefe del Dept. de Investigación Política y Social, May 26, 1942, IPS 2-1/362.4-(52)/600 II.

27. Araujo to C. Subjefe, May 26, 1942; Luis T. Tsuji to C. Secretario de Gobernación, August 10, 1943. IPS 2-1/362.4(52)1250.

28. Araujo to C. Subjefe, May 26, 1942; Luis T. Tsuji to C. Secretario de Gobernación, July 31, 1943, IPS 2-1/362.4(52)/1106.

29. Certificate by Dr. Ruperto Bretón (Manuel Masajiro Kawano), December 15, 1942, IPS 2-1/362.4(52)1128.

30. Fifty-nine-year-old Mauricio Jika Jika from Palau, Coahuila, stated that he did "not have any way to survive in this capital (as I used to do in Palau) since my right leg is paralyzed." Mauricio Jika Jika to Secretaría de Gobernación, DIPS, August 27, 1942, IPS 2-1/362.4(52)400. See also files of Pablo Jayassi, IPS 2-1/362.4(52)1349; Genaro Romero, IPS 2-1/362.4(52)1099; and Enrique Sugarawa Sugarawa, IPS 2-1/362.4(52)1355.

31. Colonia Japonesa de Mazatlán to Sr. Presidente de la República, January 17, 1942, IPS 2-1/362.4(52)/600.

32. Julio Tukunaga to C. Secretario de Gobernación, October 29, 1943. IPS 2-1/362.4(52)/1030.

33. Generals Alfredo Delgado and Ramón F. Iturbide to Lic. Don Miguel Alemán, Secretario de Gobernación, October 18, 1943, IPS 2-1/362.4 (52)/973.

34. Malaquías Huitrón to C. Oficial Mayor de la Secretaría de Gobernación, June 4, 1943, IPS 2-1/362.4(52)395.

35. Shojiro Shinomiya and Riozo Kaubayashi were arrested by military and civil officers, being incarcerated for approximately ten days in Atlixco, Puebla. Mr. Varela, their employer, had sent them to work on his ranch while their permit was being processed. Fernando Luna, Presidente Municipal de Atlixco, to C. Coronel de Caballería, Maximiano Ochoa Moreno, August 9, 1944, IPS 2-1/362.4(52)/797. Kahei Kikimura Katacha was also arrested and imprisoned. Manuel A. Guirado to Jefe DIPS, April 18, 1944, IPS 2-1/362.4(52)1880.

36. Maria Teresa Jarquín Ortega and Manuel Miño Grijalva, eds., *Historia general del Estado de Mexico* (Toluca: Colegio Mexiquense, 1998), 112.

37. Kameyama grew up in Sonora. Official Act, signed by Alejandro Ortega on December 22, 1943, IPS 2-1/362.4(52)589.

38. Report by Sadao Yamachita Yamashita [*sic*], November 18, 1943, IPS 2-1/362.4(52)/1059. See also report by Manuel S. Miyamoto, Matsimoto Toraki, Yukio Tanaka, Otakichi Kano, Kalawa Mulai Shuji, and Victor Asai Asai at the DIPS offices after their arrest on December 8, 1942, IPS 2-1/362.4(52)600.

39. José González Ortega to C. Jefe del Dept. de Investigación Política y Social, December 27, 1943, IPS 2-1/362.4(52)/600.

40. Ibid.

41. Gustavo F. Nava to C. Secretario de Gobernación, April 10, 1942, IPS 2-1/362.4(52)387.

42. Takahaski Tangi Johiro and Gral. Brigadier Sabas Hinojosa R. to C. Secretario de Gobernación, December 30, 1943, IPS 2-1/362.4(52)/1340.

43. Kaishi Kaishi Chusue Hori to C. Director General de Población, March 6, 1943, and to C. Secretario de Gobernación, May 22, 1943, IPS 2-1/362.4(52)/871. José G. Jonda, former internee at the Temixco camp, was hired by Ezequiel Padilla, minister of foreign affairs, as a gardener in his Cuernavaca home in June 1945. José G. Jonda to Secretario de Gobernación, June 9, 1945, IPS 2-1/362.4(52)/1512. Luis Manuel Moreno to C. Secretario de Gobernación, in reference to Guillermo Kono, September 13, 1945, IPS 2-1/362.4(52)/1556; Yoshimura Koshi Kumezo to H. Secretaría de Gobernación, June 2, 1943, IPS 2-1/362.4(52)/806. Another Mexican Japanese, Manuel Yofu, reported having "been brought [to Pátzcuaro, Michoacán] by General Lázaro Cárdenas who told him that he would not need any documents" to be employed at Escuela Hijos del Ejército as a cook; memorandum from Inspector 51, August 25, 1944, IPS 2-1/362.4(52)/1578.

44. Manuel Hayashi to Secretaría de Gobernación, August 1, 1942, IPS 2-1/362.4(52)843.

45. Eduardo Ampudia to C. Inspector Carlos Fontones Paz, August 4, 1943, IPS 2-1/362.4(52)1581.

46. Lic. José Lelo de Larrea to C. Inspector Carlo Saavedra, confidential letter, September 28, 1943, and undated report, IPS 2-1/362.4(52)/1604.

47. Gustavo Takano Araiza to C. Secretario de Gobernación, August 3, 1942, IPS 2-1/362.4(52)/1646; Carlos Takizawa Lara to C. Secretario de Gobernación del DF, August 3, 1942, IPS 2-1/362.4(52)/1649.

48. Hisashi Narihiro to C. Jefe de la Oficina de Información y Propaganda Política, February 20, 1943, IPS 2-1/362.4(52)/950.

49. Hisashi Narihiro to C. Ministro de Gobernación, July 8, 1942, IPS 2-1/362.4(52)/950.

50. A. S. Yoshida to Lic. Miguel Alemán, March 26, 1942, IPS 2-1/362.4(52)/600.

51. Ibid.

52. Moreno to C. Secretario de Gobernación, September 13, 1945; Kumezo to H. Secretaría de Gobernación, June 2, 1943.

53. Certificate by Dr. Eduardo González Hurtado, December 14, 1943, IPS 2-1/362.4(52)/1145.

54. G. A. Yamanouchi to C. Jefe del Depto. de Investigación Política, undated, IPS 2-1/362.4(52)/1145.

55. Luis T. Tsuji to C. Secretario de Gobernación, February 21, 1944, IPS 2-1/362.4(52)/1145.

56. Permission signed by Lic. Eduardo Ampudia, March 16, 1944, IPS 2-1/362.4(52)/1145.

57. Tokumi Tanaka to C. Jefe de la Oficina de Investigación Política, April 11, 1944, IPS 2-1/362.4(52)/1145.

58. Donaciano Ceballos to Lic. Eduardo Ampudia, August 30, 1944, IPS 2-1/362.4(52)/1145. Romualdo J. Cházaro to Lic. J. Lelo de Larrea, February 25, 1943, and to Lic. Eduardo Ampudia, August 23, 1943, IPS 2-1/362.4(52)968.

59. Ernesto Corona Ruesga, Jefe del Servicio de Inspección, to C. Oficial Mayor de la Secretaría de Gobernación, June 10, 1943, IPS 2-1/362.4(52)/1141; Ceballos to Ampudia, August 30, 1944.

60. General Miguel Martínez to C. Licenciado Miguel Alemán, November 13, 1942, IPS 2-1/362.4(52)1590. Other arrested Korean Mexican men were Antonio Kim, Pedro Kim, and José Sosa. Ricardo Lee to Sr. José Hahn, June 6, 1942, IPS 2-1/362.4(52)1331.

61. Iun Chi Kin [*sic*] to Mr. Tsun Yuan Ham, signed "December of the 23rd year of the Republic of Korea," IPS 2-1/362.4(52)1590.

62. Martínez to Alemán, November 13, 1942. Other cases of Korean men whose civil rights were canceled are in the following files: IPS 2-1/362.4(52)1082, IPS 2-1/362.4(52)1331, IPS 2-1/362.4(52)1617.

63. Agamben, *State of Exception.*

64. Earl M. Maltz, "The Fourteenth Amendment and Native American Citizenship," *Constitutional Commentary* 17, no. 3 (2000): 555–73. Guerin-Gonzales, *Mexican Workers and American Dreams*; Yasuko I. Takezawa, *Breaking the Silence: Redress and Japanese American Ethnicity* (Ithaca, NY: Cornell University Press, 1995).

65. See George Lipsitz, *The Possessive Investment in Whiteness: How White People Profit from Identity Politics* (Philadelphia: Temple University Press, 2006).

66. Corbett, *Quiet Passages*; Connell, *America's Japanese Hostages.*

Chapter 5

1. Sergio González Gálvez, "Eventos históricos de la relación México-Japón," presentation at the Ciento Veinte Años de Amistad entre México y Japón, Secretaría de Relaciones Exteriores, 2008, accessed November 7, 2009, http://www.kaikan.com .mx/kaikan/aportaciones_Colaboradores.php?id=55.
Sergio González Gálvez, "Eventos históricos de la relación México-Japón," *Revista Mexicana de Política Exterior*, no. 86 (March–June 2009): 9–17.
2. González Gálvez, "Eventos históricos" (presentation). This transcription of Sergio González Gálvez's presentation posted on the Asociación México Japonesa's website differs slightly from that published by the Mexican Foreign Ministry. For example, González Gálvez states in the version he read to the audience on December 3, 2008, which included the Japanese ambassador, that the "farm" was established during the First Great War, while in the Ministry of the Interior's publication, he refers to the war as the "Pacific War."
3. Ibid. González Gálvez, "Eventos históricos," *Revista Mexicana*.
4. González Gálvez, "Eventos históricos" (presentation).
5. Since the very first days of relocation, Japanese Mexicans were escorted with their children by soldiers who "delivered" them to officers in the regional military command in Mexico City. José Pacheco Iturribarria to C. Comandante de la Escolta del Tren Num, 6 Nocturno de Guadalajara a México, January 29, 1942, IPS 2-1/362.4(52)/600.
6. Alfonso García González to Luis Y. Shigematsu (Yoshida), January 27, 1942, IPS 2-1/362.4(52)600.
7. See Stephen R. Niblo, "Allied Policy toward Axis Interests in Mexico During World War II," *Mexican Studies/Estudios Mexicanos* 17, no. 2 (2001): 293.
8. Geoffrey C. Gunn, *New World Hegemony in the Malay World* (Lawrenceville, NJ: Red Sea Press, 2000), 192–95.
9. A Japanese association existed before World War II; however, when a presidential decree prohibited the existence of clubs or associations related to the Axis nations, the Japanese community suspended meetings, and the organization ceased to exist. García González to Shigematsu, January 27, 1942.
10. Kikumura-Yano, *Encyclopedia of Japanese Descendants*, 212–13.
11. Issei is a term that describes first-generation Japanese immigrants. Paz, *Strategy, Security, and Spies*, 37.
12. Francis Peddie, "Una presencia incómoda: La colonia japonesa de México durante la segunda guerra mundial," *Estudios de Historia Moderna y Contemporánea de México*, no. 32 (July–December 2006): 86. Abelardo Paniagua negoció on behalf of the CJAM leaders the purchase of a hacienda in Temixco. "Mexico en la guerra," *Tiempo* 1943, 11.
13. "Relation of the [*estimables*] persons and groups who donated to the 'Comité Japonés de Ayuda Mutua,'" March 4, 1942, IPS 2-1/362.4(52)/1149. Kiso Tsuru and Heiji Kato donated ten thousand pesos each.
14. Estatutos del Comité Japonés de Ayuda Mutua, undated, IPS 2-1/362.4(52)1149.
15. Fidelia Takaki de Noriega interview, Mexico City, July 16, 2006.

16. Stephanie Wössner, *Japanese American Positionality in Hawaii and on the Mainland* (Munich: GRIN Verlag), 25–26.

17. Although Stephen Niblo does not focus on corruption manifested in the relocation program, he examines mechanisms and instances of illegal or unethical deals in Mexico during World War II. See Niblo, *Mexico in the 1940s*, 254, 255.

18. Abraham H. Castellanos to C. Jefe del Depto. de Investigación Política y Social, February 8, 1945, IPS 2-1/362.4(52)785.

19. Alberto S. Yoshida to Sr. Dip. Jesús Ramírez, January 4, 1941 [*sic*]. The year is actually 1942, as Yoshida wishes Ramírez a happy new year and specifies 1942 as the current year, IPS 2-1/362.4(52)/1672.

20. Ibid.

21. The U.S. State Department had contemplated internment of Latin American Japanese since 1941. Ambassador to Panama Edwin C. Wilson negotiated the conditions under which Panama would allow the operation of concentration camps. Initially, Panama's government would run the camp under the supervision of the United States. Wilson proposed the arrest of Panamanian Japanese and their internment at Toboga Island. Internees would be classified as Panamanians being guarded by Panamanian officers. The United States agreed to cover all expenses involved in the operation of the internment and to be responsible for any claims originating from the internment. In the end, the U.S. government took over administration of the camp. Corbett, *Quiet Passages*, 140.

22. Ibid., 141; Robert M. Buffington, *Criminal and Citizen in Modern Mexico* (Lincoln: University of Nebraska Press, 2000), 98–105.

23. Romualdo J. Cházaro to Lic. J. Lelo de Larrea, February 25, 1943; Romualdo J. Cházaro to Lic. Eduardo Ampudia, August 23, 1943, IPS 2-1/362.4(52)968.

24. "Japs Must Leave Juarez in Five Days," *El Paso Herald Times*, March 27, 1942.

25. Governor Alfredo Chávez to Lic. Miguel Alemán, Srio. De Gobernación, March 16, 1942; Arturo Tamura to José Y. Sato, undated, IPS 2-1/362.4(52) 600, II Tome.

26. Japanese Mexicans from Juárez were escorted to Camargo by federal police officers under the supervision of Italian Mexican DIPS inspector Julio Ramírez Colozzi. Telegram, J. Ramírez Colozzi to Secretaría de Gobernación, April 21, 1942, IPS 2-1/362.4(52)600.

27. Tahei Ogawa and his wife and children were forced by the Jefe de Población (chief of the Immigration Office) to leave Juárez, although both parents were naturalized citizens and their children were Mexicans by birth; IPS 2-1/362.4(52)1597.

28. "List of Japanese and children of Japanese persons who remain in Tijuana for various reasons," signed by Julio Ramírez Colozzi, April 3, 1942, IPS 2-1/362.4(52)600.

29. Certificate signed by 37 residents of Cd. Juárez, January 28, 1943, IPS 2-1/362.4(52)1179.

30. "Japs Removed from Border Area," *El Paso Times*, April 1, 1942, 5; "Japs Must Leave Juarez in Five Days."

31. Merced Gómez de Okubo to C. Lic. Miguel Alemán, Secretario de Gobernación, May 21, 1942, IPS 2-1/362.4(52)1206.

32. Eighty-two residents of Camargo to C. Secretario de Gobernación, May 28, 1942, IPS 2-1/362.4(52)1577.

33. Chávez to Alemán, March 16, 1942; Tamura to Sato, undated, IPS 2-1/362.4 (52)600.

34. Camp, *Mexican Political Biographies*, 716.

35. Masterson and Funada-Classen, *Japanese in Latin America*, 126.

36. Undated list titled "Nombres de los súbditos japoneses concentrados en V. Aldama," IPS 2-1/362.4(52)600, II Tome.

37. Ernesto Hidalgo, Secretaría de Relaciones Exteriores, to C. Secretario de Gobernación, January 6, 1943, IPS 2-1/362.4(52)1179.

38. R. Tamura to Yoshio Sato, May 20, 1942, IPS 2-1/362.4(52)600, II Tome. Mr. Tamura signed as Arturo Tamura, R. Tamura, and Tamura Fumiyo Ryugo. Tamura Fumiyo Ryugo to C. Secretario de Gobernación, January 15, 1943, IPS 2-1/362.4(52)1157.

39. Adolfo Ruiz Cortines to C. Gobernador del Estado de Chihuahua, June 5, 1942, IPS 2-1/362.4(52)600, II Tome.

40. Report taken by Lic. Alfonso García González, Chief of the Departamento de Investigación Política y Social, rendered by Dr. Tsunesaburo Hasegawa Araki, Mexico City, April 2, 1942, IPS 2-1/362.4(52)/464.

41. Enedina López de Kihara and Julia R. de Ogata to C. Secretario de Gobernación, November 29, 1942, IPS 2-1/362.4(52)1179.

42. Enedina López de Kihara, Carmen L. de Komori, Carmen Fukumoto, Beatriz Harada, Emilia Tamura, and Ema Ogawa to C. Secretario de Gobernación, December 31, 1942, IPS 2-1/362.4(52)1179.

43. Enedina López de Kikara [sic] to C. Secretario de Gobernación, December 29, 1942, IPS 2-1/362.4(52)1179.

44. Ibid.

45. López de Kihara et al. to C. Secretario de Gobernación, December 31, 1942.

46. Ibid. Corroborating inflation during World War II is Niblo, *Mexico in the 1940s*, xxi, 16.

47. "Foreign Relations: To Shoe an Achilles Heel."

48. See complete file of Leonardo Arita Arita, IPS 2-1/362.4(52)/601, and Naoji Yano, IPS 2-1/362.4(52)/404, among other cases of displaced Japanese Mexican children who accompanied their parents. Yanome Mitsuo to C. Secretario de Gobernación, March 13, 1942, IPS 2-1/362.4(52)/786.

49. Middle-class Japanese Mexican children living in the borderlands experienced also a sudden change in their status when the Junta de Administración y Vigilancia de la Propiedad Extranjera (Commission for the Administration and Surveillance of Foreign Property) ordered bank accounts of Axis nationals frozen. This commission was formed in December 1942. Masterson and Funada-Classen, *Japanese in Latin America*, 60–62. Real estate and businesses often fell out of the control of Japanese Mexicans, who sold or transferred their valuables to avoid larger losses through confiscation. Colozzi to Gobernación telegram, April 21, 1942.

50. López de Kihara et al. to C. Secretario de Gobernación, December 31, 1942.

51. Ibid.

52. Oswaldo Álvarez to C. Secretario de Gobernación, January 28, 1943, IPS 2-1/362.4(52)1179.

53. Ibid.

54. Certificate signed by Eduardo Martinez and other 36 persons, January 28, 1943, IPS 2-1/362.4(52)1179.

55. Comité de Ayuda Mutua Japonesa to C. Secretario de Gobernación, June 2, 1942.IPS 2-1/362.4(52)600, II Tome.

56. Ibid.

57. A real estate agency, avenues, schools, grants, and associations are named after Tomás Valles, the owner of the hacienda that exploited the labor of Japanese Mexicans in 1942: http://webchihuahua.com/print_me.php?ckey=2974 and http://www.posadatierrablanca.com.mx.

58. Masterson and Funada-Classen, *Japanese in Latin America*, 127.

59. Although Masterson and Funada-Classen report that internees received a salary of fifty cents per day, I did not find the same evidence of wages in the DIPS files. In any case, I share the same conclusion as Masterson and Funada-Classen: Japanese Mexicans worked "virtually as slaves" on Valles property. Ibid.

60. Lamberto Ortega Peregrina to Whom It May Concern, January 18, 1943, IPS 2-1/362.4(52)/1179.

61. Yoshio Sato, former leader of the Japanese community in Ciudad Juárez was among the CJAM members who traveled with Alemán Pérez in order to pay for the expenses of the Japanese Mexicans from Villa Aldama. Adolfo Ruiz Cortines to C. Alfredo Chávez, January 2, 1942, IPS 2-1/362.4(52)465.

62. Jesús Kihara to C. Secretario de Gobernación, January 15, 1943, IPS 2-1/362.4(52)1179.

63. On July 27, 2006, Mexican president Vicente Fox attended the celebration of the fiftieth anniversary of the Asociación México Japonesa (AMJ), an association that stemmed from the CJAM and was founded in 1956 by the same board. The AMJ was financed with the funds the Mexican government confiscated from Japanese institutions operating in Mexico during World War II. In 2006, President Fox unveiled a bust of Sanshiro Matsumoto at the AMJ on the same date. Presidencia de la República, "Diversas intervenciones durante la Ceremonia Conmemorativa del 50 Aniversario de la Asociación México-Japonesa, Asociación Civil," *Presidencia de la República* (July 27, 2006), http://fox.presidencia.gob.mx/actividades/?contenido =26200.

64. Sanshiro Matsumoto had the financial means to follow some Japanese traditions, unlike many Mexican Japanese who were displaced and interned in camps. He married his wife, who adopted the name of Maria Consuelo, through the picture bride system, sending their children to Japan to be educated in his country of origin. Their daughter, Mari, returned to Mexico in one of the last commercial ships authorized to leave Japan for the North American continent during World War II. The Matsumoto family's hard work and expertise in floriculture gained them a sizable capital, and they kept their wealth throughout World War II. See "Cambian la historia del paisaje urbano," *Reforma*, April 2, 2003.

65. Matsumoto's ranch was situated in the *delegación* Magdalena Contreras, which was connected to the more populated areas of the federal district through Calzada de Tlalpan. One of the most important avenues in Mexico City, Calzada de Tlalpan was paved only in the developed area of the capital. Access to the ranch was therefore difficult, particularly for persons who were not familiar with the area, which was the case of the Japanese Mexicans evacuated from the borderlands. Gobierno del Distrito

Federal, "Las primeras colonias," Delegación La Magdalena Contreras, accessed March 7, 2015, http://www.mcontreras.df.gob.mx/historia/constitucion2.html. See also Niblo, *Mexico in the 1940s*, 29.

66. Internees at Batán's camp are included in the lists of "Japanese subjects deployed from various places." Lamberto Ortega P to C. Director General de Población, May 21, 1942, IPS 2-1/362.4(52)600, II Tome.

67. Masterson and Funada-Classen, *Japanese in Latin America*.

68. Undated list of persons of Japanese origin interned at Rancho "Batán," IPS 2-1/362.4(52)600, II Tome.

69. Anonymous telephone interview, December 15, 2009.

70. Connell, *America's Japanese Hostages*, 100.

71. See numerous permits granted to CJAM leaders to visit ranches and haciendas, IPS 2- 1/362.4(52)/600.

72. One of those partners, Kiso Tsuru, enjoyed a remarkable degree of freedom during World War II. This book explores his relationship with the Mexican state in chapter 6. The operation of the camp established in the state of Morelos is discussed in chapter 7.

Chapter 6

1. Amparo, similar to the habeas corpus recourse, did not have any effect in Mexico during World War II to protect Japanese Mexicans. See Luis Tanamachi and Ignacio Koba's file, IPS 2-1/362.4(52)/1110.

2. Ávila Camacho in "Sesión de la Cámara de Diputados Septiembre."

3. Ibid.

4. Appeal from 180 persons from Cacalotlán, with a signature from the Síndico Municipal certifying that all signatures are valid, to Carlos Ramírez, August 24, 1943, IPS 2-1/362.4(52)1061. His case, and the intervention of his wife, Herlinda Cruz de Yanagui, are described in chapter 1.

5. Ejidos are societies of peasants who own and work the land under a communal regimen and democratic administration.

6. Cacalotlán residents to Ramírez, August 24, 1943.

7. Ibid.

8. Dr. Martin Otsuka, Dr. Manuel Hiromoto, and Dr. Octavio Kazusa were among the Japanese medical practitioners who chose lifestyles very similar to those of their poor patients in rural Mexico.

9. Lic. José Lelo de Larrea, Jefe del Departamento de Investigación Política y Social, December 21, 1943, IPS 2-1/362.4(52)1061.

10. See Dr. Octavio Kazusa, Dr. Manuel Hiromoto, and Manuel Hayashi's files for cases of communities valuing medical care from Japanese Mexican medical practitioners, IPS 2-1/362.4(52)593, IPS 2-1/362.4(52)1444, and IPS 2-1/362.4(52)843.

11. Among the petitioners were the local Chamber of Commerce, Asociación Local Ganadera [Local Livestock Farmers' Association], Sociedad Mutualista Benito Juárez [Benito Juárez Mutual Society], Club de Leones [Lions' Club], Casino Camarguense [Camargo Social Club], Federación Obrera [Workers' Federation], the City of

Camargo, and the Sindicato de Doctores [Doctors' Trade Union]. See Dr. Kazusa's file, IPS 2-1/362.4(52)593. Today, there is a street in the city of Camargo named after Dr. Kazusa.

12. Juan Yoshino to C. Presidente Municipal, S. Juan de Sabinas, Coahuila, July 13, 1942, IPS 2-1/362.4(52)/1070.

13. Tetsuo Taniyama Hueda to C. Secretario de Gobernación, January 29, 1944, IPS 2-1/362.4(52)/1332.

14. Ibid.

15. Tetsuo Taniyama Hueda to C. Secretario de Gobernación, March 27, 1944, IPS 2-1/362.4(52)/1332.

16. Ibid.

17. Lic. Gilberto Lizarraga Valdez to C. Secretario de Gobernación, March 29, 1944, IPS 2-1/362.4(52)/1332.

18. Rodrigo M. Quevedo to Sr. Lic. Lelo de la Rea (sic), April 4, 1943, IPS 2-1/362.4(52)/1313. General Rodrigo M. Quevedo was a brother of federal deputy Guillermo Quevedo, who represented the state of Chihuahua. Camp, *Mexican Political Biographies*, 568.

19. General de Brigada Josué M. Benignos to Sr. Don Adolfo Ruiz Cortinez [*sic*], September 3, 1942, IPS 2-1/362.4(52)/806.

20. General Brigadier Régulo Garza to Whom It May Concern, March 5, 1943, IPS 2-1/362.4(52)/1259.

21. Robert Harland's translation from Spanish to English. Martín Tameyesu Otsuka, *Poems, Memories of My Home Town, and Chronicle of My Travels in Mexico* (Tokyo: Sumiko Otsuka Publisher, 1987), 115.

22. Shyzumi Olivia Otsuka Ordóñez de Tanaka interview, Cd. Juárez, July 17, 2006.

23. Ibid.

24. Ángel Tanaka Gómez interview, Cd. Juárez, July 17, 2006.

25. Ibid.

26. For instance, Hugo Pedro González attempted to avoid the eviction of Nakano Hideichi and Luis Tanahara from the borderlands. Although the politician acknowledged the personal suffering of two personal acquaintances, he did not attempt to cancel the relocation program in its entirety. Lic. Hugo Pedro González to C. Secretario de Gobernación, August 6, 1942, IPS 2-1/362.4(52)970.

27. A number of files in the DIPS archives show information about Japanese Mexicans from Sinaloa who did not request authorization or affidavits from Colonel Loaiza. Because these men did not have the leverage Loaiza's protégés enjoyed, they did not obtain permission from the DIPS to stay in Sinaloa, IPS 2-1/362.4(52)1355. Ernesto Mitsuo Akachi Aoki, "Los Mochis: Casa por casa, tienda por tienda," in *Los Mochis: Historia oral de una ciudad*, ed. Reba Humphries (Los Mochis: Universidad de Occidente), 167. Corl. Rodolfo T. Loaiza to C. Secretario de Gobernación, July 31, 1942, IPS 2-1/362.4(52)955.

28. During World War II several ejidos in the northern states interceded on behalf of Japanese Mexicans whom they felt were valuable members of their communities. Approximately 130 signatures appeared in this request, with the signature of Pascacio Leyva, Síndico Municipal, certifying authenticity of signatures, "neighbors of the Sindicatura de Tamazula" to C. Gobernador Constitucional del Estado, April 25, 1943, IPS 2-1/362.4(52)843.

29. Twenty-eight officers representing the ejidos of Tamazula, El Amole, Palos Verdes, Las Cañadas, La Brecha, San José de la Brecha, Las Playas, Casa Blanca, Pitahayitas, La Cuestona, Cuesta de Arriba and Cofradía de Tamazula to C. Gobernador del Estado, April 25, 1942, IPS 2-1/362.4(52)843.

30. Tomás Torres Trejo and Filomeno Sánchez C. to C. Secretario de Gobernación, April 17, 1942, IPS 2-1/362.4(52)1083.

31. Among the Japanese Mexican persons whose relocation was resisted by Colonel Rodolfo T. Loaiza are Juan Yoshio Urakami, IPS 2-1/362.4(52)1317; Manuel Nishimoto Takayama, IPS 2-1/362.4(52)1322; Fukutaro Toyohara Toyohara, IPS 2-1/362.4(52)1324; Takahashi Tangi Johiro, IPS 2-1/362.4(52)1340; Mariko Maria Ozono, IPS 2-1/362.4(52)955; Jesús Ninomiya, IPS 2-1/362.4(52)954; Alberto Nidome Shitabuke, IPS 2-1/362.4(52)952; Tomokishi Yoshida Yoshizu, IPS 2-1/362.4(52)1066; Alberto Kimura Kikuno, IPS 2-1/362.4(52)967; Alejandro Saito Saito, IPS 2-1/362.4(52)989; Seichi Matsumoto Tanaka, IPS 2-1/362.4(52)1314; and Pedro Ochiqui, IPS 2-1/362.4(52)983.

32. Toshio Shimizu to C. Secretario de Gobernación, April 12, 1942, IPS 2-1/362.4(52)591.

33. Receipt signed by Federico Márquez, June 18, 1942, IPS 2-1/362.4(52)/591.

34. Permission signed by Lic. Alfonso García González, June 25, 1942, IPS 2-1/362.4(52)/591.

35. Lic. Rafael Murillo Vidal to C. Jefe del Departamento de Investigación Política y Social, June 26, 1942, IPS 2-1/362.4(52)/591.

36. Ibid.

37. Colonel Rodolfo T. Loaiza to C. Secretario de Gobernación, June 19, 1942, IPS 2-1/362.4(52)/591.

38. See IPS 2-1/362.4(52)/1110, IPS 2-1/362.4(52)/955, and IPS 2-1/362.4(52)/1314.

39. Dr. Toshio Shimizu to C. Secretario de Gobernación, July 3, 1942, IPS 2-1/362.4(52)/591. Also Inspector PS-1 to C. Jefe del Depto. de Investigación Política y Social, August 28, 1943, IPS 2-1/362.4(436)/600.

40. Permit signed by Lic. J. L. de Larrea, July 6, 1942, IPS 2-1/362.4(52)/591.

41. Toshio Shimizu to Lic. Don Enrique Pérez Arce, July 16, 1942, IPS 2-1/362.4(52)/591.

42. Colonel Rodolfo T. Loaiza to C. Jefe de la Oficina de Población, July 14, 1942, IPS 2-1/362.4(52)/591.

43. The export of minerals to Japan was prohibited in Mexico, but Maximino Ávila Camacho, the president's brother, was involved in it. There is no evidence that Dr. Shimizu was implicated in the smuggling of any of the metals Japan was interested in. Landa was trying to obtain Alemán's support, reminding him that they were compadres. The godfather, or compadre, is obligated through this relationship to protect his grandchild's family. Rafael Landa Ruiz to Sr. Lic. Miguel Alemán, July 23, 1942, IPS 2-1/362.4(52)/591.

44. Telegram, Landa Ruiz to Depto. Investigación Política y Social, undated, IPS 2-1/362.4(52)/591.

45. Lic. J. Lelo de Larrea to Jefe Servicio Población, August 3, 1942, IPS 2-1/362.4(52)/591.

46. Colonel Rodolfo T. Loaiza to Lic. Fernando Casas Alemán, Subsecretario de Gobernación, August 6, 1942, IPS 2-1/362.4(52)/591.

47. Landa Ruiz to Investigación Política y Social, August 7, 1942, IPS 2-1/362.4(52)/591.
48. Adolfo Ruiz Cortines to Jefe del Servicio de Población in Mazatlán, Sin., August 8, 1942, IPS 2-1/362.4(52)/591.
49. Agreement sent by Oficina de Población, Mazatlán, Sin., August 17, 1942, IPS 2-1/362.4(52)/591.
50. Rafael Landa Ruiz to C. Secretario de Gobernación, August 8, 1942, IPS 2-1/362.4(52)/591.
51. Other Japanese Mexicans protected by Loaiza were harassed, and some eventually relocated to Mexico City; but none was accosted with the same persistence as Dr. Shimizu by Landa. Landa Ruiz to Alemán, July 23, 1942.
52. General Pedro Torres Ortiz to C. Secretario de Gobernación, December 21, 1942, IPS 2-1/362.4(52)/783.
53. Memorandum, without signature, undated, re: Joshio Shimizu, nac. Japonesa [*sic*], IPS 2-1/362.4(52)/591.
54. Adolfo Ruiz Cortines to H. Junta de Administración y Vigilancia de la Propiedad Extranjera, March 1, 1943, IPS 2-1/362.4(52)/591.
55. Luis Astorga, "Traficantes de Drogas," in *Vicios Públicos, Virtudes Privadas: La Corrupción en México*, ed. Claudio Lomnitz (México: Centro de Investigaciones y Estudios Superiores en Antropología Social/Porrua, 2000), 177.
56. Takaki de Noriega interview.
57. Ibid.
58. Ibid.
59. Ibid.
60. R. Nakamura Ortiz interview.
61. Ernesto Corona Ruesga, Jefe del Servicio de Inspección, to C. Oficial Mayor de la Secretaría de Gobernación, June 10, 1943; Dr. Guillermo Gaona Salazar to C. Jefe del Depto. de Investigación Política y Social, July 16, 1943, IPS 2-1/362.4(52)/1141, in regard to Haruji Yoyakama Kawada.
62. R. Candiani, Inspector 108, to C. Jefe Departamento Investigación Política y Social, September 30, 1942, IPS 2-1/362.4(52)/1442.
63. Report taken by José Lelo de Larrea, Tokuhei Hayakawa Hayakawa (Tomas Tokuhei Hayakawa), October 12, 1942, IPS 2-1/362.4(52)/1442.
64. Ibid.
65. Report by Manuel Hiromoto given on January 10, 1944, at the Ministry of the Interior, IPS 2-1/362.4(52)/1444. His name also appears as Manuel Diaz Hiromoto, Seichi Hiromoto, and Manuel Seichi Hiromoto.
66. Paz, *Strategy, Security, and Spies*, 36–38, 41–44, 82–85; Niblo, *War, Diplomacy, and Development*, 68; Masterson and Funada-Classen, *Japanese in Latin America*, 116.
67. Accordingly, Kiso Tsuru requested "permission" from the Ministry of the Interior to transfer 350 persons to a ranch in the state of San Luis Potosi to cultivate the land. Dr. Tsuru proposed that the Mexican government leave the selection and control of the inmates in the hands of the Japanese leaders. This was a separate petition from that which Yoshida addressed in December 1941. K. Tsuru to the Ministry of the Interior, August 11, 1942, IPS 2-1/362.4(52)/1339.
68. See chapter 7.
69. Paz, *Strategy, Security, and Spies*, 83.

70. Ibid., 84.

71. Memorandum in reference to Dr. Kiso Tsuru, May [n.d.], 1942, not signed, IPS 1/362.4(52)/1339.

72. Memorandum II signed by Juan Sánchez de Tagle and José R. Gracián, November 17, 1942, IPS 1/362.4(52)/1339. Paz, *Strategy, Security, and Spies,* 38.

73. "Unknown newspaper source," second section, page 14, March 16, 1943, IPS 1/362.4(52)/1339.

74. Ibid.

75. Ibid.

76. "Mexico: Flirting with Fluor Spar," *Time,* November 4, 1940.

77. K. Tsuru to C. Minister of the Interior, October 1, 1943, IPS 1/362.4(52)/1339.

78. Handwritten notes over some DIPS permits for Dr. Tsuru read "Lic. Turrent," as an explanation for granting travel authorizations. Miho Kayaba de Tsuru, Kimitaka Tsuru to C. Jefe del Departamento de Información, March 9, 1945, IPS 1/362.4(52)/1339. "Lic." is the Spanish abbreviation for *licenciado,* or lawyer.

79. Ibid.

80. Permit signed by José Lelo de Larrea, October 18, 1943, IPS 1/362.4(52)/1339.

81. Lipsitz, *Possessive Investment in Whiteness,* 112.

82. Several wives of interned husbands were already sick prior to their spouses' arrests, but others reacted involuntarily to the expulsion of their husbands with new or worsening illnesses. Among the many cases of sicknesses recorded in the DIPS files, we can cite that of María Dolores L. de Hayashi, who had four appendicitis episodes in 1942 during the time her husband, Dr. Manuel Hayashi, was relocated in Mexico City. Antonia Villanueva also reported an unspecified sickness that left her unable to take care of her seven children when her husband, Toichi Urano, was relocated. The mother of Isidro Yamamoto, whose name is not recorded in the DIPS files, suffered an unmentioned disease from which she eventually died. Her condition was aggravated by the departure of her son to Mexico City under the relocation program. In the long list of sick persons of Japanese origin during the relocation program was the case of Enrique Sugawara Sugawara, who was interned in Temixco camp due to his inability to work as a result of an also undetermined disease. Dr. Joaquín Camacho Téllez's note, September 5, 1942, IPS 2-1/362.4(52)843; Antonia Villanueva to C. Secretario de Gobernación, undated, received on August 18, 1942, IPS 2-1/362.4(52)1105; an unknown person [illegible signature] to Isidro Yamamoto, October 23, 1944, IPS 2-1/362.4(52)1049; Luis T. Tsuji to C. Secretario de Gobernación, April 4, 1944, IPS 2-1/362.4(52)1355.

83. Minoju Satiu Fugunaga [*sic*] to C. Secretario de Gobernación, September 11, 1942, IPS 2-1/362.4(52)/1158.

84. Request to cancel registration at the Registro de Extranjeros at Celaya, Guanajuato, signed by Minoju Fukunaga Satio [*sic*] and J. Jesús Ortiz Balderas, February 9, 1943, IPS 2-1/362.4(52)/1158.

85. José Lelo de Larrea to C. J. Jesús Ortiz Balderas, February 22, 1943, IPS 2-1/362.4(52)/1158.

86. José Lelo de Larrea to C. Inspector Loreto Orozco, February 24, 1943, IPS 2-1/362.4(52)/1158.

87. Jesús Ortiz Balderas to C. Presidente Municipal de Guadalajara, Jal., February 25, 1943, IPS 2-1/362.4(52)/1158.

88. Inspector IPS-65 [signed L. Orozco] to Lic. José Lelo de Larrea, "Request to cancel registration at the Registro de Extranjeros at Celaya, Gto," April 27, 1943, IPS 2-1/362.4(52)/1158.

Chapter 7

1. Eva Watanabe Matsuo interview, Mexico City, July 18, 2006.
2. Ibid.
3. Takeo Ujo Nakano, *Within the Barbed Wire Fence: A Japanese Man's Account of His Internment in Canada* (Seattle: University of Washington Press, 1981), 132–49; Greg Robinson, *A Tragedy of Democracy: Japanese Confinement in North America* (New York: Columbia University Press, 2009).
4. The Marquesado del Valle de Oaxaca given to Hernán Cortés in the sixteenth century was the first estate, or hacienda, in Mexico that rearranged an entire indigenous community to serve the needs of the Spanish conquerors. The hacienda was designed according to the economic and social requirements of the Spanish rulers: a main building, or *casco*, where the estate owner lived; quarters for the animals; quarters for the indigenous persons serving in the casco; fields for the cultivation of crops; a warehouse for the harvested crops; and a *capilla*, or church, for religious services. At a short distance, indigenous people lived in the town but were under the dominion of the hacendado. Belonging to Cortés, Temixco's hacienda originally included the land and its indigenous inhabitants. François Chevalier, *Land and Society in Colonial Mexico: The Great Hacienda*, ed. Lesley Byrd Simpson, trans. Alvin Eustis (Berkeley: University of California Press, 1963), 127.
5. González Gálvez, "Eventos históricos" (presentation).
6. Luis T. Tsuji to C. Secretario de Gobernación, November 16, 1942, IPS 2-1/362.4(52)/1141.
7. Roger Daniels, *Concentration Camps, North America: Japanese in the United States and Canada during World War II* (Malabar, FL: Krieger, 1993), 187.
8. Lic. Ernesto Escobar Muñoz, Secretario General del Gobierno de Morelos, to C. Presidente Municipal, Temixco, July 23, 1942, IPS 2-1/362.4(52)/1141. On July 13, 1942, Luis Tsuji, representing the CJAM, informed DIPS chief officer Adolfo Ruiz Cortines that the CJAM had bought the Hacienda de Temixco to "employ some Japanese men relocated in Mexico City." Although CJAM leader Sanshiro Matsumoto initiated the process to buy the hacienda, other names appeared in the title: Vicente Kadiyama Hamaguchi, Tago Tomaru Kokuro, Leji Seiguchi Seiguchi, Thuji Okamara, and Luis Tadasu.
9. Oficio 4835 (Ando Kawade Kanzichii) permit signed by Lic. J. Lelo de Larrea, August 27, 1942, IPS 2-1/362.4(52)1141; Adolfo Ruiz Cortinez, Oficial Mayor, to C. Corl. Gerardo Rafael Catalan Calvo, Guerrero Governor, July 13, 1943, IPS 2-1/362.4(52)968.
10. Adolfo Ruiz Cortines, Oficial Mayor, to Lic. Jesús Castillo López, Morelos Governor, August 27, 1942, IPS 2-1/362.4(52)1141.
11. For a discussion of the Zapatista movement in Mexico, see Samuel Brunk, *Emiliano Zapata: Revolution & Betrayal in Mexico* (Albuquerque: University of New Mexico Press, 1995).

12. José Jorge Gómez Izquierdo, *El movimiento antichino en México (1871–1934): Problemas del racismo y del nacionalismo durante la Revolución Mexicana* (México, DF: Instituto Nacional de Antropología e Historia, 1991), 148.

13. Internet communication with Alberto Ruy Sánchez, great-grandchild of Alejandro Lacy Orci, April 22, 2010. Lacy Orci's son, Alejandro Lacy, Jr., was a congressman and the director of the Anti-Chinese League. See Gerardo Cornejo Murrieta, ed., *Historia contemporánea de Sonora, 1929–1984,* vol. 5 of *Historia general de Sonora* (Hermosillo: Gobierno del Estado de Sonora, 1985), 85–86.

14. *Diario Oficial de la Federación* (Mexico City), February 19, 1944.

15. The exchange rate was 3.11 dollars for each peso. Lawrence H. Officer, "Exchange Rates Between the United States Dollar and Forty-one Currencies," *MeasuringWorth* (2009), http://www.measuringworth.com/m/datasets/exchangeglobal. Inspector PS-1 to C. Jefe del Depto. De Investigación Política y Social, September 1942. Ernesto Corona Ruesga, Jefe del Servicio de Inspección, to C. Oficial Mayor de la Secretaría de Gobernación, June 10, 1943, IPS 2-1/362.4(52)/1141.

16. Corona Ruesga to C. Oficial Mayor, June 10, 1943.

17. Alberto Ruy Sánchez, Alejandro Lacy Orci's great grandchild and renowned writer, told me that his great-grandfather had made a hurried and bad business transaction. Ruy Sánchez, Internet communication.

18. Dr. Felipe García Sánchez to Secretaría de Gobernación, December 17, 1942, IPS 2-1/362.4(52)/1141.

19. Luis T. Tsuji and Takugoro Shibayama Shibayama to C. Secretario de Gobernación, August 24, 1942, IPS 2-1/362.4(52)/301.

20. Permit signed by J. Lelo de Larrea, August 25, 1942, IPS 2-1/362.4(52)/301.

21. Minerva Yoshino Castro telephone interview, October 5, 2009.

22. Ibid.

23. Luis T. Tsuji to C. Secretario de Gobernación, September 21, 1942, IPS 2-1/362.4(52)/1141.

24. Luis T. Tsuji to C. Secretario de Gobernación, October 5, 1942, IPS 2-1/362.4 (52)/1141.

25. Permits signed by Lic. J. Lelo de Larrea, November 26, 1942, IPS 2-1/362.4(52)/1141.

26. Tanamachi Satus Utaro to C. Secretario de Gobernación, March 3, 1943; José Lelo de Larrea to Tanamachi Satus Utaro, March 17, 1943, IPS 2-1/362.4(52)/1141.

27. R. Nakamura Ortiz interview.

28. Namikawa Mitsusaki Kitaro to C. Secretario de Gobernación, June 28, 1943, IPS 2-1/362.4(52)/330.

29. Kikumura-Yano, *Encyclopedia of Japanese Descendants,* 214.

30. Oficio 4812, Lic. J. Lelo de Larrea to Whom It may Concern, in relation to Masaru Takeo and his wife and seven children, August 27, 1942, IPS 2-1/362.4(52)/1141.

31. Such was the case of Genaro Romero, born in Mexico of a Mexican mother. Genaro was "completely deaf and [could] not support himself, for which the Comité [decided to intern him in order] to provide for [him] in Temixco." Tsuji to C. Secretario de Gobernación, November 16, 1942.

32. Enrique Monterrubio to C. Secretario de Gobernación, March 13, 1944, IPS 2-1/362.4(52)/1574.

33. Juan de la C. García to C. Jefe del Departamento, August 1, 1944, IPS 2-1/362.4(52)/1574.

34. J. Lelo de Larrea to C. Inspector Romualdo J. Cházaro, December 14, 1942, IPS 2-1/362.4(52)/1141. Corona Ruesga to C. Oficial Mayor, June 10, 1943.

35. Romualdo J. Cházaro to J. Lelo de Larrea, February 25, 1943, IPS 2-1/362.4(52)/968. Romualdo J. Cházaro to J. Lelo de Larrea, May 3, 1943, IPS 2-1/362.4(52)/1141.

36. Dr. Raúl Hiromoto Yoshino telephone interview, November 7, 2006.

37. Kobayashi Somea Tsumeo to C. Secretario de Gobernación, December 11, 1942, IPS 2-1/362.4(52)/1141.

38. Alberto S. Yoshida to C. Secretario de Gobernación, December 15, 1942; permit signed by Lic. J. Lelo de Larrea, December 15, 1942, IPS 2-1/362.4(52)/1141.

39. Jotema Chojó to C. Secretario de Gobernación, August 27, 1942, IPS 2-1/362.4(52)/822.

40. Born on February 11, 1933.

41. R. Nakamura Ortiz interview.

42. Ibid.

43. Manuel M. Barrera, Rodolfo Candiani, and Romualdo J. Cházaro to C. Jefe del Departamento de IPS, January 4, 1944, IPS 2-1/362.4(52)/1141.

44. Ibid.

45. D. C. G. to C. Jefe del Depto. de IPS, August 5, 1944, IPS 2-1/362.4(52)/1141.

46. García Sánchez to Secretaría de Gobernación, December 17, 1942. Article 13 of the Geneva Convention clauses on prisoners of war states that "belligerents shall be bound to take all sanitary measures necessary to ensure the cleanliness and healthfulness of camps and to prevent epidemics. Prisoners of war shall have at their disposal, day and night, installations conforming to sanitary rules and constantly maintained in a state of cleanliness." Convention relative to Prisoners of War, July 27, 1929.

47. Yoshino Castro telephone interview.

48. List signed by Lic. R. Guzmán Araujo, October 2, 1945, IPS 2-1/362.4(52)/1141.

49. Corona Ruesga to C. Oficial Mayor, June 10, 1943.

50. Ricardo Herrera, Inspector 67, to C. Jefe del Departamento de Investigación Política y Social, February 8, 1943, IPS 2-1/362.4(52)1141.

51. Tyuta Horiuti, for example, was arrested by a civilian who delivered Horiuti to the central offices of the Mexican Army. General J. Salvador S. Sánchez to C. Secretario de Gobernación, May 29, 1942, IPS 2-1/362.4(52)/503.

52. Classified as Japanese, José Hahn Kim, of Korean descent, was detained in November 1942, accused of having a conversation with a Mexican man "contrary to democracy." Once the documents in his power were determined to be written in Korean, they were translated and provided evidence that Hahn was Korean and anti-Japanese. General Miguel Martínez, Jefe de la Policía del DF, to C. Licenciado Miguel Alemán, Secretario de Gobernación, November 13, 1942, IPS 2-1/362.4/1590.

53. Corona Ruesga to C. Oficial Mayor, June 10, 1943.

54. Luis T. Tsuji to C. Secretario de Gobernación, January 13, 1943, IPS 2-1/362.4(52)/1141.

55. Lic. José Lelo de Larrea to Luis T. Tsuji, January 29, 1943, IPS 2-1/362.4(52)/1141.

56. Yoshino Castro telephone interview.

57. Ibid.

58. Herrera to Jefe del DIPS, February 8, 1943.

59. Migashiro Otohojin to C. Secretario de Gobernación, March 8, 1943; Nakao Nakao Saburo to C. Jefe del Departamento de Investigación Política y Social, March 28, 1943, IPS 2-1/362.4(52)/1141. Notsuka Shiraki Manabu to C. Secretario de Gobernación, March 4, 1943, IPS 2-1/362.4(52)/1141; Saburo Ueda Fujimori to C. Secretario de Gobernación, March 5, 1943, IPS 2-1/362.4(52)/1141.

60. As in U.S. concentration camps, World War II internees in Mexico were detained in the zones they were excluded from or ordered to leave. Luis T. Tsuji, to C. Secretario de Gobernación, June 3, 1943, IPS 2-1/362.4(52)/1141.

61. "General List of Japanese who used to live in Hacienda Temixco, now out of the facilities with the permission of this department," by Inspector PS-57, DCG, August 15, 1944, IPS 2-1/362.4(52)/1141.

62. List of internees in the Hacienda Temixco, July 21, 1943, IPS 2-1/362.4(52)/1141.

63. Declaration rendered by Zintaro Matzu Nacagawa [*sic*] on August 28, 1944, IPS 2-1/362.4(52)1463. Nakagawa's name was spelled Juntaro, Jyuntaro, and Zintaro in different documents.

64. Report signed by Alejandro Ortega in reference to Santiago Cobayasi [*sic*], August 21, 1942, IPS 2-1/362.4(52)1446.

65. Elie Wiesel reported a similar tendency among internees within the death camps in Europe to detach themselves from other inmates, erasing signs of empathy. Under extreme hunger, exhaustion, and psychological abuse, Jewish inmates would consider their weakened beloved ones "an encumbrance which could lessen [their] own chances of survival." Of course, the difference in treatment of inmates between the Mexican internment camps and the death camps in Europe is huge; Japanese Mexicans did not reach such a level of dehumanization. See Elie Wiesel, *Night* (New York: Hill and Wang, 1960), 87.

66. Illegible signature at the end of the official resolution concerning Zintaro Matzu Nacagawa [*sic*], August 30, 1944, IPS 2-1/362.4(52)/1463.

67. Adolfo Nobuo Yoshioka to C. Secretario de Gobernación, September 14, 1944, IPS 2-1/362.4(52)/1463.

68. Ibid.

69. Yoshino Castro telephone interview; see also file IPS 2-1/362.4(52)1444.

70. Tomás Hayakawa, Isaac Sasaki, Ernesto Saito, Ernesto Naito, José Yshida, and other illegible signatures, to Luis Tsuji, April 10, 1943, IPS 2-1/362.4(52)/1149.

71. Report taken by Lic. Alfonso García González, Chief of the Departamento de Investigación Política y Social, rendered by Dr. Tsunesaburo Hasegawa Araki in Mexico City, April 2, 1942, IPS 2-1/362.4(52)/464.

72. Yoshino Castro telephone interview.

73. García González report, April 2, 1942.

74. Dr. Kianshi Atsumi and Luis T. Tsuji to Excmo. Señor Dr. Otto Wuntwyler, June 8, 1945, IPS 2-1/362.4(52)/1149. Report titled "Información General De la Sección Médica correspondiente al mes de febrero de 1945," signed by Dr. Tsunesaburo

Hasegawa, which includes patients in Mexico City, Batán, and Temixco, March 6, 1945, IPS 2-1/362.4(52)/1149.

75. Corona Ruesga to C. Oficial Mayor, June 10, 1943. Donaciano Ceballos to Lic. Eduardo Ampudia, August 30, 1944, IPS 2-1/362.4(52)/1141.

76. The parasite that causes malaria is transmitted through the bite of the *Anopheles* mosquito. It attacks the liver to feed on red blood cells, multiplying at a fast pace, and the sickness it causes is associated with poverty and thus with the lack of sanitary living quarters. Kenneth F. Kiple, "Malaria: Poverty, Race, and Public Health in the United States," *Journal of Southern History* 69, no. 3 (2003): 682. Corona Ruesga to C. Oficial Mayor, June 10, 1943.

77. The CJAM hired Chori Fujii Morinosuke, an expert in agriculture, to direct the production. The technician resided in the hacienda for three months at the end of 1943 and the beginning of 1944. Luis T. Tsuji to C. Secretario de Gobernación, December 9, 1943, IPS 2-1/362.4(52)/1141.

78. Report by Alejandro Ortega, August 21, 1943, IPS 2-1/362.4(52)/1146.

79. Yoshino Castro telephone interview.

80. Ibid. Hiromoto Yoshino telephone interview.

81. See file of Felix Miyazaki Murallama, particularly the report taken by Lic. Eduardo Ampudia in relation to the bribe IPS officials asked from Miyazaki Murallama, August 11, 1944, IPS 2-1/362.4(436)/747.

82. Kikumura-Yano, *Encyclopedia of Japanese Descendants*, 214.

83. Barrera, Candiani, and Cházaro to C. Jefe del Departamento de IPS, January 4, 1944.

84. *Diario Oficial*, February 19, 1944.

85. Donaciano Ceballos and Oscar Olvera Villafana to C. Jefe del DIPS, March 6, 1944, IPS 2-1/362.4(52)/1141.

86. Donaciano Caballero to C. Jefe del DIPS, March 15, 1944, IPS 2-1/362.4(52)/1141.

87. Pedro Chavarría (Tierra y Justicia) to C. Inspector de la Secretaría de Gobernación comisionado en Hacienda Temixco, October 20, 1944, IPS 2-1/362.4(52)/1141.

88. Ibid.

89. Donaciano Ceballos González to C. Licenciado Eduardo Ampudia, October 24, 1944, IPS 2-1/362.4(52)/1141.

90. *Diario Oficial*, February 19, 1944.

91. Ricardo Trujillo to C. Lic. Jefe del Departamento, November 6, 1944, IPS 2-1/362.4(52)/1141.

92. Ibid.

93. Lic. Eduardo Ampudia V. to C. C. Pedro Chavarría and Efrén Domínguez, November 23, 1944, IPS 2-1/362.4(52)/1141.

94. *Diario Oficial*, February 19, 1944.

95. Masterson and Funada-Classen, *Japanese in Latin America*, 129.

96. Other Latin American Japanese used the same recourse to avoid their expulsion from the American republics and their internment in U.S. concentration camps. Connell, *America's Japanese Hostages*, 159.

97. Francisco T. Shibayama to Eduardo Ampudia, Jefe del Depto. de Investigaciones, Pol. Y Soc, January 16, 1945, IPS 2-1/362.4(52)/301.

98. Handwritten note on letter in ibid.

99. Ex Hacienda de Temixco Parque Acuatico, http://www.temixcoacuatico .com.

100. Copy of Public Proclamation No. 21, December 17, 1944, by the Office of the Commanding General, Presidio of San Francisco, California, OM-1886, in IPS 2-1/362.4(52)/600.

101. Mae M. Ngai, *Impossible Subjects: Illegal Aliens and the Making of Modern America* (Princeton, NJ: Princeton University Press, 2004), 276.

102. Inmates and released persons of Japanese ancestry did not have the rights that whites enjoyed during the postwar period anyway. The prohibition against Asian immigrants naturalizing remained, and with it the restrictions on buying and renting land. The statute prohibiting nonwhites from naturalizing was repealed in 1952, opening the door for Japanese immigrants in the United States to become landowners. Ibid.

103. Rodolfo Perdomo to Sr. Dr. Héctor Pérez, Secretaría de Gobernación, January 9, 1946, IPS 2-1/362.4(52)/1141.

104. Lic. Pablo Campos Ortiz to Subsecretario Encargado del Despacho, Secretaría de Gobernación, June 9, 1945, IPS 2-1/362.4(52)/600, II Tome.

105. Gral. Emilio Baig Serra to C. Secretario de Relaciones Exteriores, July 24, 1945, IPS 2-1/362.4(52)/600, Tome II.

106. Lic. Pablo Campos Ortiz to C. Secretario de Gobernación, June 30, 1945, IPS 2-1/362.4(52)/1142.

107. Ibid.

108. Document Number 8281, Department of Justice in regard to Japanese internees, September 4, 1945, submitted to the Ministry of the Interior on November 5, 1945, IPS 2-1/362.4(436)/600.

109. Telegram, Dr. Héctor Pérez Martínez to General Emilio Baig Serra, October 1, 1945, IPS 2-1/362.4(52)/1142.

110. Act signed by Lic. Roberto Guzmán Araujo and Adalberto Ortega, October 2, 1945, IPS 2-1/362.4(52)/1141.

111. Message from the Director of the War Relocation Authority, undated, D. S. Myer, IPS 2-1/362.4(52)/600.

112. General Eulogio Ortiz, Commander of the Seventh Military Zone, to General Emilio Baig Serra, October 8, 1945, IPS 2-1/362.4(52)/1141.

113. Act signed by Araujo and Ortega, October 2, 1945.

Chapter 8

1. L. T. McCollister, Acting Officer in Charge, to W. J. Harmon, Bureau of Customs at El Paso, Texas, April 2, 1947, file 940/15, Immigration and Naturalization Service Archives, National Archives and Records Administration, Washington, DC (hereafter INS NARA).

2. Report of Alien Enemy, United States Department of Justice, Immigration and Naturalization Service, Office of Crystal City, Texas, District No. 940/15, Alien No. 4895135, April 15, 1947, file 940/15, INS NARA.

3. Application for Repatriation (By alien of enemy nationality under jurisdiction of Immigration and Naturalization Service), Denhichiro Gushiken, Crystal City, Zavala, Texas, undated, file 940/15, INS NARA. See also J. L. O'Rourke to Principal of Emilio Carranza School in Cd. Juárez, undated, file 940/15, INS NARA.

4. Ethnicities and nationalities, such as German and Italian, determined the place and length of internment for many residents of the United States and of Latin American countries. See Corbett, *Quiet Passages*.

5. Ibid.

6. Grover C. Page, cashier at Federal Reserve Bank of Dallas, El Paso Branch, to L. T. McCollister, Acting Officer in Charge, U. S. Department of Justice, Alien Internment Camp, Crystal City, Texas, January 3, 1943, file 940/15, INS NARA. Denkei Gushiken's store address in El Paso was 700 E. Overland St. Report of Alien Enemy, April 15, 1947.

7. Frances L. Rand, State Department of Public Welfare, El Paso, Texas, to Mr. N. D. Collaer, Supervisor of Alien Detention, Crystal City, Texas, April 7, 1943, file 940/15, INS NARA.

8. L. T. McCollister, Acting Officer in Charge, Crystal City, Texas, to El Paso Branch Federal Reserve Bank, December 30, 1943 (In reference to the "monies, etc. taken from Den Produce Co"), file 940/15, INS NARA.

9. Tetsuden Kashima, "American Mistreatment of Internees during World War II: Enemy Alien Japanese," in *Japanese Americans: From Relocation to Redress*, ed. Roger Daniels, Sandra C. Taylor, and Harry H. L. Kitano (Seattle: University of Washington Press, 1991), 52–56; Everett M. Rogers and Nancy R. Bartlit, *Silent Voices of World War II: When Sons of the Land of Enchantment Met Sons of the Land of the Rising Sun* (Santa Fe, NM: Sunstone Press, 2005), 152.

10. Yasutaro (Keiho) Soga, *Life Behind Barbed Wire: The World War II Internment Memoirs of a Hawai'i Issei* (Honolulu: University of Hawaii Press, 2007), 113.

11. Rand to Collaer, April 7, 1943.

12. Ibid.

13. Mrs. Mary Romo's address was C. Moctezuma, 514. Undated list of correspondence from the Gushiken family in Crystal City, file 940/15, INS NARA. Rand to Collaer, April 7, 1943.

14. Page to McCollister, January 3, 1943; Mrs. Frances L. Rand, Field Worker from the State Department of Public Welfare, to Mr. N. D. Collaer, INS, Crystal City, Texas, October 25, 1943, file 940/15, INS NARA.

15. Denkei Gushiken earned a total of $576.20 while interned in the concentration camps of Lordsburg and Crystal City. Certificate by L. Tatum McCollister, Acting Officer in Charge, United States Department of Justice, INS, Crystal City, Texas, March 20, 1947, file 940/15, INS NARA.

16. Tsune Gushiken to "Beloved husband," from Cd. Juárez, Chih., April 13, 1943, file 940/15, INS NARA.

17. See Gardiner, *Pawns in a Triangle of Hate*, 21.

18. Denkei Gushiken to Commissioner, INS, Department of Justice, Washington, DC, July 6, 1943, file 940/15, INS NARA.

19. On December 12, the first internees, a group of Germans, arrived and began the construction of additional facilities. Originally, the camp had 159 buildings, but it had expanded to 694 by the end of the war. Kashima, *Judgment without Trial*, 120;

Ronald Nakasone, ed., *Okinawan Diaspora* (Honolulu: University of Hawaii, 2002), 105–6.

20. Max Paul Friedman, *Nazis and Good Neighbors: The United States Campaign against the Germans of Latin America in World War II* (Cambridge: Cambridge University Press, 2003), 153–54.

21. Connell, *America's Japanese Hostages.*

22. T. Gushiken to "Beloved husband," April 13, 1943.

23. J. L. O'Rourke, Officer in Charge of the Alien Internment Camp at Crystal City, Texas, to Collector of Customs, United States Custom Service, El Paso, TX, October 25, 1943, file 940/15, INS NARA.

24. Ibid.

25. W. F. Kelly, Assistant Commissioner for Alien Control, to District Director, Immigration and Naturalization Service, El Paso, TX, August 14, 1943, file 940/15, INS NARA.

26. Since November 24, 1942, the U.S. embassy had provided a list of fifty-eight individuals and families in Mexico who would be transported to the United States in an exchange of civilians with Japan. Ernesto Hidalgo to C. Secretario de Gobernación, November 24, 1942, IPS 2-1/362.4(52)/600. See also Miguel Z. Martínez to Lic. Miguel Alemán, May 28, 1942, in regard to Gan Miyasaka, IPS 2-1/362.4(52)/600.

27. H. S. B., United States Embassy, to the Secretaría de Relaciones Exteriores, in relation to Toshimi Hidano and her newborn, Katsumi Hidano, as well as to Tsune Gushiken and her three children, May 23, 1943, IPS 2-1/362.4(52)/1540.

28. Corbett, *Quiet Passages*, 113.

29. Dr. Enrique García González, August 23, 1943, and Manuel Tello, August 24, 1943, to C. Secretario de Gobernación, IPS 2-1/362.4(52)/600.

30. D. Gushiken to Commissioner, July 6, 1943; fingerprint record card for Tsune Gushiken, from Alien Internment Camp, Crystal City, Texas, undated, file 940/15, INS NARA. According to article 5 of the 1929 Geneva Convention, "Prisoners of war may be interned in a town, fortress, camp, or other place, and bound not to go beyond certain fixed limits."

31. O'Rourke to Collector of Customs, October 25, 1943.

32. Form I-111, Record of Hearing before a Board of Special Inquiry held at El Paso, TX, August 20, 1943, El Paso file 3900/38406, file 940/15, INS NARA.

33. Ibid.

34. Ibid.

35. Ibid. Capital letters in original text.

36. Ibid. Capital letters in original text.

37. Gardiner, *Pawns in a Triangle of Hate.*

38. Ibid.

39. H. B. Mathews, Assistant District Director, El Paso District, United States Department of Justice, INS, U.S. Courthouse, to the Officer in Charge, Alien Internment Camp, Crystal City, Texas, August 21, 1943, files 940/15 and 930/M, INS NARA.

40. Gardiner, *Pawns in a Triangle of Hate.*

41. Frances L. Rand, Field Worker at the State Department of Public Welfare, El Paso, Texas, to Mr. N. D. Collaer, INS, Crystal City, Texas, September 23, 1943, file 940/15, INS NARA.

42. Form I-111, August 20, 1943.

43. Lowe, *Immigrant Acts*, 6, 26, 29, 71–80, 211–16.

44. Historian C. Harvey Gardiner considers endogenous marriages, and "exclusive Japanese schools and societies," as contributing to the anti-Japanese sentiment that allowed deportation. Historian Thomas Connell explains that although Peruvians had isolated Japanese immigrants, "the cultural chasm between the Japanese and 'native' Peruvians, never smooth, was exacerbated by the 'clannish' behavior of the Peruvian Japanese." Additionally, Connell states that in Costa Rica, "the closed nature of the Japanese colonies drew great suspicion from others." Although Japanese immigrants continued to practice some elements of their culture, this was not the main reason for their seizure and deportation: Latin American and U.S. political and economical elites determined their uprooting and transfer to the United States. Connell, *America's Japanese Hostages*, 24–25; Donald E. Collins, *Native American Aliens: Disloyalty and the Renunciation of Citizenship by Japanese Americans during World War II* (Westport, CT: Greenwood Press, 1985), 5; Gardiner, *Pawns in a Triangle of Hate*, 9.

45. President Manuel Ávila Camacho, referring to Japanese immigrants, publicly declared that the war had taught Mexicans to rigorously select immigrants according to their race. According to Ávila Camacho, race defined the capability of immigrants to assimilate in Mexico. Ávila Camacho, "Tercer Informe."

46. Kikumura-Yano, *Encyclopedia of Japanese Descendants*.

47. Fingerprint record card, INS Form 8-73 undated, file 940/15, INS NARA. According to Denhichiro Gushiken's fingerprint record card, he arrived in the United States through Mexico.

48. Mrs. Fern Aument, Otero County Director, State of New Mexico, Department of Public Welfare, to Mr. J. L. O'Rourke, INS, Alien Internment Camp, Crystal City, NM, November 22, 1944, file 940/15, INS NARA.

49. Denkei Gushiken to Mr. J. L. O'Rourke, Officer in Charge, Alien Internment Camp, Crystal City, Texas, October 24, 1944, NARA INS 950/15.

50. J. L. O'Rourke, INS, Crystal City, Texas, to Grover C. Wilmoth, District Director, INS, El Paso, Texas, January 26, 1945, file 950/15, INS NARA.

51. Karen Lea Riley, *Schools behind Barbed Wire* (Lanham, MD: Rowman and Littlefield, 2002), 33; James J. Barnes and Patience P. Barnes, *Nazi Refugee Turned Gestapo Spy: The Life of Hans Wesemann, 1895–1971* (Westport, CT: Praeger, 2001), 156; Friedman, *Nazis and Good Neighbors*, 146–48.

52. Riley, *Schools behind Barbed Wire*, 33; Barnes and Barnes, *Nazi Refugee Turned Gestapo Spy*, 156; Friedman, *Nazis and Good Neighbors*, 146–48.

53. Connell, *America's Japanese Hostages*, 131–32.

54. Ibid.

55. Heidi Gurcke Donald, *We Were Not the Enemy* (New York: iUniverse, 2006), 56.

56. Connell, *America's Japanese Hostages*, 132.

57. Seiichi Higashide, *Adios to Tears: The Memoirs of a Japanese-Peruvian Internee in U.S. Concentration Camps* (Seattle: University of Washington Press, 2000), 71.

58. Riley, *Schools behind Barbed Wire*, 33; Gardiner, *Pawns in a Triangle of Hate*, 87; Connell, *America's Japanese Hostages*, 129–31; Donald, *We Were Not the Enemy*, 57; Arthur D. Jacobs, *The Prison Called Hohenasperg: An American Boy Betrayed by His Government during World War II* (Parkland, FL: Universal Publishers, 1999).

59. Donald, *We Were Not the Enemy*, 57.

60. Karen Lea Riley cites contact among Japanese and German children; however, their schools were separated, and most of the time, the "American" school had an overwhelming number of Japanese children. See Riley, *Schools behind Barbed Wire*. Heidi Gurcke Donald, a child internee of German descent at Crystal City camp, does not record interactions with Japanese children or adults. Ibid.

61. Friedman, *Nazis and Good Neighbors*, 137–41; Kashima, *Judgment without Trial*, 120; Riley, *Schools behind Barbed Wire*, 33.

62. Richard Drinnon, *Keeper of Concentration Camps: Dillon S. Myer and American Racism* (Berkeley: University of California Press, 1987), 47, 64–65. For racism against Mexican Americans in Crystal City during World War II and their perception that Japanese Americans were treated in the same way, see Antonia Castañeda, "'Que Se Pudieran Defender' (So You Could Defend Yourselves): Chicanas, Regional History, and National Discourses," *Frontiers: A Journal of Women's Studies* 22, no. 3 (2001): 116–42.

63. Castañeda, "Que Se Pudieran Defender."

64. Gardiner, *Pawns in a Triangle of Hate*, 97–98.

65. Drinnon, *Keeper of Concentration Camps*; Geneva Convention 1929, article 12.

66. Gardiner, *Pawns in a Triangle of Hate*, 97–98; Connell, *America's Japanese Hostages*, 130–31.

67. Rogers and Bartlit, *Silent Voices*, 170.

68. Mrs. Tsuruyo Moda, at the Colorado River Relocation Center, was denied her application to reunite with her husband, Kinsaburo Noda, who was in Mexico. W. Kelly, Assistant Commissioner for Alien Control, to Mrs. Tsuruyo Noda, August 3, 1944, 16-29-01-1-1, box 2426, 85-580734, 56125/64E, INS NARA.

69. Gardiner, *Pawns in a Triangle of Hate*, 106–7.

70. Connell, *America's Japanese Hostages*, 122; Riley, *Schools behind Barbed Wire*, 32; Kashima, *Judgment without Trial*, 119–21.

71. Drinnon, *Keeper of Concentration Camps*, 43–47.

72. Ibid., 43.

73. Connell, *America's Japanese Hostages*, 174.

74. Form signed by Denkei Gushiken, February 4, 1944, file 950/15, INS NARA.

75. Ibid.

76. Masterson and Funada-Classen, *Japanese in Latin America*, 170; Gardiner, *Pawns in a Triangle of Hate*, 117–22.

77. Application for Non-Repatriation, by Tsune Gushiken, signed on February 26, 1946, file 950/15, INS NARA.

78. Application for Repatriation, by Denhichiro Gushiken, INS, February 26, 1946.

79. L. T. McCollister, Acting Officer in Charge, Crystal City, Texas, to District Director, INS, El Paso, Texas, June 11, 1946, file 940/15, INS NARA.

80. J. L. O'Rourke, Officer in Charge Crystal City Internment Camp, to Grover C. Wilmoth, District Director, INS, El Paso, Texas, June 24, 1946, file 940/15, INS NARA.

81. Application for Repatriation, by Tsune Gushiken, June 26, 1946, file 940/15, INS NARA.

82. Application for Repatriation, by Denkei Gushiken, June 26, 1946, file 940/15, INS NARA.

83. Friedman, *Nazis and Good Neighbors*, 165–66; Connell, *America's Japanese Hostages*, 192–217.

84. Higashide, *Adios to Tears*, 166.

85. Clinical Record, Form 1946A, July 24, 1946, file 940/15, INS NARA.

86. Purchase request from Denkei and Tsune Gushiken to the Financial Officer, INS, Crystal City, January 22, 1947, file 940/15, INS NARA.

87. W. J. Harmon, Supervising Customs Agent, to Mr. Denkei Gushiken, March 14, 1947, file 940/15, INS NARA.

88. Mike Dipp, owner of City Market, to the United States Government, March 14, 1947; memorandum and routing form signed by "MPA," undated, file 940/15, INS NARA.

89. Joseph L. Brownlow, Agent, United States Secret Service, to Supervising Customs Agent, El Paso, Texas, March 7, 1947, file 940/15, INS NARA.

90. Report of Alien Enemy, April 15, 1947.

91. Denkei Gushiken to Mr. McCollister, May 12, 1947, Okinawa, Japan, file 940/15, INS NARA.

92. Dr. Bernardo Batiz to Hachiro Uyeji, May 23, 1946, IPS 2-1/362.4(52)/1039; Manuel Palacio to C. Secretario de Gobernación, August 6, 1946, IPS 2-1/362.4(52)/385.

93. Mexican ambassador Sergio González Gálvez stated on December 8, 2008, that "while the Japanese residing in Central America were arrested to be taken to the United States, Mexico did not give away even one Japanese to the neighbor country." González Gálvez, "Eventos históricos" (presentation). In August 1943, thirty-three persons of Japanese origin were deported to the United States. The Mexican state claimed they were part of an "exchange between nationals of the American Republics for Japanese residents of the same republics." No records of Mexican nationals exchanged for the Mexican residents of Japanese origin listed here were found in the course of this research. Tello to C. Secretario de Gobernación, August 24, 1943.

94. García González, August 23, 1943 and Tello, August 24, 1943, to C. Secretario de Gobernación.

Bibliography

Archives

Dirección General de Investigaciones Políticas y Sociales Archives. Archivo General de la Nación, Ciudad de México.
Immigration and Naturalization Service Archives. National Archives and Records Administration, Washington, DC.

Interviews

Fujigaki Lechuga, María (Mexico City), July 12, 2006.
Hiromoto Yoshino, Raúl (Temixco), July 20, 2006.
Hiromoto Yoshino, Raúl (Temixco), telephone interview, November 7, 2006.
Kobashi Sánchez, Susana (Mexico City), July 10, 2006.
Nakamura Ortiz, Diamantina (Monterrey), telephone interview, October 6, 2009.
Nakamura Ortiz, Rodolfo (Mexico City), July 25, 2006.
Otsuka de Tanaka, Shyzumi Olivia (Cd. Juárez), July 17, 2006
Ruy Sánchez, Alberto (Mexico City), Internet communication, April 22, 2010.
Sánchez Cisneros, Hermilo (Tijuana), telephone interview, January 3, 2010.
Takaki de Noriega, Fidelia (Mexico City), July 16, 2006.
Tanahara Romero, Mahatma (Monterrey), telephone interview, March 27, 2010.
Tanaka Gómez, Ángel (Cd. Juárez), July 17, 2006.
Watanabe Matsuo, Eva (Mexico City), July 18, 2006.
Watanabe Matsuo, Eva (Mexico City), telephone interview, December 15, 2009.
Yoshino Castro, Minerva (Cuernavaca), telephone interview, October 5, 2009.

Other Primary Sources

Ávila Camacho, Manuel. *Informes presidenciales*. Mexico City: Cámara de Diputados LX Legislatura, 1942. http://www.diputados.gob.mx/sedia/sia/re/RE-ISS-09
-06-09.pdf.
——. "Tercer informe del presidente Manuel Ávila Camacho." *500 años de México
en documentos* (1943). http://www.biblioteca.tv/artman2/uploads/1943.pdf.
"Believe Japs Reported on U.S. Units." *El Paso Times*, March 22, 1942.
Convention Between the United States of America and Other Powers, Relating to Pris-
oners of War, July 27, 1929. Geneva Convention of 1929. Yale Law School, 1929.
Convention Relative to the Treatment of Prisoners of War. Geneva, July 27, 1929. *In-
ternational Committee of the Red Cross*. http://www.icrc.org/ihl.nsf/FULL/305
?OpenDocument.
"Foreign News: Trotsky, Stalin & Cardenas." *Time*, January 25, 1937.
"Foreign Relations: To Shoe an Achilles Heel." *Time*, January 26, 1942.
Ichihashi, Yamato. *Japanese Immigration: Its Status in California*. San Francisco: Mar-
shall Press, 1915.
"Japanese Aliens Moved into Mexico." *El Paso Herald Post*, March 21, 1942.
"Japanese Buy Big Areas of Valley Lands," *El Paso Herald*, October 19, 1920.
"Japs May Colonize in State of Chihuahua." *El Paso Herald*, November 11, 1907,
5:07.
"Japs Must Leave Juarez in Five Days." *El Paso Herald Times*, March 27, 1942.
"Japs Removed from Border Area." *El Paso Times*, April 1, 1942, 5.
"Juarez Japs Put on U.S. Blacklist." *El Paso Herald Post*, December 26, 1941.
"Mexico Agrees to Colonization by Jap Farmers." *El Paso Herald*, January 31–February 1,
1920.
"México en la guerra." *Tiempo*, 1943.
"México: Flirting with Fluor Spar." *Time*, November 4, 1940.
"New President, Old Job." *Time*, December 9, 1940.
Organization of American States. "Consultative Meeting of Foreign Ministers of the
American Republics." In "Official Documents," supplement, *American Journal of
International Law* 34, no. 1 (1940): 1–20.
——. *Final Act of the Third Meeting of the Ministers of Foreign Affairs of the Ameri-
can Republics*. Rio de Janeiro: Organization of American States, 1942.
Presidencia de la República. "Diversas intervenciones durante la Ceremonia Conmem-
orativa del 50 Aniversario de la Asociación México-Japonesa, Asociación Civil."
Presidencia de la República (July 27, 2006). http://fox.presidencia.gob.mx/actividades
/?contenido=26200.
"Real Estate in Mexico." *Dunn's International Review* 11 (1907).
"Second Meeting of Ministers of Foreign Affairs of the American Republics." In "Official Documents," supplement, *American Journal of International Law* 35, no. 1
(January 1941): 1–32.
"Sesión de La Cámara de Diputados Efectuada El Dia 2 de Junio 1942." *Diario de los
Debates de la Cámara de Diputados del Congreso de los Estados Unidos Mexicanos*. México, DF: Cámara de Diputados del Congreso de los Estados Unidos Mexi-
canos, 1942. http://cronica.diputados.gob.mx/DDebates/38/2do/Extra/19420602
.html.

"Sesión de la Cámara de Diputados Efectuada el Dia 1o. de Septiembre de 1942." *Diario de los Debates de la Cámara de Diputados del Congreso de los Estados Unidos Mexicanos*. México, DF: Cámara de Diputados del Congreso de los Estados Unidos Mexicanos, 1942. http://cronica.diputados.gob.mx/DDebates/38/3er/Ord/19420901.html.

Thompsons, Craig. "Fears Revolution in the Philippines: Theodore Roosevelt Deplores Independence in Talk Before the Science Academy." *New York Times*, April 3, 1938.

Treat, Payson Jackson. "Immigration and the 'Gentlemen's Agreement.'" In *A League of Nations*, 449. Boston: World Peace Foundation, 1917–1918.

U.S. Senate. *Investigation of Mexican Affairs: Hearing Before a Subcommittee of the Committee on Foreign Relations* (testimony of Henry Lane Wilson). 66th Cong., 1st sess. Washington, DC: Government Printing Office, 1920.

"'Yellow Peril' Plot Detected." Editorial. *El Paso Herald*, August 9, 1921.

Secondary Sources

Aceves, Antonieta Kiyoko Nishikawa. "La inmigración japonesa a Ensenada durante la primera mitad del siglo XX." *Revista Meyibó/Instituto de Investigaciones Históricas* 1, no. 1–8 (2004). http://iih.tij.uabc.mx/iihDigital/Calafia/Contenido/Vol-I/Numero1-8/Lainmigracion.htm.

Agamben, Giorgio. *Homo Sacer: Sovereign Power and Bare Life*. Stanford, CA: Stanford University Press, 1998.

———. *State of Exception*. Chicago: University of Chicago Press, 2005.

Almaguer, Tomás. "Racial Domination and Class Conflict in Capitalist Agriculture: The Oxnard Sugar Beet Workers Strike of 1903." *Labor History* 23, no. 3 (1984): 325–50.

Amati, Escipión. *Historia de la embajada de Idate Masamune al Papa Paulo V (1613–1615)*. Madrid: Doce Calles, 2011.

Anderson, Emily. "Containing Voices in the Wilderness: Censorship and Religious Dissent in the Japanese Countryside." *Church History* 83 (2014): 398–421.

Anderson, Gary Clayton. *The Conquest of Texas: Ethnic Cleansing in the Promised Land, 1820–1875*. Norman: University of Oklahoma Press, 2005.

Anzaldúa, Gloria. *Borderlands/La Frontera: The New Mestiza*. San Francisco: Spinsters/Aunt Lute, 1987.

Aoki, Ernesto Mitsuo Akachi. "Los Mochis: Casa por casa, tienda por tienda." In *Los Mochis: Historia oral de una ciudad*, edited by Reba Humphries, 153–81. Los Mochis: Universidad de Occidente, 1986.

Ashby, Joe C. *Organized Labor and the Mexican Revolution under Lázaro Cárdenas*. Chapel Hill: University of North Carolina Press, 1967.

Asociación México Japonesa A.C. "Las migraciones de japoneses a México." *Asociación México Japonesa A.C.* (2009). http://www.kaikan.com.mx/kaikan/aportaciones_Migraciones.php?id=302.

Astorga, Luis. "Traficantes de Drogas." In *Vicios Públicos, Virtudes Privadas: La Corrupción en México*, edited by Claudio Lomnitz. México: Centro de Investigaciones y Estudios Superiores en Antropología Social/Porrúa, 2000.

Azuma, Eiichiro. *Between Two Empires: Race, History, and Transnationalism in Japanese America.* New York: Oxford University Press, 2005.

——. "Japanese Immigrant Settler Colonialism in the U.S.-Mexican Borderlands and the U.S. Racial-Imperialist Politics of the Hemispheric 'Yellow Peril.'" *Pacific Historical Review* 83, no. 2 (2014): 255–76.

Baily, Samuel L., and Eduardo José Míguez. *Mass Migration to Modern Latin America.* Wilmington, DE: Scholarly Resources, 2003.

Balderrama, Francisco E., and Raymond Rodríguez. *Decade of Betrayal: Mexican Repatriation in the 1930s.* Albuquerque: University of New Mexico Press, 2006.

Bangarth, Stephanie D. "Religious Organizations and the 'Relocation' of Persons of Japanese Ancestry in North America: Evaluating Advocacy." *American Review of Canadian Studies* 34, no. 3 (2004): 511–40.

Bantjes, Adrian A. *As If Jesus Walked on Earth: Cardenismo, Sonora, and the Mexican Revolution.* Wilmington, DE: Scholarly Resources, 1998.

Barnes, James J., and Patience P. Barnes. *Nazi Refugee Turned Gestapo Spy: The Life of Hans Wesemann, 1895–1971.* Westport, CT: Praeger, 2001.

Bashō, Matsuo. *Sendas de Oku.* Translated by Octavio Paz and Eikichi Hayashiya. Barcelona: Seix Barral, 1981.

Benería, Lourdes, and Shelley Feldman, eds. *Unequal Burden: Economic Crises, Persistent Poverty, and Women's Work.* Boulder, CO: Westview, 1992.

Bloch, Avital, and Servando Ortoll. "The Anti-Chinese and Anti-Japanese Movements in Cananea, Sonora, and Salt Lake River, Arizona, during the 1920 and 1930s." *Americana: E-journal of American Studies in Hungary* 6, no. 1 (2010). http://americanaejournal.hu/vol6no1/bloch-ortoll.

Brunk, Samuel. *Emiliano Zapata: Revolution & Betrayal in Mexico.* Albuquerque: University of New Mexico Press, 1995.

Buffington, Robert M. *Criminal and Citizen in Modern Mexico.* Lincoln: University of Nebraska Press, 2000.

Calvo, Thomas. "Japoneses en Guadalajara: 'Blancos de honor' durante el seiscientos mexicano." *Revista de Indias* 43, no. 172 (1983): 531–47.

"Cambian la historia del paisaje urbano." *Reforma*, April 2, 2003.

Camp, Roderic Ai. *Mexican Political Biographies, 1935–1993.* 3rd ed. Austin: University of Texas Press, 1995.

Carrera, Magali Marie. *Imagining Identity in New Spain: Race, Lineage, and the Colonial Body in Portraiture and Casta Paintings.* Austin: University of Texas, 2003.

Carrigan, William D. "The Lynching of Persons of Mexican Origin or Descent in the United States, 1848 to 1928." *Journal of Social History* 37, no. 2 (2003): 411–38.

Castañeda, Antonia. "'Que Se Pudieran Defender' (So You Could Defend Yourselves): Chicanas, Regional History, and National Discourses." *Frontiers: A Journal of Women's Studies* 22, no. 3 (2001): 116–42.

——. "Women of Color and the Rewriting of Western History: The Discourse, Politics, and Decolonization of History." *Pacific Historical Review* 61, no. 4 (1992): 501–33.

Chan, Sucheng. "Against All Odds: Chinese Female Migration and Family Formation on American Soil during the Exclusion Era." In *Chinese American Transnationalism: The Flow of People, Resources, and Ideas between China and America during the Exclusion Era*, edited by Sucheng Chan, 34–135. Philadelphia: Temple University Press, 2005.

Chassen de López, Francie R. *From Liberal to Revolutionary Oaxaca: The View from the South, Mexico, 1867–1911*. University Park: Pennsylvania State University Press, 2005.

Chaunu, Pierre, "Le galion de Manille. Grandeur et décadence d'une route de la soie." *Annales: Economies, Sociétiés, Civilisations* 4 (1951): 447–62.

———. *Les Philippines et le Pacifique des Ibériques (XVIe, XVIIe, XVIIIe siècles)*. Paris: SEVPEN, 1960.

Chávez, Ernesto. *The U.S. War with Mexico: A Brief History with Documents*. New York: Bedford/St. Martin's, 2007.

Chevalier, François. *Land and Society in Colonial Mexico: The Great Hacienda*. Edited by Lesley Byrd Simpson. Translated by Alvin Eustis. Berkeley: University of California Press, 1963.

Chew, Selfa. "Mexicanidades de la Diáspora Asiática: Considerations of Gender, Race and Class." *Chicana/Latina Studies: The Journal of Mujeres Activas en Letras y Cambio Social* 14, no. 1 (Fall 2014): 56–87.

Cicero, Jorge. "International Law in Mexican Courts." *Journal of Transnational Law* 30, no. 5 (1997): 1035–86.

Coatsworth, John H. "Measuring Influence: The United States and the Mexican Peasantry." In *Rural Revolt in Mexico: U.S. Intervention and the Domain of Subaltern Politics*, edited by Daniel Nugent, 65–72. Durham, NC: Duke University Press, 1995.

Coerver, Don M., and Linda B. Hall. *Tangled Destinies: Latin America and the United States*. Albuquerque: University of New Mexico Press, 1999.

Collins, Donald E. *Native American Aliens: Disloyalty and the Renunciation of Citizenship by Japanese Americans during World War II*. Westport, CT: Greenwood Press, 1985.

Conn, Stetson, and Byron Fairchild. *U.S. Army in World War II—the Western Hemisphere: The Framework of Hemispheric Defense*. Washington, DC: Department of the Army, 1960.

Connell, Thomas. *America's Japanese Hostages: The World War II Plan for a Japanese Free Latin America*. Westport, CT: Praeger, 2002.

Connelly, Marisela, and Romer Cornejo Bustamante. *China-América Latina: Génesis y desarrollo de sus relaciones*. México, DF: Colegio de México, 1992.

Corbett, P. Scott. *Quiet Passages: The Exchange of Civilians between the United States and Japan during the Second World War*. Kent, OH: Kent State University Press, 1987.

Cornejo Murrieta, Gerardo, ed. *Historia contemporánea de Sonora, 1929–1984*. Vol. 5 of *Historia general de Sonora*. Hermosillo: Gobierno del Estado de Sonora, 1985.

Corona Baeza, Javier Amado. "La inmigración coreana/The Korean Immigration." In *Henequén: Leyenda, historia y cultura/Its Legend, History and Culture*, edited by Maureen Ransom Carty, 168–73. Mérida: Instituto de Cultura de Yucatán, 2006.

Corral Rodríguez, Fortino. "Génesis del relato fantástico en México." In *Ruta crítica: Estudios sobre literatura hispanoamericana*, edited by Fortino Corral Rodríguez, 97–116. Hermosillo: Universidad de Sonora, 2007.

Daniels, Roger. *Asian America: Chinese and Japanese in the United States since 1850*. Seattle: University of Washington Press, 1988.

------. *Concentration Camps, North America: Japanese in the United States and Canada during World War II*. Malabar, FL: Krieger, 1993.

------. *The Politics of Prejudice: The Anti-Japanese Movement in California and the Struggle for Japanese Exclusion*. Berkeley: University of California Press, 1978.

Deere, Carmen Diana. "Rural Women's Subsistence Production in the Capitalist Periphery." In *Peasants and Proletarians: The Struggles of Third World Workers*, edited by Robin Cohen, Peter C. W. Gutkind, and Phyllis Brazier, 133–48. New York: Monthly Review Press, 1979.

De Genova, Nicholas P. "Migrant 'Illegality' and Deportability in Everyday Life." *Annual Review of Anthropology* 31 (2002): 419–47.

Dickter, Arturo Grunstein. "In the Shadow of Oil: Francisco J. Múgica vs. Telephone Transnational Corporations in Cardenista Mexico." *Mexican Studies/Estudios Mexicanos* 21, no. 1 (2005): 1–32.

Donald, Heidi Gurcke. *We Were Not the Enemy*. New York: iUniverse, 2006.

Doode Matsumoto, Olga Shoko. *Los claro-oscuros de la pesquería de la sardina en Sonora: Contradicciones y alternativas para un desarrollo equilibrado*. Zamora: El Colegio de Michoacán, 1999.

Drinnon, Richard. *Keeper of Concentration Camps: Dillon S. Myer and American Racism*. Berkeley: University of California Press, 1987.

Emmerson, John K. *The Japanese Thread: A Life in the U.S. Foreign Service*. New York: Holt, Rinehart and Winston, 1978.

Espiritu, Yen Le. *Asian American Women and Men: Labor, Laws, and Love*. The Gender Lens, edited by Judith Howard, Barbara Risman, and Joey Sprague. Thousand Oaks, CA: Sage, 1997.

Ettinger, Patrick. *Imaginary Lines: Border Enforcement and the Origins of Undocumented, 1882–1930*. Austin: University of Texas Press, 2009.

Falck Reyes, Melba, and Héctor Palacios. *El japonés que conquistó Guadalajara: La historia de Juan de Páez en la Guadalajara del siglo XVII*. Guadalajara: Universidad de Guadalajara, 2010.

Fein, Seth. "Myths of Cultural Imperialism and Nationalism in Golden Age Mexican Cinema." In *Fragments of a Golden Age: The Politics of Culture in Mexico since 1940*, edited by Anne Rubenstein, Gilbert Michael Joseph, and Eric Zolov, 159–98. Durham, NC: Duke University Press, 2001.

Fernández-Kelly, Patricia, and Douglas S. Massey. "Borders for Whom? The Role of NAFTA in Mexico-U.S. Migration." *Annals of the American Academy of Political and Social Science*, vol. 610, *NAFTA and Beyond: Alternative Perspectives in the Study of Global Trade and Development* (March 2007): 98–118.

Fox, Claire F. *The Fence and the River: Culture and Politics at the U.S.-Mexico Border*. Minneapolis: University of Minnesota Press, 1999.

Friedman, Max Paul. *Nazis and Good Neighbors: The United States Campaign against the Germans of Latin America in World War II*. Cambridge: Cambridge University Press, 2003.

Garcia, Jerry. *Looking Like the Enemy: Japanese Mexicans, the Mexican State, and U.S. Hegemony, 1897–1945*. Tucson: University of Arizona Press, 2014.

Gardiner, C. Harvey. *Pawns in a Triangle of Hate: The Peruvian Japanese and the United States*. Seattle: University of Washington, 1981.

Geiger, Andrea. *Subverting Exclusion: Transpacific Encounters with Race, Caste, and Borders, 1885–1928.* New Haven, CT: Yale University Press, 2011.

Gobierno del Distrito Federal. "Las primeras colonias." *Delegación La Magdalena Contreras.* Accessed March 7, 2015. http://www.mcontreras.df.gob.mx/historia /constitucion2.html.

Gómez Izquierdo, José Jorge. *El movimiento antichino en México (1871–1934): Problemas del racismo y del nacionalismo durante la Revolución Mexicana.* México, DF: Instituto Nacional de Antropología e Historia, 1991.

González, Deena J. *Refusing the Favor: The Spanish-Mexican Women of Santa Fe, 1820–1880.* Oxford: Oxford University Press, 1999.

González Gálvez, Sergio. "Eventos históricos de la relación México-Japón." Presentation at the Ciento Veinte Años de Amistad entre México y Japón, Secretaría de Relaciones Exteriores, 2008. Accessed November 7, 2009. http://www.kaikan.com .mx/kaikan/aportaciones_Colaboradores.php?id=55

———. "Eventos históricos de la relación México-Japón." *Revista Mexicana de Política Exterior,* no. 86 (March–June 2009): 9–17.

González Oropeza, Manuel. "La discriminación en México: El caso de los nacionales chinos." In *La problemática del racismo en los umbrales del siglo XXI,* chapter 2. México, DF: Universidad Nacional Autónoma de México, Instituto de Investigaciones Jurídicas, 1997.

Guerin-Gonzales, Camille. *Mexican Workers and American Dreams: Immigration, Repatriation, and California Farm Labor, 1900–1939.* New Brunswick, NJ: Rutgers University Press, 1994.

Gruzinski, Serge. *The Eagle and the Dragon: Globalization and European Dreams of Conquest in China and America in the Sixteenth Century.* Malden, MA: Polity, 2014.

Gunn, Geoffrey C. *New World Hegemony in the Malay World.* Lawrenceville, NJ: Red Sea Press, 2000.

Haney-López, Ian. *White by Law: The Legal Construction of Race.* New York: New York University Press, 1997.

Harris, Charles H., III, and Louis R. Sadler. *The Texas Rangers and the Mexican Revolution: The Bloodiest Decade, 1910–1920.* Albuquerque: University of New Mexico Press, 2007.

Hart, John Mason. *Revolutionary Mexico: The Coming and Process of the Mexican Revolution.* Berkeley: University of California Press, 1997.

———. "Social Unrest, Nationalism, and American Capital in the Mexican Countryside, 1876–1920." In *Rural Revolt in Mexico: U.S. Intervention and the Domain of Subaltern Politics,* edited by Daniel Nugent, 72–88. Durham, NC: Duke University Press, 1998.

Hatamiya, Leslie T. *Righting a Wrong: Japanese Americans and the Passage of the Civil Liberties Act of 1988.* Stanford, CA: Stanford University Press, 1993.

Hatfield, Shelley Bowen. *Chasing Shadows: Indians Along the United States-Mexico Border, 1876–1911.* Albuquerque: University of New Mexico Press, 1998.

Hayashiya, Eikichi. "Los japoneses que se quedaron en México en el siglo XVII: Acerca de un samurai en Guadalajara." *México y la Cuenca del Pacífico* 6, no. 18 (2003): 10–17.

Hernández Galindo, Sergio. *La guerra contra los japoneses en México durante la Segunda Guerra Mundial: Kiso Tsuru y Masao Imuro, migrantes vigilados.* México, DF: Itaca, 2011.

Higashide, Seiichi. *Adios to Tears: The Memoirs of a Japanese-Peruvian Internee in U.S. Concentration Camps.* Seattle: University of Washington Press, 2000.

Horne, Gerald. *Black and Brown: African Americans and the Mexican Revolution, 1910–1920.* New York: New York University Press, 2005.

Hu-DeHart, Evelyn. "Indispensable Enemy or Convenient Scapegoat? A Critical Examination of Sinophonia in Latin America and the Caribbean, 1870s to 1930s." In *The Chinese in Latin America and the Caribbean,* edited by Walton Look Lai and Tan Chee-Beng, 65–102. Leiden, Netherlands: Brill Academic Publishers, 2010.

Huggins, Martha K. *Political Policing: The United States and Latin America.* Durham, NC: Duke University Press, 1998.

Instituto Nacional de Estadística, Geografía e Informática (INEGI). *Los extranjeros en México.* Aguascalientes, México: INEGI, 2007. http://www.inegi.gob.mx/prod _serv/contenidos/espanol/bvinegi/productos/estudios/sociodemografico/ext_en _mex/extraen_mex.pdf.

Jacobs, Arthur D. *The Prison Called Hohenasperg: An American Boy Betrayed by His Government during World War II.* Parkland, FL: Universal Publishers, 1999.

Jarquín Ortega, Maria Teresa, and Manuel Miño Grijalva, eds. *Historia general del Estado de México.* Toluca: Colegio Mexiquense, 1998.

Johnson, Benjamin. "The Plan de San Diego Uprising and the Making of the Modern Texas-Mexican Borderlands." In *Continental Crossroads,* edited by Samuel Truett and Elliott Young, 273–98. Durham, NC: Duke University Press, 2004.

Jones, Halbert. *The War Has Brought Peace to Mexico: World War II and the Consolidation of the Post-Revolutionary State.* Albuquerque: University of New Mexico Press, 2014.

Kashima, Tetsuden. "American Mistreatment of Internees during World War II: Enemy Alien Japanese." In *Japanese Americans: From Relocation to Redress,* edited by Roger Daniels, Sandra C. Taylor, and Harry H. L. Kitano, 52–56. Seattle: University of Washington Press, 1991.

———. *Judgment without Trial: Japanese American Imprisonment during World War II.* Seattle: University of Washington Press, 2003.

Katz, Friedrich. *La guerra secreta en México.* México, DF: Ediciones Era, 2005.

———. *The Life and Times of Pancho Villa.* Stanford, CA: Stanford University Press, 1998.

Kawakami, Kiyoshi Karl. *Japan in World Politics.* New York: MacMillan, 1919.

Kellogg, Susan. "Depicting Mestizaje: Gendered Images of Ethnorace in Colonial Mexican Texts." *Journal of Women's History* 12, no. 3 (2000): 69–92.

Kikumura-Yano, Akemi, ed. *Encyclopedia of Japanese Descendants in the Americas: An Illustrated History of the Nikkei.* Walnut Creek: AltaMira Press, 2002.

Kim, Hyung-chan, ed. *Asian Americans and the Supreme Court: A Documentary History.* Westport, CT: Greenwood Press, 1992.

Kiple, Kenneth F. "Malaria: Poverty, Race, and Public Health in the United States." *Journal of Southern History* 69, no. 3 (2003): 682.

Krauze, Enrique. *Mexico: Biography of Power—A History of Modern Mexico, 1810–1996.* New York: Harper Perennial, 1998.

Lee, Erika. *At America's Gates: Chinese Immigration during the Exclusion Era, 1882–1943.* Chapel Hill: University of North Carolina Press, 2003.

——. "Orientalisms in the Americas: A Hemispheric Approach to Asian American History." *Journal of Asian American Studies* 8, no. 3 (October 2005): 235–56.

Levario, Miguel Antonio. *Militarizing the Border: When Mexicans Became the Enemy.* College Station: Texas A&M University Press, 2012.

Leyva, Yolanda Chávez. "'There Is Great Good in Returning': A Testimonio from the Borderlands." *Frontiers: A Journal of Women's Studies* 24, no. 2/3 (2003): 1–9.

Lim, Julian. "Chinos and Paisanos: Chinese Mexican Relations in the Borderlands." *Pacific Historical Review* 79, no. 1 (2010): 50–85.

Ling, Huping. *Surviving on the Gold Mountain: A History of Chinese Women and Their Lives.* Albany: State University of New York Press, 1998.

Lipsitz, George. *The Possessive Investment in Whiteness: How White People Profit from Identity Politics.* Philadelphia: Temple University Press, 2006.

Lovell Banks, Taunya. "Mestizaje and the Mexican Mestizo Self: No Hay Sangre Negra, So There Is No Blackness." *Southern California Interdisciplinary Law Journal* 15, no. 199 (2006): 199–234.

Lowe, Lisa. *Immigrant Acts: On Asian American Cultural Politics.* Durham, NC: Duke University Press, 1996.

Luibhéid, Eithne. *Entry Denied: Controlling Sexuality at the Border.* Minneapolis: University of Minnesota Press, 2002.

Lytle Hernández, Kelly. *Migra!: A History of the U.S. Border Patrol.* Berkeley: University of California Press, 2010.

Maltz, Earl M. "The Fourteenth Amendment and Native American Citizenship." *Constitutional Commentary* 17, no. 3 (2000): 555–73.

Markiewicz, Dana. *The Mexican Revolution and the Limits of Agrarian Reform, 1915–1946.* Boulder, CO: Lynne Rienner, 1993.

Márquez, John D. *Black and Brown Solidarity: Racial Politics in the New Gulf South.* Austin: University of Texas Press, 2013.

Martínez, Oscar J., ed. *U.S.-Mexico Borderlands: Historical and Contemporary Perspectives.* Wilmington, DE: Scholarly Resources, 1996.

Masterson, Daniel M., and Sayaka Funada-Classen. *The Japanese in Latin America.* Urbana: University of Illinois Press, 2004.

Maviglia, Sandra F. "Mexico's Guidelines for Foreign Investment: The Selective Promotion of Necessary Industries." *American Journal of International Law* 80, no. 2 (1986): 281–304.

Mecham, J. Lloyd. *The United States and Inter-American Security, 1889–1960.* Austin: University of Texas Press, 1961.

Medina, Rubén. "El mestizaje a través de la frontera: Vasconcelos y Anzaldúa." *Mexican Studies/Estudios Mexicanos* 25, no. 1 (2009): 101–23.

Meyers, William K. *Forge of Progress, Crucible of Revolt: Origins of the Mexican Revolution in La Comarca Lagunera, 1880–1911.* Albuquerque: University of New Mexico Press, 1994.

Mohl, Raymond A. "Asian Immigration to Florida." *Florida Historical Quarterly* 74, no. 3 (1996): 261–86.

Montejano, David. *Anglos and Mexicans in the Making of Texas, 1836–1986.* Austin: University of Texas Press, 1987.

Mora, Carl J. *Mexican Cinema: Reflections of a Society, 1896–1980.* Berkeley: University of California Press, 1989.

Mufwene, Salikoko S. "Race, Racialism, and the Study of Language Evolution in America." In *Lavis III—Language Variety in the South: Historical and Contemporary Perspectives*, edited by Michael D. Picone and Catherine Evans Davies, 449–74. Tuscaloosa: University of Alabama Press, 2006.

Nakano, Takeo Ujo. *Within the Barbed Wire Fence: A Japanese Man's Account of His Internment in Canada*. Seattle: University of Washington Press, 1981.

Nakasone, Ronald, ed. *Okinawan Diaspora*. Honolulu: University of Hawaii, 2002.

Ngai, Mae M. *Impossible Subjects: Illegal Aliens and the Making of Modern America*. Princeton, NJ: Princeton University Press, 2004.

Niblo, Stephen R. "Allied Policy toward Axis Interests in Mexico During World War II." *Mexican Studies/Estudios Mexicanos* 17, no. 2 (2001): 351–73.

——. "Allied Policy toward Germans, Italians and Japanese in Mexico During World War II." Paper presented at the Latin American Studies Association conference, Chicago, 1998.

——. *Mexico in the 1940s: Modernity, Politics, and Corruption*. Wilmington, DE: Scholarly Resources Books, 1999.

——. *War, Diplomacy, and Development: The United States and Mexico, 1938–1954*. Wilmington, DE: Scholarly Resources, 1995.

O'Connor, Brendon, ed. *Anti-Americanism: Comparative Perspectives*. Vol. 3 of *Anti-Americanism: History, Causes, Themes*. Oxford: Greenwood World Publisher, 2007.

Okihiro, Gary Y. *Cane Fires: The Anti-Japanese Movement in Hawaii, 1865–1945*. Philadelphia: Temple University Press, 1991.

——. *The Columbia Guide to Asian American History*. New York: Columbia University Press, 2005.

Okihiro, Gary Y., and David Drummond. "The Concentration Camp and Japanese Economic Losses in California Agriculture, 1900–1942." In *Japanese Americans: From Relocation to Redress*, edited by Roger Daniels, Sandra C. Taylor, and Harry H. L. Kitano, 168–75. Seattle: University of Washington Press, 1991.

O'Malley, Ilene V. *The Myth of the Revolution: Hero Cults and the Institutionalization of the Mexican State, 1920–1940*. New York: Greenwood Press, 1986.

Omi, Michael, and Howard Winant. *Racial Formation in the United States: From the 1960s to the 1980s*. New York: Routledge, 1986.

Ota Mishima, María Elena. *Siete migraciones japonesas en México, 1890–1978*. México, DF: El Colegio de México, 1982.

Otsuka, Martín Tameyesu. *Poems, Memories of My Home Town, and Chronicle of My Travels in Mexico*. Tokyo: Sumiko Otsuka Publisher, 1987.

Painter, Nell Irvin. *The History of White People*. New York: Norton, 2010.

Pascoe, Peggy. *What Comes Naturally: Miscegenation Law and the Making of Race in America*. Oxford: Oxford University Press, 2009.

Paz, María Elena. *Strategy, Security, and Spies: Mexico and the U.S. as Allies in World War II*. University Park: Pennsylvania State University, 1997.

Peddie, Francis. "Una presencia incómoda: La colonia japonesa de México durante la segunda guerra mundial." *Estudios de Historia Moderna y Contemporánea de México*, no. 32 (July–December 2006): 73–102.

Peña Delgado, Grace. *Making the Chinese Mexican: Global Migration, Localism, and Exclusion in the U.S.-Mexico Borderlands*. Stanford, CA: Stanford University Press, 2012.

Pérez, Emma. *The Decolonial Imaginary: Writing Chicanas into History*. Bloomington: Indiana University Press, 1999.

Petras, James, ed.. *Latin America: From Dependence to Revolution*. New York: Wiley, 1973.

Rankin, Monika A. *¡México, La Patria!: Propaganda and Production during World War II*. Lincoln: University of Nebraska Press, 2010.

Rénique, Gerardo. "Región, raza y nación en el antichinismo sonorense." In *Seis expulsiones y un adiós: Despojos y exclusiones en Sonora*, edited by Aarón Grageda Bustamante, 231–89. México, DF: Universidad de Sonora/Editorial Plaza y Valdés, 2003.

Riley, Karen Lea. *Schools behind Barbed Wire*. Lanham, MD: Rowman and Littlefield, 2002.

Robinson, Daniel. "Planning for the 'Most Serious Contingency': Alien Internment, Arbitrary Detention, and the Canadian State 1938–39." *Journal of Canadian Studies* 28, no. 2 (1993): 5–20.

Robinson, Greg. *A Tragedy of Democracy: Japanese Confinement in North America*. New York: Columbia University Press, 2009.

Rogers, Everett M., and Nancy R. Bartlit. *Silent Voices of World War II: When Sons of the Land of Enchantment Met Sons of the Land of the Rising Sun*. Santa Fe, NM: Sunstone Press, 2005.

Ruiz, Vicki L. *From Out of the Shadows: Mexican Women in Twentieth-Century America*. New York: Oxford University Press, 1999.

Russell, James W. *Class and Race Formation in North America*. Toronto: University of Toronto Press, 2009.

Sánchez Aguilar, Federico. *El lago español: Hispanoasia*. Madrid: Fuenlabrada, 2003.

Said, Edward W. *Orientalism*. New York: Vintage Books, 1979.

Sandoval, Chela. "U.S. Third World Feminism: The Theory and Method of Oppositional Consciousness in the Postmodern World." *Genders* 10 (spring 1991): 2–24.

Schiavone Camacho, Julia María. *Chinese Mexicans: Transpacific Migration and the Search for a Homeland, 1910–1960*. Chapel Hill: University of North Carolina Press, 2012.

Schuler, Friedrich E. *Mexico between Hitler and Roosevelt: Mexican Foreign Relations in the Age of Lázaro Cárdenas, 1934–1940*. Albuquerque: University of New Mexico Press, 1998.

Secretaría de Relaciones Exteriores. "Comunicado 357." *Sala de Prensa del Gobierno Federal* (2008). http://portal.sre.gob.mx/imr/pdf/8601glezgalvez.pdf.

Seijas, Tatiana. *Asian Slaves in Colonial Mexico: From Chinos to Indians*. New York: Cambridge University Press, 2014.

Shah, Nayan. *Contagious Divides: Epidemics and Race in San Francisco's Chinatown*. Berkeley: University of California Press, 2001.

Showman, Richard K., and Lyman S. Judson, eds. *The Monroe Doctrine and the Growth of Western Hemisphere Solidarity*. New York: H. W. Wilson, 1941.

Slack, Edward R., Jr. "Sinifying New Spain: Cathay's Influence on Colonial Mexico via the *Nao de China*." In *The Chinese in Latin America and the Caribbean*, edited by Walton Look Lai and Tan Chee-Beng, 7–34. Leiden, Netherlands: Brill Academic Publishers, 2010.

Sofsky, Wolfgang. *The Order of Terror: The Concentration Camp*. Translated by William Templer. Princeton, NJ: Princeton University Press, 1997.

Soga, Yasutaro (Keiho). *Life Behind Barbed Wire: The World War II Internment Memoirs of a Hawai'i Issei*. Honolulu: University of Hawaii Press, 2007.

SRE. "Portal." Secretaría de Relaciones Exteriores. Accessed June 3, 2009. http://portal .sre.gob.mx/imr/popups/articleswindow.php?id=78.

Stacy, Lee. "Cananea Mines." In *Mexico and the United States*, edited by Lee Stacy, 514. Tarrytown, NY: Marshall Cavendish, 2003.

Starr, Kevin. *Embattled Dreams: California in War and Peace, 1940–1950*. New York: Oxford University Press, 2003.

Stern, Alexandra Minna. *Eugenic Nation: Faults and Frontiers of Better Breeding in Modern America*. Berkeley: University of California Press, 2005.

Sugiman, Pamela. "Memories of Internment: Narrating Japanese Canadian Women's Life Stories." *Canadian Journal of Sociology* 29, no. 3 (2004): 359–88.

Takezawa, Yasuko I. *Breaking the Silence: Redress and Japanese American Ethnicity*. Ithaca, NY: Cornell University Press, 1995.

Tanaka, Michiko. "Seki Sano and Popular Political and Social Theatre in Latin America." *Latin American Theatre Review* 27, no. 2 (1994): 53–69.

Taylor, Quintard. *In Search of the Racial Frontier: African Americans in the American West, 1528–1990*. New York: Norton, 1998.

tenBroek, Jacobus, Edward N. Barnhart, and Floyd W. Matson. *Prejudice, War, and the Constitution*. Vol. 3 of *Japanese American Evacuation and Resettlement*. Berkeley: University of California Press, 1954.

Thompson, John Herd, and Stephen J. Randall. *Canada and the United States: Ambivalent Allies*. 4th. ed. Athens: University of Georgia Press, 2008.

Torres-Rodríguez, Laura J. "Diseños asiáticos: Orientalismo y modernidad en México." PhD diss., University of Pennsylvania, 2012.

Trueba Lara, José Luis. *Los chinos en Sonora: Una historia olvidada*. Hermosillo: Universidad de Sonora, 1990.

Trujillo Muñoz, Gabriel. *Entrecruzamientos: La cultura bajacaliforniana, sus autores y sus obras*. Mexicali: Universidad Autónoma de Baja California, 2002.

van Dijk, Teun A. "Elite Discourse and the Reproduction of Racism." In *Hate Speech*, edited by Rita Kirk Whillock and David Slayden, 1–27. Thousand Oaks, CA: Sage, 1995.

Vasconcelos, José. *La raza cósmica*. Translated by Didier Tisdel Jaén. Baltimore, MD: Johns Hopkins University Press, 1997.

Velázquez-Morales, Catalina. "Inmigrantes japoneses en Baja California, 1939–1945." *Clío* 6, no. 35 (2006): 81–101.

Wasserman, Mark. *Capitalists, Caciques, and Revolution: The Native Elite and Foreign Enterprise in Chihuahua, Mexico, 1854–1911*. Chapel Hill: University of North Carolina Press, 1984.

Welles, Sumner. *The Time for Decision*. New York: Harper, 1944.

———. *The World of the Four Freedoms*. New York: Columbia University Press, 1943.

Wiesel, Elie. *Night*. New York: Hill and Wang, 1960.

Wiley, Peter Booth. *Yankees in the Land of the Gods: Commodore Perry and the Opening of Japan*. New York: Viking, 1990.

Wössner, Stephanie. Japanese American Positionality in Hawaii and on the Mainland. Munich: GRIN Verlag, 2002.

Yanaga, Chitoshi. *Japan since Perry.* New York: McGraw Hill, 1949.

Zhao, Xiaojian. *Asian American Chronology: Chronologies of the American Mosaic.* Santa Barbara, CA: Greenwood Press/ABC-CLIO, 2009.

Index

About the Author

Selfa A. Chew holds a bachelor's degree in communication science from Universidad Nacional Autónoma de México. She received an MFA in creative writing, and her PhD in borderlands history from the University of Texas at El Paso. She is an editor for *Border Senses Literary Review*. Her work (poetic, graphic, narrative, and editorial) has been published in Peru, Spain, Argentina, Mexico, the Netherlands, and the United States. She teaches at the University of Texas at El Paso and New Mexico State University.